*At
My
Best*

At My Best

365 Meditations for Physical, Spiritual and Emotional Well-Being

By the Author of
A New Day and
A Time to Be Free

BANTAM BOOKS

NEW YORK • TORONTO • LONDON • SYDNEY • AUCKLAND

AT MY BEST

A Bantam Book / July 1992

Library of Congress Cataloging-in-Publication Data

At my best : 365 meditations for physical, spiritual and emotional
  well-being / Anonymous.
      p.   cm.
  Includes index.
  ISBN 0-553-35337-3
  1. Devotional calendars.
BL624.2.A8   1992
291.4'3—dc20   91-40741
                                                         CIP

Published simultaneously in the United States and Canada

PRINTED IN THE UNITED STATES OF AMERICA

QPK   10987

At My Best

No man ever wetted clay and then left it, as if there would be bricks by chance and fortune.

—Plutarch

The physical, emotional, and spiritual components of well-being are not unlike the legs of a tripod. Each contributes to the balance and solidity of the whole. When we fail to attend to any one, the structure of our life soon becomes shaky and insecure.

That's why it is important each day to set our personal priorities and to follow through with disciplined and consistent actions. We know from experience what happens when we do otherwise. To be sure, numerous examples are still fresh in our minds. . . .

When we gave up exercising for an entire month, without a good reason, we lost much of the cardiovascular fitness we had attained. When we regressed and for a time stopped being honest and open with our feelings, we soon began to feel angry and alienated. When we lost interest and temporarily abandoned our spiritual search, God suddenly seemed remote and impersonal.

We've learned, and probably will have to learn again, that consistency and discipline—a day at a time—are absolutely essential if we are to maintain the well-being we've worked so hard to achieve.

THOUGHT FOR TODAY: What important actions will I take today to enhance my well-being?

January 2

None of us has a patent on being right.
—Millard E. Tydings

For many years of my life it was vitally important for me to always be right. I would go to any length to defend the rightness and validity of my actions and opinions. Even when I suspected or knew that I was wrong, something compelled me to prove I was right.

I certainly didn't see it at the time, but I've come to realize that my immaturity in this regard was a way of compensating for strong feelings of inadequacy. To make matters worse, I had no humility but, instead, was driven by pride.

Since I expended so much energy defending my "rightness," it was all but impossible to grow psychologically and spiritually. Because I was always fighting someone or something, my relationships were severely strained. I was perpetually tied up in emotional knots.

I matured slowly. As I became more secure within myself and developed a growing sense of self-worth, I became less prideful and more open-minded.

Now that I no longer have to defend my rightness, I'm so much more at ease. Even when I know I'm right, I'm not driven to prove it. These days, what's most important is being right with myself.

THOUGHT FOR TODAY: Do I always have to have the last word?

January 3

Nothing can bring you peace but yourself.
— Ralph Waldo Emerson

In the past, it wasn't often that we experienced a sense of well-being. When we did, it was as if we were receiving a precious gift. Those fleeting moments were serendipitous, and almost always resulted from circumstances that had somehow lined up favorably—an extraordinary sunset, for example, or even unexpected praise at work. Hardly ever did such intervals of serenity come from within.

Today, in contrast, emotional well-being is an undercurrent of our daily lives. It flows steadily through our thoughts, actions, and experiences. It arises largely from within ourselves, and has little to do with outside forces.

How is it that something once so rare and ephemeral is now an abiding part of our existence? The answer is that we've developed self-knowledge, and as the result have learned what actions to take or avoid in order to attain a sense of well-being.

We no longer have to wait passively for peace of mind to come to us, but can actively pursue it. In addition, we now trust that God will always love and care for us, and this in itself provides us with great inner peace.

THOUGHT FOR TODAY: Serenity is no less precious, but ever more abundant.

January 4

The first problem for all of us, men and women, is not to learn, but to unlearn.

—Gloria Steinem

Change eluded some of us for a long, long time. It's not that we didn't want to change, or didn't try. The opposite was true. Changing the way we looked, felt, and acted was just about all we ever thought about and desired.

The problem was, we were so intolerant of ourselves that we felt life wouldn't be worthwhile unless we changed radically and completely. Needless to say, our intolerance—our total inability to accept ourselves, even partially—created enormous and unrelenting pressure to change. And this virtually guaranteed failure.

As it turned out, we first had to learn to accept ourselves as we were—unhealthy, depressed, addicted, laden with character defects, whatever—before it became possible to change. We had to develop enough self-acceptance to honestly believe, "If this is the best I can do at this point in my life, it's okay."

Only then did the tremendous pressure we had put on ourselves for so long begin to lift. We soon started going out of our way to be supporting and encouraging of ourselves, for we had come to realize that these qualities are essential to personal change.

THOUGHT FOR TODAY: Self-acceptance is not an ending, but a beginning.

Truth is such a rare thing, it is delightful to tell it.
—Emily Dickinson

This time it feels like it's for real—we've finally started doing something constructive about our compulsive overeating. We've joined a support group, we're following a recommended diet, and we've begun to exercise. Best of all, we've actually lost five pounds in the first month and a half.

But suddenly our old archenemy, *impatience*, takes over. We feel that the weight isn't coming off fast enough, that our exercise program isn't doing any real good. Practically overnight, we become discouraged and depressed. We're ready to blow the whole thing.

If ever there was a time to be gentle and fair to ourselves, this is it! To overcome our disillusionment, it's vitally important that we actively encourage ourselves—as often and as specifically as we can.

First and foremost, we need to honestly acknowledge the progress we've already made, and give ourselves credit for that. Next, we ought to take stock of the most recent 24-hour period. Did we stick to our diet? Did we exercise? Did we do the very best we were able to do?

If the answers are yes, we should then ask the most important question of all: What more can we possibly expect from ourselves?

THOUGHT FOR TODAY: I will treat myself as I would a dear friend—with patience and encouragement.

January 6

Patience and time do more than strength or passion.
　　　　　　　　　　　—Jean de La Fontaine

Hardly a month goes by when each of us is not taken aback by adversity of some kind. Whatever it may be—financial setback, business dispute, family crisis—it frequently takes us by surprise, or is the opposite of what we had hoped for or expected.

Unless we are in the habit of denying reality or shirking responsibility, chances are we'll try to tackle the problem head on, with all the emotion, energy, and willfulness we can muster. We may become consumed with the problem, and find no peace until it is resolved.

When we steamroll our way through life like this, we may be quite successful in overcoming problems, or at least smoothing them over. But at what price? None of us needs to be reminded that a life fueled by adrenaline and stress will soon catch up with us physically and emotionally.

We do need to be reminded, however, that we will be far more successful—in solving problems as well as preserving our health—if we calmly and sanely do what we can, then let go and allow things to work themselves out as they always do.

THOUGHT FOR TODAY: I choose patience and self-preservation.

Love consists in desiring to give what is our own to another and feeling his delight as our own.
                                        —Emanuel Swedenborg

It seems that almost every week I read about medical advances which hold promise to cure illnesses that are now incurable. These discoveries are amazing and heartwarming, absolutely, and hopefully their development will accelerate in the years to come. As far as I'm concerned, however, love will always remain the most potent healing force of all.

From my own experience I am convinced that the more love I have in my life, the more quickly I heal, the more likely I am to remain well, the better I feel. I sense also that the more love I give to others, the better they feel.

God works through people in many ways. To me, the most special way is His transmission of love from one person to another. Love is the ultimate expression of God's healing power.

Love is free and available to everyone. We don't need to go through any kind of training or develop any particular aptitude; all we need to do is open our hearts. God has provided each of us with an endless source of people to love.

THOUGHT FOR TODAY: Through our own pain, we are often led to others we can love and heal.

January 8

Health is the vital principle of bliss, and exercise of health.

—James Thomson

Those of us who exercise regularly will extol its virtues at the drop of a hat. But not everybody feels that way. In fact, most people don't like to exercise. They see it as an inconvenient and even painful chore.

If you are someone who doesn't exercise, even though you know you should, you may find new incentive by considering these advantages. . . .

Exercise will improve your cardiovascular system—it will strengthen your heart and expand your lung capacity. You will be able to walk, play, and stay active for longer periods without feeling breathless.

Exercise can help with weight control. Not only will you burn calories, but your appetite will actually be suppressed. If you work out regularly, your body will become toned and your metabolism will become more efficient.

The health and strength of your muscles, ligaments, tendons, and bones also will be enhanced by exercise.

Exercise offers many emotional advantages as well. It relieves stress, relaxes you, and often results in a sense of euphoria. If you haven't yet experienced the "natural high" that exercise can bring, you have something wonderful in store.

THOUGHT FOR TODAY: I now exercise because I want to, not because I need to.

Safeguard the health of both body and soul.
                                    —Cleobulus

I affirm that I am an important priority in my own life. This day and every day, I will take the time and devote the energy toward achieving improved health and well-being.

Not long ago, I was easily detoured by the demands of others. Almost always, I would put their needs ahead of my own. But in recovery I have learned to put my personal priorities first—to respect and honor myself with the attention and care I deserve.

It is not an option, but a loving obligation to tend to the needs of my body. So I will carefully choose and prepare the foods that are right for me, and I will schedule adequate time for exercise, recreation, and rest.

It is not a luxury, but a necessity to care for my emotional health. I will be sure to talk with close friends, sharing my feelings, experiences, and concerns. I will reduce the stress of unfulfilled obligations by meeting my commitments and taking care of my responsibilities.

It is not a duty, but a life-affirming choice to enrich my spiritual being. Today, in my own time and in my own way, I will draw closer to my Creator.

THOUGHT FOR TODAY: Am I giving my physical, emotional, and spiritual priorities the "first things first" attention they require?

January 10

Do not turn back when you are just at the goal.
> —Publilius Syrus

On a vacation one summer, a friend and I went fishing and hiking in the Sawtooth Mountains of Idaho. One day our destination was a remote lake at the end of a steep foot trail. It was a grueling climb. Three-quarters of the way up, I sent my companion ahead without me. I'd had enough.

As I sat and waited, two men came bounding up the trail. They wore heavy backpacks, and must have been in their late seventies. They waved cheerfully as they passed by, and suffice it to say I was embarrassed for having given up so easily. Later, I thought about other times and ways I had shortchanged myself by quitting, even when it was well within my capability to meet the challenge at hand.

Once in a while, we're all tempted to give up too soon. At such times we can seek support and encouragement from our friends—or, as I learned that day, inspiration from strangers. We can also reach down deeper within ourselves. The truth is that most of the time we fail to realize just how much we have inside—not just in stamina, strength, and courage, but also in knowledge and creativity.

THOUGHT FOR TODAY: Do I still have "halfway to go"? Or am I already halfway there?

Nothing in the affairs of men is worthy of great anxiety.

—Plato

We know how damaging stress can be, not only emotionally, but also physically. It has become a continuing priority to temper our negative reactions and learn to cope with stressful situations in the best ways possible.

Of course, this is rarely as simple as it sounds. At times it can be extremely difficult to remain calm, especially when stress-producing interactions are unavoidable. How can we alter our response and reduce harm to ourselves when we are involved in such situations?

When we feel stress building, we can try to remember that the less intense our reaction, the less damage we will do to our emotions, immune system, and spirit. We might ask ourselves, at that early stage, if an unrestrained reaction on our part will be worth the price we'll ultimately have to pay.

We can also try to change our perception of the person or circumstance triggering our anxiety. Events that at first seem threatening and even disastrous are often less so when we take a more objective look.

Finally, we can try to stop "fighting" whatever it is that's upsetting us. We may find that surrender is the best possible solution.

THOUGHT FOR TODAY: Stress control is damage control.

A fresh mind keeps the body fresh. Take in the ideas of the day, drain off those of yesterday.
—Edward George Bulwer-Lytton

The old ideas that have influenced our attitudes and actions for years don't magically disappear when we make a commitment to improve our health and well-being. Old ideas can haunt and harm us long after we think they are buried.

If we don't want the destructive echoes of the past to limit our freedom and progress today, we have to identify and neutralize them as soon as they surface. An effective way is to take a moment to examine the old idea, then come up with an alternative more in line with our new objectives. Here are some examples. . . .

Old idea: I don't have time for myself. I'm too busy to exercise and meditate. *New idea:* My health and well-being must become a top priority. I'll set aside time no matter what.

Old idea: It's too hard. The very prospect of making major changes in my lifestyle is overwhelming. *New idea:* I'm going to take it as slowly as I need to, and be satisfied with gradual change.

Old idea: The only thing I really need in order to change is enough willpower. *New idea:* I also need to be committed, disciplined, and willing to seek help from others and God.

THOUGHT FOR TODAY: I need not follow yesterday's script.

We shall all be changed, in a moment, in the twinkling of an eye.
>   —New Testament: I Corinthians, xv, 51, 52.

I smoked for years and years and years—high tar, low tar, no tar. Even after I had been diagnosed with heart disease and was told that cigarettes would kill me, I still couldn't quit.

Eventually I wanted to stop smoking more than anything. I thought about it all the time, to the point of obsession. I tried. I failed. I tried and failed again and again. I became frustrated and disgusted.

I waited for a month, or maybe it was a year, then tried again with the same results. No matter what I did, nothing changed except my health. It continued to deteriorate.

Then one day, when I least expected it—at the wrong time and in an inappropriate place—it all changed. The objective that for so long I had tried to achieve—to *will*, to *force*—actually occurred. I became a nonsmoker.

Later, I tried to figure out what was different this time, why all of a sudden I had succeeded. The answer didn't come right away. Gradually, however, I realized that I had finally experienced a state of rock-bottom surrender, combined with a sincere willingness to be changed. And that's when God stepped in to do the rest.

THOUGHT FOR TODAY: I accept my powerlessness; I acknowledge God's power.

January 14

We cannot too often think, that there is a never sleeping eye that reads the heart, and registers our thoughts.

—Francis Bacon

There are times in all of our lives when we feel completely alone. We go to our friends with our problems, but don't seem to get what we need from them. It's not that they don't care; rather, they are involved with their own lives, and in reality are quite powerless to help or even understand what we are going through. Or so it seems.

But we have one friend who has all the time in the world for us. No problem or concern in our life is too large or too small for God's attention and care. When we talk to God, and ask Him for guidance and solutions, He listens with infinite patience. He listens as no one else can, so that ultimately He may graciously show us the way.

God is never far away, but always readily available to attend to our every need. The answers may not come as quickly as we might hope, but we can be assured that they will come at the right time, in accordance with His plan for our ultimate good.

THOUGHT FOR TODAY: I am never alone, never friendless, never without a receptive ear.

*He who reigns within himself, and rules his passions,
desires, and fears is more than a king.*
—John Milton

When my internal pressure gauge used to shoot up
into the red "danger" zone, which it often did, I
compulsively turned to rituals that temporarily as-
suaged my pain and gave me solace. I went out and
got drunk. I bought a quart of ice cream and ate it in
one quick sitting. I squandered money I didn't have
on things I would never use.

The problem, of course, was that such behavior
did little to reduce the stress, and in fact ended up
intensifying it. In addition to any hangover, weight
gain, or financial embarrassment I suffered, I inevitably also felt guilty, ashamed, and more anxiety-ridden
than before.

Like many people in recovery, I've learned over
time to seek out positive and growth-enhancing ways
to overcome stressful feelings. Instead of picking up a
drink, I pick up the telephone and call an understanding friend. Instead of going on an overeating binge, I
go for a walk, swim, or bike ride. Instead of turning to
my checkbook or credit cards, I turn to God and ask
Him for serenity, acceptance, and guidance.

THOUGHT FOR TODAY: Am I finding constructive
rather than destructive ways to deal with stress?

*Our doubts are traitors, and make us lose the good we
oft might win by fearing to attempt.*
                                        —William Shakespeare

One of the priorities of our new lifestyle is to stop
judging ourselves so harshly. In fact, a long-term
objective is to try to eliminate self-judgment entirely.
We're making progress along these lines, and have
found that we're at our physical, emotional, and
spiritual best—flexible, creative, and spontaneous—
when we "let ourselves be."

Because we are human, however, the likelihood
is that we're bound to judge ourselves in some way
from time to time. On those occasions, we might try
to do so on what could be called a "best efforts" basis.

In our exercise program, for example, we may
wish we had worked harder or made more progress
during a particular month. We can temper that
judgment by resolving to be more disciplined, rather
than merely berating ourselves. We can also keep our
priorities in order by refusing to allow temporary
discouragement to mushroom into stronger feelings of
failure and defeat. We do our best—period.

We used to criticize ourselves unmercifully for
even the slightest mistake or misstep. It's such a relief
to now accept setbacks as part of an ongoing process
that brings us ever closer to our wellness goals.

THOUGHT FOR TODAY: I will accept rather than
judge myself; I will be encouraging rather than
critical.

Yet still we hug the dear deceit.

—Nathaniel Cotton

For those of us who have successfully reached and maintained an ideal weight, it's hard not to sometimes feel regret for the denial that kept us in the shadows. Yet as painful as it is to look back, it's important to be reminded of the way we used to live, and of how far we've come.

In order to avoid even thinking about our weight problem, we refused to discuss it with family members or close friends. We averted our eyes when we passed full-length mirrors. We avoided scales entirely, and put off shopping for new clothes.

We were able to surrender to the gravity of our problem only after some serious soul-searching. We took a hard look at how overeating adversely affected almost every area of our life. We could see a myriad of important reasons to lose weight. At last we became willing to put our denial and rationalizations aside, and explore avenues for change.

How good it is to walk in the sunlight and have control of our life! What a relief to accept who we are and how we look. How freeing it is to be open with our loved ones, and to lead a joyful, lively life.

THOUGHT FOR TODAY: Denial prolongs the pain.

January 18

To tired limbs and over-busy thoughts,
Inviting sleep and soft forgetfulness.
—William Wordsworth

Sleep was not one of my priorities. When I was a teenager, I tried to get by with as little as possible. As a practicing alcoholic, I more often passed out than turned in. Frequently I would "come to" in the small hours, tormented by some omission or commission, and remain awake until morning. In early recovery, I'd stay up half the night.

I don't do that to myself anymore, thankfully. My priorities have shifted sharply, and as each day comes to an end I look forward to a good night's sleep.

Sleep allows me to take a break from my conscious mind—not only from my own thoughts and speculations, but also from the myriad images and stimuli of the outside world and my responses and reactions to them.

Sleep allows me to heal. It brings regeneration and peace to my body, mind, and spirit. Following a restful night, I'm invariably more productive, patient, and even-tempered. For all of these reasons—for all the good it does me—these days I treat the sleep I require with the respect it deserves.

THOUGHT FOR TODAY: Sleep calms, heals, rejuvenates.

We are all of us imaginative in some form or other, for images are the brood of desire.

—George Eliot

At one time or another, we all have used imagination to "transport" ourselves out of difficult, stressful, or otherwise painful situations. We closed our eyes and visualized ourselves in happier and more tranquil circumstances—at a different time, in a different place, in a personal memory setting of our own choosing.

Whether we realized it or not, we were practicing mental imagery as a relaxation technique. Many of us have since learned how to use this liberating tool more frequently, more effectively, and with more versatility.

In essence, mental imagery helps us creatively express, pursue, and achieve positive expectations. We begin by making a clear and decisive image of our goal. By repeating the image in our mind, we create an expectation that the goal will be met. Eventually, we automatically begin to act in ways that help turn the goal into a reality.

A writer, for example, might repeatedly visualize a stream of thoughts flowing from his brain to a computer screen. A person who is apprehensive about meeting an estranged family member might visualize a tension-free, loving reunion. A person beginning a diet might visualize the way he will look when he has reached the weight-loss objective.

THOUGHT FOR TODAY: I have the power to channel my imagination into life-affirming pursuits.

January 20

Imagination is more important than knowledge.
—Albert Einstein

The more we practice mental imagery, the more evident it becomes that there are few limits to the positive impact it can have on the quality of our lives.

Mental imagery can be used to reduce anxiety and stress, to alleviate fear in any number of areas, and to help us regain a sense of control. It can enable us to communicate with our subconscious and change our attitudes and beliefs. In the process, mental imagery can bring about sharpened skills, improved physical health, and strengthened emotional security.

Let's say, for example, that we want to improve our tennis serve. Over and over again, we picture in our mind's eye a perfect swing and follow-through, with the ball going exactly where we aim.

In a health-related application, a person with an infection can augment medical treatment by visualizing the body's healing agents traveling to the site and vigorously attacking the bacteria or virus.

Mental imagery can also be used to help us maintain our composure in difficult social or work situations. By repeatedly visualizing ourselves as a poised and self-confident participant in an upcoming event, for example, we may be able to reduce or even prevent our usual self-consciousness and anxiety.

THOUGHT FOR TODAY: Mental imagery is a multipurpose wellness tool that is always at my disposal.

What a thing friendship is, world without end!
                                    —Robert Browning

Even more powerful than our fear of people *per se* was our fear of what they would think of us and how they would treat us once they got to know us. So we developed a formidable array of defenses: behavioral trip wires to shock and frighten off "the enemy," physical and emotional camouflage of every variety to make us less noticeable.

While such barriers effectively shut out much anxiety and pain, they also sealed us off from fun, loving feelings, understanding, and support—all the good things that flow from closeness with others.

The degree to which we lower our defenses and allow others into our life is a good measure of our progress in recovery. Each time we permit ourselves to be vulnerable in some way, and let another person know who we really are, our self-assurance grows.

Today, as the result of this growth process, we are beginning to emerge from hiding; we've learned to reach out, and to experience the world in a new, nonthreatening way. Our fears are diminishing, and we feel comfortable around other people. It gives us a deep sense of well-being to share our lives with trusted and loving friends.

THOUGHT FOR TODAY: Are my defenses still holding me captive?

January 22

All walking is discovery. On foot we take the time to see things whole.

—Hal Borland

One of my most useful discoveries when I first visited the countries of western Europe was the extent and frequency with which people walked. The streets were always filled, day and night. People walked to school and work; they walked home for lunch and then back again; they walked to distant markets and department stores.

Before and after dinner, entire families promenaded for hours. Perhaps it was my imagination—although I don't think so—but it seemed, overall, that very few of the walkers were overweight.

Within a week, I too had become an enthusiastic walker. I soon thought nothing of walking three or more miles to a museum, restaurant, or park, forsaking taxis and buses. And it didn't take long for me to develop the habit of strolling for several hours each evening, along with the locals.

The benefits were quickly evident: I felt terrific; I soaked up character and details at a most personal level; I sampled foods to my heart's content without concern, returning home a few pounds thinner and as fit as when I had left.

THOUGHT FOR TODAY: I can walk for health, pleasure, and serenity.

Whenever you are sincerely pleased, you are nourished.

—Ralph Waldo Emerson

Recreation and pleasure have become a welcome and natural part of our lives, but there was a time when many of us had convoluted ideas about these necessities. Some of us, for example, had fallen into the habit of working such long hours that breaks for pleasure didn't seem right; whenever we took time out to enjoy ourselves we felt guilty. Others believed that pleasure ought to be considered a reward—it had to be earned. And there were those of us with low self-esteem; we felt that we didn't deserve pleasure.

But all of that is behind us. We have come to believe that life is not meant to be a vale of tears, but rather, that God's plan for us includes an abundance of happiness and lightheartedness.

We no longer question whether we are "deserving enough" to have a full measure of enjoyment in our lives. And while we are by no means perfect, that doesn't mean we have to punish ourselves by withholding joy.

These days, we feel that recreation and pleasure are no less important than work and responsibility. In our view, life is meant to be fully lived and enjoyed, not to be survived or endured.

THOUGHT FOR TODAY: Joy is not a fringe benefit; it's part of the package.

I celebrate myself, and sing myself . . .
—Walt Whitman

I recently attended a dinner party at the home of a business associate. All the other guests had come as couples, but I happened to be by myself. During the evening, it occurred to me that an unattached person at such a gathering could easily feel "less than," "apart from," and even be filled with self-pity.

Actually, there have been periods in my life when I had such feelings because I was without a partner. As a single person, I felt isolated, undesirable, and somehow inadequate. Those were painful times.

I've learned—and doubtless the learning process will be lifelong—that my emotional well-being can't be contingent on whether or not I'm in a relationship. A true sense of wholeness and inner security can only come from within. If that sense is lacking, or has diminished, there are actions I can take on my own and with the help of God to restore it.

It's wonderful to be in a relationship, to have a partner, to be close to someone in that special way. But such a connection is by no means an essential ingredient for emotional well-being.

THOUGHT FOR TODAY: I am already complete.

Though losses and crosses be lessons right severe,
there's wit there ye'll get there, ye'll find no other
where.

—Robert Burns

They usually seem to come out of nowhere, like an
unexpected blow that knocks the wind out of us. We
describe them as crises, disasters, exigencies. No
matter what we call them, they demand our immediate attention and cause great distress. We become
frantic and overwhelmed, and don't see how we will
possibly survive.

At such times we can of course turn to God and
our close friends for comfort. In addition, we can
pause and think back to other times in our lives that
were no less calamitous and frightening.

Each of us will surely be able to recall one or
more major illnesses, the breakup of a long-term
relationship, a devastating financial loss, or a painful
siege of depression. If we think about any one of these
events, even briefly, it will become clear that it is
behind us, that we did in fact *survive*.

By focusing not on the details of the past crisis,
but on our survival, we can put hard-earned experience to good use. We can be reassured that we do
indeed have the faith, courage, and capability to
transcend anything that is put in front of us.

THOUGHT FOR TODAY: I have overcome before; I
can and will overcome again.

January 26

Nothing will ever be attempted if all possible objections must be first overcome.

—Samuel Johnson

One of the surest ways to stay stuck where we are—unhealthy and unfulfilled—is to blame other people and other things for our condition: "Stress is killing me, I'll be the first one to admit it. But if you had my schedule, you'd be a wreck too." "I was such a fat baby! My parents forced food on me when I was little. That's why I can't lose weight." "I'd like to work out, sure, but I'm afraid I'll hurt myself; I have a bad back."

As farfetched as these excuses may sound, practically every one of us has fallen back on them or similar ones at one time or another. By doing so, we gave ourselves permission to avoid taking responsibility, to sit back, to do nothing, and to feel sorry for ourselves.

Nobody said it would be easy to stick with an exercise program, shed excess pounds, or reduce stress in our lives. The reality is that we all have past histories and present-day obstacles to overcome as we strive to achieve health and fitness goals. So the sooner we stop looking for excuses, inventing rationalizations, and blaming others, the sooner we're likely to find success.

THOUGHT FOR TODAY: Overcoming the challenge adds to the achievement.

Come what may, I have been blessed.
—George Gordon Byron

It's hard to imagine gaining anything of value from a serious injury or illness. When we are incapacitated, fearful, and in pain, the last thing we are likely to be thinking about is what we can learn from our ordeal. Nevertheless, many of us who have undergone such difficulties have benefited greatly.

For example, our perspective changed significantly during recovery from illness or injury. We began to appreciate our loved ones and blessings in a whole new way. We no longer took our good fortune and overall good health for granted.

We gained a new sense of life's timetable, and as the result stopped putting things off. We began to zero in on joy, making choices that allow us to be as happy as possible right now, rather than at some unspecified future date.

We learned to save our emotional energy for the really important things—living and loving. We stopped letting ourselves get caught up in pettiness and trivialities.

Of course, it's possible to learn these very same lessons without suffering in any way, and many people do. But sometimes it takes an illness or injury to open our eyes and renew our gratitude.

THOUGHT FOR TODAY: Do I appreciate my blessings while I'm enjoying them?

Passion costs too much to bestow it on every trifle.
—Thomas Adams

When two of my friends recently had a heated disagreement, each tried to win my support. I refused to take sides. Rather than risk alienating either of them, and getting caught up in the emotional turmoil of their argument, I remained neutral.

I felt good about the way I handled the situation, because there was a time when I couldn't be neutral about anything. I held vociferous, unyielding beliefs, and would get emotionally involved in office politics, other people's relationships, you name it.

My passionate opinions kept me in a state of siege. I was always on the brink, ready to lash out or defend my position. I was constantly upset and angry.

When stress reduction became a vital objective in my life, I had to change my behavior along these lines. I had to learn to recognize my powerlessness in most areas. I've found that it's a boon to my emotional well-being when I can remain neutral.

This is not to say that I don't take stands and have opinions. I exercise my right to vote, and do what I can to improve the world around me. But I hardly ever let my opinions get the better of me.

THOUGHT FOR TODAY: Neutrality is strength, not weakness.

It is necessary to the happiness of man that he be mentally faithful to himself.

—Thomas Paine

We knew that our lack of self-acceptance was undermining every facet of our lives. We wanted to become more self-accepting, there was no question about that, but it took us time to develop an understanding of what self-acceptance involves.

Self-acceptance, we've learned, means accepting every bit of ourselves exactly as we are. This includes not only what we sometimes perceive as liabilities—such as physical limitations and character defects—but also the qualities we don't always acknowledge as assets—body coordination, or teachability, for example.

Self-acceptance means honoring and treasuring ourselves as we are at this very moment. It goes far beyond a half-hearted concession that we'll never be what we once were, or become what we once hoped to be.

More than anything, self-acceptance comes from valuing our inner self. But first we have to get to know that part of our being. We have to discover or rediscover the very special qualities that make us who we are—such as our capacity for compassion and love, our resilience, or our creative talents.

When we achieve this kind of total and multidimensional self-acceptance, it becomes possible to stop judging ourselves harshly.

THOUGHT FOR TODAY: Self-acceptance is the pathway to inner freedom.

January 30

Character, that sublime health which values one moment as another, and makes us great in all conditions.

—Ralph Waldo Emerson

By now we've become convinced that regular physical workouts can help us with weight control, cardiovascular fitness, and overall body strength and flexibility. However, there are also a number of less obvious benefits—from sports, in particular—that can carry over into all areas of our lives.

In any sport, to begin with, we face risks, difficulties, and our own fears. By overcoming these challenges through actual experience, we develop greater self-confidence.

Team sports enable us to become less self-centered, to move from isolation to interaction, and to become part of something worthwhile. In the process, we learn to get along with others, and to be mutually supportive as we work for the greater good.

Sports activities also help us develop grace and coordination while putting us in harmony with our natural surroundings. We learn to "go with the flow" rather than resist outside forces.

Since sports require a great deal of focused attention, participation teaches us to clear our minds, ignore distractions, and sharpen our senses. These capabilities can be transferred to studying, reading, and communication, as well as to our expressions of creativity.

THOUGHT FOR TODAY: My goal is balanced fitness—body, mind, and spirit.

God to me is that creative Force, behind and in the universe, who manifests Himself as energy, as life, as order, as beauty, as thought, as conscience, as love.
—Henry Sloane Coffin

When my life seems complicated and tumultuous, I can always regain perspective by looking beyond myself to the natural order of the world around me. I can always become centered by reflecting on this reality: God's Divine Order is the underlying foundation of stability and harmony within all people and all things.

I know from experience that feelings of confusion and unrest will fade when I connect again with that same source of Divine Order within myself. At any time, I can return to my inner source through prayer and meditation.

I can also regain stability by observing the evidences of Divine Order that are everywhere present. Looking seaward, I will be awed and comforted by the regularity of the tides—by the amazing symmetry and perfection of all God's creatures, from the smallest diatom to the largest whale.

Looking skyward, I will be reassured by the predictability of sunrises over countless millennia, by the precision of planetary orbits, by the synchronicity of distant galaxies. Then, as thoughts of Divine Order return me to poise and serenity, I will give thanks to God.

THOUGHT FOR TODAY: Everything is in order; everything is as it should be.

February 1

After these two, Doctor Diet and Doctor Quiet, Doctor Merryman is requisite to preserve health.
—James Howell

We've learned a lot about the psychological and physiological aspects of nutrition and weight control. We know what to eat, how much to eat, and what happens if we eat the wrong foods.

But a frequently overlooked area of nutritional wellness is our mealtime environment—that is, the physical and emotional conditions under which we prepare and eat the foods we have so carefully selected. Many of us with families eat our meals in a setting not unlike a three-ring circus. People pop up and down, arguments rage, music blares, chaos reigns.

Similarly, those of us who live alone may eat while watching the television news, ingesting a plateful of gloom and doom along with dinner. We frequent noisy restaurants, eat standing up, and wolf down our meals.

What happens under these circumstances? Certainly we don't enjoy our food as we should, nor do we properly digest it. Stressful eating environments cause headaches, indigestion, and other problems.

Granted, we don't always have a choice. But usually we can make decisions that allow us to relax at mealtimes in quiet, tension-free environments. Each of us can determine the "house rules" that work best, and then do what's necessary to put them into effect.

THOUGHT FOR TODAY: Are my mealtimes pleasant times?

Whatever comes, this too shall pass away.
                              —Ella Wheeler Wilcox

There are times in our lives when it seems that all the world's clocks and calendars have stopped. We are in a distressing situation—a severely strained relationship, an impossible workload, a lingering illness. And we feel as trapped as a fly in amber.

What can we do to change our perspective and prove to ourselves that our life is indeed in motion? We can think back to some of the worst times of the past, reviewing how they began, how long they actually lasted, and how they ended. This simple mental exercise can convince us that there will in fact be a resolution of our present difficulties.

Another way to bring about a more realistic outlook is to take a determined action that points us toward change, or at least symbolizes change. We can update our job résumé, for example. We can see a doctor, or get a second opinion. We can write down the pros and cons or specific problems we have, or decisions we must make. It doesn't matter how small or seemingly premature the action is, so long as it helps change the way we're feeling.

THOUGHT FOR TODAY: Is it really true that what's going on right now will last forever?

February 3

If it is well with your belly, your back, and your feet,
regal wealth can add nothing greater.

—Horace

The other night I had a dream so stressful that I
awakened with physical symptoms. My heart was
beating rapidly, I was perspired, and my muscles
were tense.

In the morning, thinking about the dream and
my anxiety, I remembered something. For years,
because of the reckless and irresponsible way I lived,
stress-induced symptoms were a constant in my life.
A chronically self-destructive lifestyle, including decades of addictive drinking and smoking, took a
tremendous toll on my health. I rarely gave thought
to the needs of my body, or the ways I was abusing it.
I took my health for granted, and that attitude almost
killed me.

I've since worked very hard to regain my health.
Today I'm healthier and more physically fit than ever
before, and of course I'm extremely grateful. As one
who has been there and back, I can say from once
painful but now joyous experience that good health is
paramount to a quality life. Good health means far
more than any amount of money, property, or prestige. Next to my relationship with God, I put it above
all else.

THOUGHT FOR TODAY: Good health is my most
precious asset.

The noontide sun is dark, and music discord, when the heart is low.

—Edward Young

We feel quite good these days. We're well on our way toward solving our major problems, we've taken care of unfinished business, and we generally feel right with ourselves and the world. But every so often our mood plummets. We become irritable, disgusted, and depressed. When friends ask us what's wrong, we snap at them, "I'm just in a bad mood."

More often than not, we can slip into such a state of mind without having the foggiest notion why. It certainly seems major. However, if we take just a few moments to analyze our thoughts and feelings at such times, we may find that our mood has deteriorated over something insignificant or even silly. Once we recognize that the incident or thought is hardly worth a ruined day, it becomes relatively easy to switch emotional gears.

In addition, we often can elevate our mood by taking a simple action—going for a walk, making a phone call, spending some time alone, even changing clothes. We can also improve our mood and take the power away from negative thoughts by writing about them, or saying them out loud to ourselves.

THOUGHT FOR TODAY: I have the power within me to alter my mood.

February 5

What is noble can be said in any language, and what is mean should be said in none.

—Maimonides

It's hard to know how to react when we are being teased, or we are the target of someone's cynical humor. We may be terribly hurt, yet remain silent because we don't want to appear overly sensitive. We may want to lash out at the person who is needling us. Or, we may simply want to flee because we feel vulnerable and anxious as we wait for the next barb.

If teasing, sarcasm, and innuendo affects us in these ways, why do we sometimes dish it out ourselves? In all honesty, most of us do. We joke insensitively about someone's new hairstyle or weight gain, and then say, "Just kidding!" We mock another person's point of view, and then make it even worse by saying sarcastically, "Well, everyone's entitled to their opinion."

The next time we are tempted to tease someone or be sarcastic, we might want to recall what such jibes do to our own well-being when we're on the receiving end. We might also remind ourselves that this sort of so-called humor drives people away from us, and eventually extinguishes love.

THOUGHT FOR TODAY: I will rely on the language of kindness and love.

One thorn of experience is worth a whole wilderness of warning.

—James Russell Lowell

Once, on an ocean fishing trip, our excursion boat drifted over a school of sculpin. As my fellow anglers and I began catching them, the captain warned us about their venomous spines. "They're great eating," he shouted, "but don't let yourself get stung!"

Five minutes later, disregarding the admonition, the man next to me reached into his sack to examine the sculpin he had caught. He was stung instantly and suffered excruciating pain all afternoon.

I couldn't help thinking about the pain I suffered for years because of *my* reckless and willful ways. My arrogance was such that I refused to learn from the experiences of others. My rebelliousness was such that when someone steered me one way, I would automatically head in the opposite direction. My immaturity was such that I always felt my case was different.

That day on the boat, while helping my fellow fisherman get through the pain of the sculpin's sting, I felt grateful for having become more teachable over the years. Because I'm now willing to listen to others and learn from their experiences, I'm frequently spared unnecessary pain.

THOUGHT FOR TODAY: Do I still sometimes insist that my case is different?

February 7

Alas! must it ever be so?
Do we stand in our own light, wherever we go,
And fight our own shadows forever?
                              —Owen Meredith

Even after a substantial period of growth, we can sometimes be overcome by a sense of uneasiness, unworthiness, and even impending doom.

Our relationships have been secure and loving, yet all at once we feel nervous around our friends, and distrustful of them. We have become financially secure, but suddenly fear that our material prosperity will somehow be taken from us. We are in excellent health, and have had more peace of mind than we ever thought possible, yet we can't help thinking that emotional and physical catastrophe is just around the corner.

We used to be riddled with such feelings, day in and day out. But at least now, thank God, these fears and phantoms arise only occasionally, and are short-lived.

We have worked hard to achieve health and harmony in our lives, and for the most part feel deserving of our blessings. We have grown accustomed to life running smoothly; the well-being we enjoy certainly seems far more natural than the discord and despair we used to know. These days, we expect and welcome harmony, good health, and loving relationships.

THOUGHT FOR TODAY: If a shadow briefly crosses my mind, that doesn't mean I am destined to live in darkness.

Prevention is so much better than healing.
—Thomas Adams

We've come to believe from our very personal experiences that many of the solutions to our physical and emotional problems lie within. Some of us call this healing force *inner wisdom,* others call it the *inner physician* or the *mind-body connection.*

In order to get in touch with the innate wisdom of our bodies, we often have to first quiet our minds. That way we can concentrate on the present moment and clear the channel to the power within. The practice of meditation has proven to be a most effective way to accomplish this.

In a place free from noise and other distractions, we focus our thoughts on how we feel, targeting the specific malaise or injury that is causing difficulty. We concentrate on self-healing, opening ourselves to direction from within.

We may learn during the meditation that our body needs more physical exercise, for example, or more rest, or less stress-producing activity. We may realize that we need to take more quality time for ourselves. Whatever the message, we are almost certain to benefit in some way.

THOUGHT FOR TODAY: Is my body trying to tell me something?

February 9

An excuse is a lie guarded.

—Jonathan Swift

Of all the ingredients necessary for successful weight loss, none has been more important than self-honesty. We needed a strong support system, but also needed to acknowledge that we are sometimes obsessed and almost always powerless over food. We had to find the food plan that is right for us, but also had to admit it when we temporarily returned to overeating.

At a deeper level, self-honesty has enabled us to unmask the roles and rationalizations that gave us "permission" to overeat. Some of us fancied ourselves as authorities on fine foods, for example. We knew the best restaurants and latest food trends. We used our gourmet image as an excuse to overeat.

Others among us thought of ourselves as "big people" who require a lot of food to sustain them. Our "big bones and big appetite" was our excuse to overeat. We were also "expert cooks." Since we spent hours in the kitchen, we deserved to enjoy the fruits of our talent and labor.

Only when we became honest enough to see through these roles—and willing enough to give them up once and for all—could we make steady progress toward our goal.

THOUGHT FOR TODAY: Denial delays progress; self-honesty destroys denial.

It is better to wear out than to rust out.
—Richard Cumberland

During the years I've been working out and participating in sports, I've had my share of minor injuries.
My initial reaction, almost invariably, is to become
angry and disappointed that I can't follow my regular
exercise program.

But my self-pity is usually short-lived. When I
think it through, I'm able to be more accepting of the
pulled muscle or tendinitis, as well as the necessary
recovery period. I'm even able to feel grateful for the
lifestyle that brings about such inevitabilities.

I consider, for example, that cycling, swimming,
and hiking—with their attendant risks—are infinitely
more rewarding than "rusting out" on a barstool. I
remind myself that occasional minor injuries are a
very small price to pay for the satisfaction, self-
esteem, and health benefits I derive from a physically
active life.

All of this is not to say that I am nonchalant about
my injuries. I try to learn from each one, in order to
prevent a reoccurrence. I do what's necessary to
accelerate the healing process and try not to be
impatient. And I try to use my downtime produc-
tively, while looking forward to the day when I will be
fully active again.

THOUGHT FOR TODAY: Life is activity and move-
ment; life is joy.

February 11

There's nothing constant in the universe,
All ebb and flow, and every shape that's born
Bears in its womb the seeds of change.

—Ovid

During the dawn of my new life, when rebirth and renewal began to seem possible, I frequently asked myself, "What do I need to change?" Since I carried with me a lengthy list of imperfections, character flaws, and bad habits, the overwhelming answer was, "Almost everything!"

By admonishing myself in that way, I created an increasingly heavy emotional burden. My overblown expectations not only set me up for failure, but caused great stress.

I eventually learned that a far more constructive question to ask myself was (and still is), "How can I let myself grow?" When I ask that question, my focus is less on flaws and self-improvement, and more on self-expansion. When I ask that question, it helps me think about the things I am doing that may be inhibiting my growth.

These days, I seldom ask myself, "What do I need to change?" That outdated question predicates change by *my* force of will, *my* capability alone. It excludes my most valuable resource for the kind of growth and change I desire. That resource is the grace and power of God.

THOUGHT FOR TODAY: I need not expect too much too soon.

*In the course of time, we grow to love things we once
hated and hate things we loved.*
                              —Robert Louis Stevenson

The meaning we give to events flows out of our sense
of self—how we see and value the person we are.
Indeed, our levels of self-awareness, self-acceptance,
and spiritual enlightenment determine not only our
reaction to individual events, but our outlook on life
in general.

   The breakup of a love relationship, for example,
could have various meanings. We could see it as one
more defeat, one more failure. We could even see it
as a sign that we are destined to be alone forever. Or,
the breakup could mean that we're ready to start
fresh, and make some overdue changes. It could offer
the opportunity to learn something new about ourselves.

   That's why it's so important to become ever more
aware of the kinds of meanings we attach to the
situations and circumstances that arise in our daily
lives. Clearly, our interpretation and reaction to these
events can be a major influence on our sense of
well-being, either strengthening or weakening it.

   From that standpoint, it's largely up to us
whether the path through life will be rutted and
rocky, or smooth and easily navigable.

THOUGHT FOR TODAY: I determine the significance of events.

Faith and works are like the light and heat of a candle; they cannot be separated.

—Joseph Beaumont

We all know people—in some cases, *ourselves*—who have had spiritual awakenings or spiritual experiences which signaled the onset of major transformations in their lives. However, few if any of us have been suddenly "struck" with faith that remains permanent and unwavering.

To be kept alive, faith has to be nurtured. To remain vital, faith has to be renewed regularly through prayer and meditation.

It is axiomatic that faith without works is dead. This means we keep our faith strong through willingness and actions. We put our faith into practice each day by relying on God for guidance and strength in all areas of our lives—doing what we can do on our own, and letting Him do for us what we are unable to do for ourselves.

Just as we express and renew our faith on a daily basis, that is how we reap its rewards. A daily affirmation of faith enables us to vanquish fear and doubt during that day. It affords us a clear and secure pathway through confusion. It brings us not only Divine guidance, but also the acceptance, courage, and power to carry out God's will.

THOUGHT FOR TODAY: As I act to strengthen my faith, my faith acts to strengthen me.

Loyalty to petrified opinion never yet broke a chain or freed a human soul.

—Mark Twain

It is said that pain has no memory. As far as physical pain is concerned, that's been mostly true in my life. I remember emotional pain more clearly; it is still traumatic to remember, for example, what it was like to feel boxed in and trapped month after month and year after year.

I truly believed at the time that I *was* trapped, that my life could never change for the better. And I blamed outside forces—other people, places, and things—for my circumstances.

In reality I was confined and limited by my own fears and closed-mindedness. I was unwilling to try anything new for fear that it wouldn't work out, or that I wouldn't look good. I was afraid of making mistakes. On top of that, I was full of pride; I had my own preconceived ideas and refused to listen to anyone else's opinions or suggestions.

That's why nothing really changed for so long, and therein lies one of my most painful memories. It was only when I realized that I was imprisoned by my own inflexible beliefs and habitual ways of responding that I began to find freedom.

THOUGHT FOR TODAY: Thank God, I'm free at last from self-confinement.

February 15

Be not too zealous; moderation is best in all things.
—Theognis

Those of us with "addictive personalities"—we know who we are—could never get enough of anything. Our entire lives revolved around excess of one kind or another—alcohol, drugs, food, destructive relationships, gambling.

Even in recovery, while making progress on the road to wellness, many of us still find it difficult to do things in moderation. When we find something we like, we almost always go overboard. No sooner do we discover a new sport or form of entertainment than we become obsessive participants or fans. We become fanatics about our diet or specific foods. We exercise till we drop.

The problem, of course, is that whenever we go to extremes in this way, we are bound to suffer. We neglect our responsibilities; relationships become tense; we begin to feel really uncomfortable.

When that happens, we need to remind ourselves what wellness and emotional sobriety are all about. Our goal is to enjoy rather than punish ourselves, to expand rather than restrict our lives. If this personal reminder isn't enough to turn us around, then perhaps it's time to reapply the same principles that enabled us to recover from our more serious addictions.

THOUGHT FOR TODAY: Is it time to admit I'm powerless over my obsession, and to ask for God's help?

The lively force of his mind has broken down all barriers, and has made its way far beyond the glittering walls of the Universe.

—Lucretius

We used to think that only in fairy tales could dreams become reality. But today we believe we can transform expectations into actualities by harnessing our innate capabilities—the positive energy of the mind and the determination of the spirit.

Let's say that our heart's desire is learning how to ski, or traveling abroad, or building a new career. We can focus our mental and emotional energy toward fulfillment of the goal by visualizing the details as we wish them to be.

For example, we can experience the exhilaration of speeding down a ski slope. We can enjoy the sensory images of a faraway destination. Or we can picture the pomp and ceremony of graduation and the rewards of our new vocation. All of these mental actions can be taken with the conviction that we are planting and nurturing a seed, that it will grow, that nothing can stop it from blooming.

Fears and doubts may surface. Rather than resist, we allow them to flow through us, without negative influence. If our mental images have enough positive energy behind them, they will surely inspire us to find creative ways to transcend any obstacles that may stand in our way.

THOUGHT FOR TODAY: The power of my mind and spirit can help turn aspirations into actualities.

February 17

The great art of learning, is to undertake but little at a time.

—John Locke

I have a friend who runs like the wind. She has a special grace and enthusiasm that is magnetic. As she follows her regular course on roads and beach paths near my home, people sometimes call out, "I wish I could run like you!" And she always calls back, "But you can!"

At one point, I had thoughts of becoming a runner myself, and I asked my friend how to get started. She began by telling me what not to do. Most people have a tendency to start out with overblown expectations of their mind and body, she said. They do too much too soon; they quickly become frustrated and discouraged, and may even injure themselves. They expect to quickly acquire a level of skill that only comes with training, patience, and experience, she added.

My friend and I agreed that in any new sport, there are several keys to becoming skillful and finding long-term fulfillment. It's usually helpful to get instruction, and it's also a good idea to prepare one's body with stretching exercises in order to develop flexibility and strength. Above all, it's essential to gradually ease into the sport rather than plunge in all at once.

THOUGHT FOR TODAY: I can take all the time I need to learn and grow in my sport.

*If you would learn self-mastery, begin by yielding
yourself to the One Great Master.*
—Johann Friedrich Lobstein

Many of us continue to have difficulty with the
spiritual concept of surrender. We know intellectually
that surrender is a positive rather than a negative
action, a pathway to transcendence and renewal.
We've seen the act of surrender bring about dramatic
changes in other people's lives. Yet we're still fighting
our own seemingly insoluble problems and dilemmas.

If we find ourselves in this position, we might want
to think about the French term for surrender—*se
rendre*. Its literal translation is "to give oneself over,"
which is certainly different than giving in or giving up.

To what or to whom can we give ourselves over
when we surrender in this manner?

We stop trying through willpower and stubborn
determination to quench our raging obsessions and
give ourselves over to spiritual solutions.

We stop clashing with others by trying to mold
them to our ideals; we *give ourselves over* to the
reality that, with God's help, we can only change
ourselves.

We accept our own powerlessness and *give ourselves over* to the power of God.

THOUGHT FOR TODAY: I will stop fighting the
problem and give myself over to the solution.

Everything without tells the individual that he is nothing; everything within persuades him that he is everything.

—Xavier Doudan

It's hard not to compare ourselves—our looks, our capabilities, our personal style—with "paragons of perfection." We know who they are: models, actors, sports figures, celebrities of one kind or another. No matter where we turn, we are bombarded with visual and editorial superlatives about them.

Needless to say, we fall short in these comparisons. We always have and always will. For most of us, "falling short" in this regard may not be devastating, but it certainly can result in a subtle and steady erosion of our self-image and self-confidence.

In order to strengthen our self-image, we have to develop respect for our uniqueness and individuality. The culture may define beauty in terms of a particular body shape or facial structure, but what qualities do we find attractive? What about traits other than physical ones?

Current fashion may try to dictate the styles and colors of the clothing we buy, but what do we like to wear? What looks best on us?

The point is, we need to define and aspire to our own sense of what is beautiful, successful, stylish. We need to determine and hold fast to what's right for us individually.

THOUGHT FOR TODAY: I am unique, positively so.

I've shut the door on yesterday
And thrown the key away—
Tomorrow holds no fears for me,
Since I have found today.

—Vivian Yeiser Laramore

People who grow up in dysfunctional families—who are mistreated, ignored, or abused—often enter the world lacking not only self-esteem, but trust. If we can't trust our mothers and fathers, how can we trust anyone else?

Lack of trust is but one example of how negative past experiences can define and even create present and future experiences. With the darkness of the past shadowing every thought and action, one can hardly gain inner security and personal freedom.

In order to live joyously and freely today, we first must come to terms with the past. We can do this in many ways, and with many avenues of support.

When we do, we will learn that just because we couldn't trust our parents, that doesn't mean we can't trust ourselves and our friends today. We will learn that just because we grew up financially insecure, that doesn't mean we have to forever fear not having enough. We will learn that just because we were once abandoned physically or emotionally, that doesn't mean we will be unappreciated and alone all the days of our lives.

THOUGHT FOR TODAY: These moments and hours are mine, to shape and live anew.

February 21

Every stroke our fury strikes is sure to hit ourselves at last.

—William Penn

The longer I live, and the more I try to improve the quality of my life, the more aware I am of the negative power of certain emotions. I stand guard against anger in particular. From years of painful experience, I know full well its potential for destructive impact on my body, mind, and spirit.

When I allow the spark of anger to flare, there is an adrenaline rush. My heart pumps rapidly, blood pulses furiously, and my entire body tenses into a high-stress "fight or flight" mode.

When anger takes over, I quickly lose perspective and see everything in extremes. My rationality suffers, as does my emotional equilibrium. I may act impulsively and unrestrainedly, saying or doing things that will cause still greater harm.

When anger displaces acceptance, I forget about my inability to change other people's behavior or the course of events. I forget about the spiritual principles I try to live by—tolerance, understanding, compassion. I develop tunnel vision, revert to extreme self-centeredness, and temporarily lose whatever humility I've gained.

THOUGHT FOR TODAY: In all my thoughts, actions, and interactions, self-restraint will be the watchword.

Gratitude is the memory of the heart.
—Jean Baptiste Massieu

Thanks to God's loving goodness, our lives are richly blessed. We are healthy and whole in mind and body. We have warm, caring friendships and feel connected to our fellows. There is a sense of purpose and direction in our lives.

We've learned to trust ourselves. Our intuitive voices have become stronger and more clear, enabling us to make the choices and decisions that lead to a successful life. Most of the time we are at peace with ourselves. We have a growing sense of self-esteem.

The most meaningful and satisfying way to express our gratitude to God, we've found, is to share our blessings. We try to live our lives as channels for God's goodness, sharing our gifts by reaching out in friendship, by being available when needed, by offering experience, empathy, and encouragement. We give of ourselves by showing interest and enthusiasm in the lives of others, especially our own family members.

Above all, we try to be kind and loving with no strings attached, in the spirit of God's unconditional kindness and love toward us.

THOUGHT FOR TODAY: The more I give, the more I receive.

February 23

Action may not always bring happiness, but there is no happiness without action.

—Benjamin Disraeli

It's not that we've sat back and passively watched our world deteriorate. For months—in our relationship, job, or living situation—we've tried to communicate our unhappiness, and have encouraged the others involved to respond in some constructive way.

We've firmly stated our case, offering possible solutions and compromises. We've prayed to be more accepting and resilient. We've done a lot of soul-searching, examining our attitudes, reactions, and motives; we've asked ourselves, "Is the situation as bad as it seems, or is it just me?"

In short, we've done all we can, but to no avail. The person we're dealing with hasn't given an inch, or made the slightest effort to work with us. We've reached an emotional bottom; our suffering is beyond endurance. In the interest of our health and sanity, it's clearly time to make a major change—to leave the relationship, or resign from the job.

What we must now do ranks among the most difficult and heart-wrenching actions we've ever had to take. We know deep down, however, that God didn't intend us to live this way. So we ask for His help, for the courage and strength to move forward to a better life.

THOUGHT FOR TODAY: With God in my life, I always have what it takes to do what is necessary.

The heart has always the pardoning power.
—Madame Swetchine

At a concert one summer, a friend and I turned to each other with knowing looks when the unmistakable odor of marijuana smoke drifted into our area.

"I smoked that stuff for a long time," my friend said ruefully. "After I got clean and sober, I read a report that said that long-term marijuana use causes irreversible brain damage. I still remember one quote: 'It will make a bright student average, and an average student dull.'

"That really upset me," she continued. "For a while I was terribly angry at myself for damaging my mind, for thwarting my potential."

I told her that I had experienced similar feelings. Decades of alcohol and drug use had unquestionably resulted in a certain amount of brain damage. I, too, had been angry at myself.

We talked about it some more, agreeing that self-forgiveness was essential in coming to terms with our past behavior. Fortunately, we both accepted those years of illness-related self-destructiveness as part of our destiny.

What helped us most was the gratitude we felt for our sobriety and that we had stopped drinking and using when we did—before causing even greater damage.

THOUGHT FOR TODAY: Self-forgiveness can heal the wounds of my past.

February 25

He who considers too much will perform little.
        —Johann Christoph Friedrich von Schiller

Saturday dawns clear and crisp—a perfect morning for tennis. We begin to play, but half an hour into the first set we start thinking about the other things we could have done, or should have done.

Many of us do that; we make a choice, then almost immediately begin nibbling away at ourselves with doubts. Before long we are so distracted that it's impossible to enjoy what we're doing, whether it's tennis, shopping, or working in the garden.

With life's normal pressures, it's difficult enough to make the right choices and follow through with them; our tentativeness springs from too many options, too much advice, too little time, plus in some cases a lack of self-confidence. But when we second-guess ourselves *after* we've finally made a choice, it's doubly difficult.

If we take a moment to think about it, it's clear that most of our feelings of happiness, enjoyment, and satisfaction come in relatively short bursts. All the more reason to savor what we are doing while we are doing it. All the more reason to accept each choice we've made and fully surrender to the experiences it brings.

THOUGHT FOR TODAY: I will trust the decisions and choices I've worked so hard to make.

We may give advice but we do not inspire conduct.
—Duc de La Rochefoucauld

It's natural to want to pass along what we have learned. Indeed, that is one of the mainstays of our new life: The more we give of ourselves, the more we receive. So we don't hesitate to tell our close friends and family members what we have discovered, what we have achieved, and how our lives have been transformed.

We are such grateful nonsmokers, for example, that we eagerly encourage our loved ones to follow our example in order to benefit as we have. We feel so much better since we've changed our eating habits that we can't resist urging our spouse or partner to do the same. We have gained so much inner peace by following spiritual principles that it's all we can do to avoid proselytizing our friends.

Lest we become disappointed or even annoyed at others for not following our lead, we need to remember that each person makes life-affirming choices in his or her own time, not our time. We can give advice based on our own success, and perhaps we can inspire by example, but we can't cause others to act until they are ready and willing to do so.

THOUGHT FOR TODAY: Am I coming on too strong?

February 27

Only a mediocre person is always at his best.
— William Somerset Maugham

I really messed up yesterday. To begin with, I ate all the wrong foods; I don't know what possessed me, but I made a real pig out of myself. On top of that, I was moody and irritable. At one point I snapped at a dear friend, bringing her to the verge of tears. My boorishness dragged on all day, and I didn't do a thing to bring myself out of it.

For the first hour after I awakened this morning, I compounded it all by mercilessly beating myself up for my rotten attitude and behavior. Indeed, my guilt and remorse threatened to bring out the worst in me all over again. I had to get off my case, and quickly.

Don't get me wrong. I'm not about to take yesterday's actions lightly; I'm quite ashamed. In fact, my first order of business is to apologize to the people I offended.

I'm hardly perfect, nor can I be at the top of my form every single day. But what I can do, starting right now, is learn something from yesterday's events. I can also try to forgive myself, put it behind me, and concentrate on making the very best out of today.

THOUGHT FOR TODAY: I can punish myself for missteps of the past—or I can try to benefit from them.

We live amid surfaces, and the true art is to skate well on them.

—Ralph Waldo Emerson

When overeating was a problem in our lives, any number of triggers would set off the compulsion. None, however, was more threatening and insistent than stress. Along these lines, an occasional glance at the past can go a long way toward keeping us on track in the present.

There was the time we were laid off from work, and then the time our car was rear-ended. Events like those invariably resulted in a weight gain. Come to think of it, to be perfectly honest, even minor stresses such as a bank error or a lost earring could send us rushing to the refrigerator for solace.

Over time, we've become keenly aware of the kinds of stressors that can bring on overeating relapses. It took a lot of trial and error, but eventually we learned new ways to handle stress that *didn't* involve eating. Now when we are upset, we "take five"; we talk about our feelings; we make an entry in our "stress diary"; we say a prayer.

These days, in short, we try to make certain that the motivating factors for *when* and *what* we eat are positive rather than negative in nature.

THOUGHT FOR TODAY: Eating because of stress only causes more stress.

March 1

Nothing is so easy as to deceive one's self, for what we wish we readily believe; but such expectations are often inconsistent with the reality of things.
—Demosthenes

I postponed giving up smoking for many reasons, but none was more compelling than the fear that I might gain a lot of weight.

My vanity was such that the prospect of putting on even a few pounds, and becoming "less attractive," was unthinkable. Besides that, I reasoned, everyone knows that excess weight is a proven detriment to health. So what's the point of trading one health hazard for another?

Of course, all of this was not only negative projection, it was pure rationalization—just one more excuse to avoid facing and dealing with my addiction.

When I eventually became completely ready to give up smoking, part of my willingness was accepting the possibility that I would gain weight. Willingness led to surrender: With God's help I was able to face and get through those early weeks of withdrawal and irritability.

As it turned out, I didn't gain any weight. This is not to say that everyone will have the same experience. In terms of health priorities, however, most rational people will agree that it's far more important to give up smoking than to put it off to avoid a temporary weight gain.

THOUGHT FOR TODAY: Has my addiction convinced me that it's the lesser of two evils?

I am erecting a barrier of simplicity between myself and the world.

—André Gide

We're sitting on a park bench on a sunny afternoon. Nearby a group of children are romping in the grass. We can't help smiling at the sound of their laughter and the sight of their high-spirited antics. And we can't help feeling a little envious of their carefree, uncomplicated lives.

Then we sigh, thinking, "Childhood is over, and now I'm an adult. My life has to be more complicated. That's just the way it is."

True, adulthood brings new goals and difficult challenges, as well as myriad responsibilities of all kinds. However, spirit-numbing complexity and confusion need not be part of the package. Indeed, for the most part our lives are as complicated as we make them.

All too often, we make choices which are bound to bring on complications. We rent an apartment or buy a house we can barely afford financially. We commit ourselves to a job or relationship we can barely afford emotionally. Before long we are overwhelmed, wondering why our life is all work and no play.

But it's never too late to make courageous new choices that can turn things around. Life is too short and precious to do otherwise.

THOUGHT FOR TODAY: I'll try to keep it simple.

March 3

Simplicity, simplicity, simplicity. I say, let your affairs be as two or three, and not a hundred or a thousand. . . . Simplify, simplify.

—Henry David Thoreau

It's taken quite a while and caused us much emotional anguish, but we've finally decided to somehow simplify our life. Year after year everything has become increasingly complex. We've been paying an unwanted toll of health-threatening and life-shortening stress.

What are some of the choices we can make to reduce the pressures of an overly complicated existence? What can we actually do?

To begin with, we can try to simplify our needs overall. For example, we can try to avoid unnecessary debt by not buying things we can't afford. We can try to limit our use of charge cards and high-interest revolving accounts. In other words, we can shift life's emphasis from quantity to quality.

We can think about redefining and reestablishing personal goals. We can try not to overschedule our days. We can stop taking on too much, constantly disappointing our friends and ourselves.

Another way to reduce complexity and confusion is to avoid being overly analytical. If, instead, we look for simple answers and solutions to our day-to-day living problems, life will surely become less stressful and more pleasurable.

THOUGHT FOR TODAY: Complexity or simplicity—I really do have a choice.

For he who much has suffered, much will know.
                                                              —Homer

Like most people who have been physically, emotionally, or spiritually bankrupt, I've learned a great deal from suffering. Suffering taught me to ask for and accept help from others and God. I also gained understanding, empathy, and compassion for my fellows. Above all, I learned not to take anything for granted—neither health, love, nor material possessions. I learned to be grateful for today's blessings.

But I've also come to understand that suffering has no intrinsic value, even though at times I feel and act otherwise. For example, suffering doesn't help me atone for past wrongs by "evening the score," nor does it free me of guilt.

By the same token, suffering doesn't enhance my self-esteem or increase my prestige; it doesn't make people think more highly of me. And although there are many myths and legends to the contrary, suffering doesn't sharpen my creative powers.

While suffering brought me to my knees and into the arms of God, I believe with all my heart that it is not necessary for me to suffer further in order to continue receiving His boundless love.

THOUGHT FOR TODAY: Pain is sometimes a catalyst for change, but it is not a necessary ingredient for ongoing progress.

March 5

Forgiveness saves the expense of anger, the cost of hatred, the waste of spirits.

—Hannah More

Why do some of us still have trouble practicing forgiveness? Why is it so difficult to make this spiritual tool work for us?

One reason is that we may not yet be willing to give up our imagined "edge" over those who wronged us. By withholding forgiveness, we feel that we are punishing them in some way, that they still "owe us," and therefore, we have control.

Another possible reason is a lack of understanding of what forgiveness is, and how it actually works. One common misapprehension is that forgiveness will somehow weaken us—that it will be an admission that the wrong committed against us was "okay," or that we deserved to be harmed.

In light of the serious damage that ongoing resentments cause, there can be no valid reason for postponing forgiveness. Indeed, forgiveness is one of the most emotionally freeing and spiritually uplifting actions we can take.

We may be powerless in many areas of our lives, but the act of forgiveness gives us considerable power to become free of resentments, to come to terms with the past, to repair damaged relationships, and to get on with our lives.

THOUGHT FOR TODAY: By forgiving you, I heal myself.

The whole trouble is that we won't let God help us.
—George MacDonald

When our character defects or old habit patterns occasionally surface these days, as they are bound to, they usually do so in relatively minor ways. We may exhibit a bit of selfishness; our temper may flare, and we may briefly seethe with resentment. Or we may temporarily seek comfort from food during a trying time.

Such shortcomings are hardly grave, nor do they necessarily cause real damage to us or anyone else. Nevertheless, they certainly have the potential to spoil a nice day, to cause tension in a relationship, and to do serious harm if allowed to continue.

One would think that such minor flaws and frailties could easily be handled and put to rest. But obviously that's not the case, since they reemerge in spite of our best efforts to keep them under control.

God doesn't expect us to become rid of our flaws on our own. This is true not only with difficult and life-threatening behavior patterns, but also with ones that are simply annoying and frustrating. God's help is always available. All we need to do is become completely willing to have our character defects removed, and then humbly ask Him to do so.

THOUGHT FOR TODAY: Do I turn to my Higher Power only for the "big" things?

March 7

An acre of performance is worth the whole world of promise.

—Jeremiah Brown Howell

I have a friend who is notoriously lax about keeping her commitments. She promises to call, to meet me, or to take care of something, but almost invariably doesn't follow through. Later, there is always a phone call and profuse apology; I can tell that she has suffered more than I have because of her irresponsibility.

In a way her behavior keeps me on track. It reminds me of the pain I once caused myself and others by failing to keep commitments. If I close my eyes I can still hear accusing voices from the past: "Where were you—you were supposed to be here hours ago!" "How come you didn't call?" "We missed the deadline—thanks to you."

Now that I've become a more responsible and dependable person, I feel so much better about myself. Each time I keep a promise, fulfill a commitment, or show up on time, I gain that much more self-respect.

There's no question that failure to fulfill commitments (no matter how seemingly inconsequential) hurts no one more than one's self. But an equally important truth is that the pattern is completely reversible, with commensurately positive results.

THOUGHT FOR TODAY: Can others depend on me? Can I depend on myself?

I am suffocated and lost when I have not the bright feeling of progression.

—Margaret Fuller

Those of us who have come to thrive on regular exercise know how important it is to choose and follow a varied, balanced program. By cross-training—that is, combining several activities such as walking, cycling, and swimming—we are able to minimize boredom and possible injury while maximizing satisfaction and total fitness.

We've found that an exercise diary is an excellent way to track the balance and schedule that's right for us. We keep a daily written record of the type of sport or workout, the time of day, and the number of minutes spent exercising.

There are other advantages to such a diary. It's a quick and accurate measure of progress. Moreover, if we feel discouraged or self-critical, it can be uplifting to turn back the pages and review our past efforts.

Some of us record our mental and emotional state following each workout. That way we're better able to understand what makes us enthusiastic and energetic one day, and lackadaisical and awkward the next. Overall, our exercise diary helps us remain consistent, improve our performance, and further our progress.

THOUGHT FOR TODAY: Look what I've accomplished! I'm proud of it.

March 9

We know the truth, not only by the reason, but by the heart.

—Blaise Pascal

When at long last we became open-minded, it was truly inspiring to read and hear about the power of spirituality. It was hard not to be moved when people described how they were freed of their resentments by practicing forgiveness, and how much more comfortable and harmonious their lives had become.

Each time someone exulted about the sense of purpose and fulfillment they received by being of service, our own long-standing reluctance to serve others faded a little more. Who could remain unaffected by so many examples of lives transformed through the power of prayer and the living principles of kindness, tolerance, and love?

These and other spiritual principles have existed throughout the ages, and have become available in many forms and from many sources. Yet each of us must discover them in our own time and our own way.

As we learn, we come to believe that the principles are indeed true and valuable; but only when we begin practicing them do we come to *know* their full value. Only when we apply them to the circumstances of our own lives do they become a part of us.

THOUGHT FOR TODAY: Have my beliefs become my way of life?

I travel not to go anywhere, but to go.
—Robert Louis Stevenson

Soon after I began taking long walks, a friend gave me an electronic pedometer. It shows me the distance I've walked, the number of steps I've taken, the time that has elapsed, and so on.

After using the pedometer for several days, I determined that I walk at an average rate of four miles per hour. My first reaction was disappointment. Four miles an hour didn't seem very fast; I couldn't cover much ground at that speed.

But then I started looking at it in a different way. When I travel in cars or on airplanes, the world goes by in a blur; there is little intimacy or involvement with my surroundings. I can get from one place to another quickly, to be sure, but a lot is lost in the process.

When I'm cruising along on foot, in contrast, I regain my identity and become part of the world around me. I am aware of myself as an individual, and not just one of a multitude on a 300-passenger jet or in a stream of speeding cars.

Just by taking a walk, I can reduce the world's speed to four miles per hour. It's reassuring to have that choice.

THOUGHT FOR TODAY: Walking allows me to gear down and regain my serenity.

March 11

Thought is deeper than all speech,
Feeling deeper than all thought.

— Christopher Pearse Cranch

We were forever battling our feelings. Some of us had been taught that they were unacceptable and ought to be kept hidden. Others among us made that choice on our own, fearing the consequences of intense emotions set free.

In either case, we were tormented; we came to see our passionate feelings as embarrassing or in some way dangerous. So we stuffed them deep inside, where they constantly gnawed away at us.

In recovery, we learned from others how to come to terms with our feelings—how to understand and deal with them. Little by little, we learned to accept and embrace our feelings instead of fearing or disowning them.

As we continue to grow and mature, our feelings are becoming increasingly positive in nature. We feel love far more often than anger, and serenity far more often than turmoil.

When we occasionally experience an onslaught of negative emotions these days, we know they won't last forever. Moreover, we've learned that we don't have to isolate ourselves or bury our negative feelings for fear that people will shun us. Even when we are resentful, confused, or filled with self-pity, our friends will accept and love us.

THOUGHT FOR TODAY: My emotional well-being is greatly influenced by my attitude and approach to my feelings.

A judicious friend is better than a zealous one.
　　　　　　　　　　　—James Sheridan Knowles

We've learned a lot about the valuable principle of detachment. We know from experience that we can't "fix" other people, or even solve their problems. We also know how futile it is to take responsibility for someone else's actions or attitudes. In short, we've come to accept our powerlessness over others and learned to detach ourselves emotionally.

Yet when someone we're close to is entangled in personal problems or facing adversity of one kind or another, it's hard not to absorb their stress. Because we care so much about the person, it's difficult not to become overly involved emotionally.

What happens when we take on someone else's stress? First, we unnecessarily create stress for ourselves. Second, we diminish our ability to be helpful and supportive. And third, we may lose our objectivity while adding fuel to the fire.

Yet if we practice detachment, we can stay clear of another person's emotional whirlpool. Detachment also enables us to retain our individuality, and fortify ourselves during times of crisis, so that we can be truly helpful to a friend or loved one in need.

THOUGHT FOR TODAY: To empathize with someone is to "walk in their shoes"—not take on their pain or stress.

March 13

His madness was not of the head, but heart.
—George Gordon Byron

It is still embarrassing to admit, but feelings of self-loathing governed my thoughts and actions practically all my life. Those feelings were so intense that they forced me into a chronically self-destructive lifestyle.

In recovery, I began to realize that my perception of myself was absolutely false. My mind was feeding me erroneous information; the fact that I not only believed it, but continued to act on it, was sheer insanity.

I further realized that not a single friend or family member had feelings toward me remotely similar to my own. I alone saw myself as a despicable person. It became quite clear that my lifelong view of myself was a total distortion of reality.

It was a major psychological and spiritual breakthrough to understand my self-loathing as a form of insanity. Because then I was able not only to become aware of the true magnitude of the problem, but also to acknowledge that it was far too serious to overcome without God's help.

These days when I am occasionally threatened by self-hate, I don't try to wish or will those thoughts and feelings away. I ask God to restore me to sane thinking and sane actions.

THOUGHT FOR TODAY: Is my perception of myself grounded in reality?

*Practice yourself, for heaven's sake, in little things;
and thence proceed to greater.*

—Epictetus

There was a time when we hardly ever tried to learn anything new. We felt comfortable sticking with the familiar, with activities and avocations we already could do well. So we turned our backs on new sports, art forms, hobbies, and even career opportunities.

To be sure, we had our dreams. Some of us wanted to become actors, musicians, skiers, or tennis players, but our egos prevented us from following through. Our immaturity was such that if we couldn't do something well in the first ten minutes, we didn't want to do it at all.

One of the most important things we've learned in recovery is that there's far more to life than winning approval and looking good. As time goes by, those self-centered needs mean less and less to us.

Recovery is all about expansion and enrichment. We're becoming more open to taking risks, to trying new pursuits. We're becoming willing to start out slowly, to make mistakes, to fall down and then get up again. Little by little and step by step, we're realizing our fondest dreams.

THOUGHT FOR TODAY: Am I willing to be a beginner?

March 15

This world has been harsh and strange;
Something is wrong; there needeth a change.
—Robert Browning

A good friend of mine owns a restaurant and occasionally I stop by for a snack. Even when business is slow he seems rushed, and his greeting is little more than a friendly wave.

On a recent visit, my friend took the time to have a cup of coffee with me. Caught by surprise, I asked, "Is something wrong?"

He laughed and went on to explain that he was making a major effort to be more relaxed, not just on his day off, but at work.

"I know how uptight I've always been, you don't have to remind me," he said. "But I just felt that if I went about things in a relaxed way, I'd lose control of this place. If I relaxed, I thought, I'd be less motivated and productive. If I even appeared to be relaxed, my employees wouldn't take me seriously.

"Behaving like that," he continued, "there was no pleasure left here. I was at the point where it was either change, or sell. Now that I'm learning to relax, I can't believe how much more productive and motivated I am. My employees are more responsive too. Best of all, I have energy and time to spare."

THOUGHT FOR TODAY: Am I reluctant to relax, for fear of losing control?

It is a folly to expect men to do all that they may reasonably be expected to do.

—Richard Whately

Our expectations of other people have the potential to cause us great pain; that is one of the most valuable and practical lessons we're learning in our new life. Plainly and simply, we are powerless over the actions or inactions of everyone except ourselves.

Of course, learning a principle is one thing, and regularly putting it to use is quite another. Because we are human, it's all too easy for our fond hopes to turn into expectations, especially in close relationships. That's why, when we feel disappointed by a family member or loved one, it can be helpful to uncover and then discard any unrealistic expectations we may have developed.

Perhaps we *expect* our grown children to be more ambitious or successful. Perhaps we *expect* our partner or spouse to be more understanding or giving. Or perhaps we *expect* our parents to start treating us in a whole new way, because *we* have changed and progressed in recovery.

The point is, it's not the actions or inactions of others that usually cause us emotional distress, but our unrealistic and unfulfilled expectations of others.

THOUGHT FOR TODAY: It's easier on everyone when I accept others as they are.

The greater part of progress is the desire to progress.
—Seneca

How do we know we are making progress on the road to physical, emotional, and spiritual well-being? How do we know we're growing? As children we could stand against a doorjamb and our parents would measure us, so they could mark and compare our growth year by year. But what about today?

We know we are growing because there is stability and serenity in our life. For many years we knew only erratic swings—euphoric highs, depressing lows, unending stress.

We know we are making progress because we have become more self-confident and assertive, and less self-conscious and fearful.

We know we've changed for the better because we have an increasingly clear idea of who we are, of our capabilities and limitations, of our wants and needs, of where we are going.

We know we are growing because we now care deeply about our health, and over time have dramatically altered our lifestyle in order to enhance and preserve it.

We know we are moving at the right pace, on the right path, because we feel a true sense of oneness with others and our Creator.

THOUGHT FOR TODAY: My growth is clearly evident in the way I think, the way I act, the way I live.

Do not live to eat, but eat that you may live.
—Dionysius

During a ten-year span of my life, I was substantially overweight. Periodically, after ignoring my condition for as long as I could, something would push me back into dieting. The impetus could be a year-end resolution, or a tailor telling me that my pants couldn't be let out any more.

I usually chose hard-core diets which severely limited my calorie intake. I favored shakes taken in place of meals, although I recall once trying something called "The Drinking Man's Diet."

The outcome was always the same. I'd lose ten or fifteen pounds; then within several months I would regain all of it and sometimes more.

I've since learned that there's much more to losing weight and keeping it off than ingesting fewer calories. For me, success in weight control has meant a change in lifestyle. I've had to learn about nutrition and make gradual yet eventually dramatic and permanent changes in my eating habits.

I've also had to change my relationship with food. Where once I used food as a reward, as a source of comfort, or as a means of celebration, for example, I now eat for the right reason—to promote and maintain my physical well-being.

THOUGHT FOR TODAY: I can best change my outside by changing from the inside.

March 19

It is one of the beautiful compensations of life that no man can sincerely try to help another, without help-ing himself.

—Gamaliel Bailey

At one time or another, each of us is called upon to care for an ill family member or dear friend. Invari-ably, we spring into action without a second thought. We gladly and unhesitatingly attend to every need, actual or anticipated.

When the crisis has passed, the expressions of gratitude are effusive. "I don't know what I would have done without you," we are told. Naturally, we feel good about ourselves for having been there, and we are glad our friend or loved one is on the mend.

Following such an experience, we might ask our-selves if we're in the habit of "rewarding" illness—with our attentiveness, patience, and warmth—to a greater extent than we reward health. True, those we're close to need us more when they are sick, but they also require and value our care and support when trying to stay healthy.

How can we reward our friends' and loved ones' pursuit of health? We can express our encouragement and love by taking an active interest in their exercise or food plans, by complimenting them on discipline and progress, and by reminding them how well they look and how much better they are feeling.

THOUGHT FOR TODAY: Do I ration my love and save it for emergencies?

Nothing in the world so solid as a thought.
—Ralph Waldo Emerson

There are days when I focus on everything I don't like about myself—my job, where I live, even my recreational activities. When I think in these terms, the energy is drawn right out of me. I wear a scowl and feel hateful and depressed.

Today, with God's help, I will make a supreme effort to think loving thoughts about myself and the people and situations that affect me personally. Instead of noticing and becoming preoccupied with the imperfect aspects of individuals and circumstances, I will try to think generous and accepting thoughts.

If I am even partially successful, I am bound to derive greater satisfaction from all that I experience, and to feel good about myself again. I will feel buoyant, uplifted, and joyful; I will bring these positive emotions into everything I do.

Today I will strive for love and harmony among myself, my fellows, and the circumstances of my life. Through my words, thoughts, and deeds, I can become a channel for God's goodness. His love inspires me, and hopefully my loving thoughts and actions will in turn influence and even inspire others.

THOUGHT FOR TODAY: Loving thoughts can bring on loving feelings.

March 21

Happiness grows at our own firesides, and is not to be picked in strangers' gardens.

—Douglas Jerrold

Despite everything we have learned, at times we unwittingly resurrect the old idea that other people, places, or things will bring us the happiness and fulfillment that is sometimes lacking in our lives.

We may meet someone new and be swept away by the belief that this person is the answer to our loneliness, boredom, or depression. Or perhaps we become suddenly captivated by an expensive piece of jewelry or article of clothing that we feel can somehow bring us out of the emotional doldrums.

In truth, whenever we enter into a relationship with such unrealistic expectations, that relationship will more than likely fail. Similarly, whenever we acquire something material in the belief that it will make us content and whole, we are bound to be disappointed and left feeling emptier than before.

Happiness comes only from within. It comes from thinking and acting in ways that make us feel good and right. It comes from being responsible and finishing what we've started. It comes from treating others as we would like to be treated. Most of all, it comes from feeling grateful for the blessings in our lives.

THOUGHT FOR TODAY: I am responsible for my own happiness.

The business of life is to go forward.
—Samuel Johnson

As a young man, before I had yet faced any hardships, I believed that health, happiness, and security would come automatically. It didn't occur to me that I would have to learn *how* to live, and work for physical and emotional well-being.

The most perplexing part of this misconception was that my life during those years was anything but carefree and fulfilled. To the contrary, it was complicated, deadly serious, and shot through with fear. What a rude awakening I had when I crashed and burned in my early twenties for the first time.

It has been a slow, evolutionary process, but my beliefs along these lines have changed 180 degrees since then. Yes, I believe that each of us has a Divine birthright, that God intends us to be happy, joyous, and free. But I also believe with equal fervor that achieving a quality life and sense of well-being requires a great deal of willingness, commitment, and *effort* on our part.

God's gifts have always been freely available—there is no question in my mind about that. But I will continue receiving them only by continuing to seek them and work for them on a daily basis.

THOUGHT FOR TODAY: The gifts of life are in plain view, but I must do the footwork to attain them.

Change is not made without inconvenience, even from worse to better.

—Richard Hooker

When we became committed to changing our lifestyle and improving our health, one of our first challenges was to break away from old routines. Of course, this was easier said than done. Many regular activities, familiar places, and even times of day had for years been closely linked with habits harmful to our health.

Day after day, for example, we skipped breakfast and ate processed food at the same lunch stand. Each evening we came home from work and just sat around. We had fallen into the habit of rewarding ourselves, on the slightest pretext, with high-calorie, high-fat desserts.

It took not only awareness and willingness, but also a considerable amount of discipline on our part to break old routines and create new ones. However, we soon became accustomed to waking up earlier to eat a nutritious breakfast and fix lunch. Once we got into the habit of exercising after work, we looked forward to it.

On a broader scale, we started each day with a period of reflection or meditation. We practiced the art of saying, "No, thank you" during times of temptation, and we stayed in close touch with the people who were supportive of our positive efforts.

THOUGHT FOR TODAY: Changing old routines can move me more quickly along the road to health.

My mind's my kingdom.

—Francis Quarles

No one can disagree that the human mind has incredible power. In countless ways it directly influences the way we feel, leading us to the heights of elation or the depths of despair. As we well know, the mind also affects our physical health and can play a decisive role in whether an illness abates or lingers.

In the past, many of us stood by helplessly as our minds deceived us and eroded our sense of well-being. But now, thank God, we're able to put all that behind us. It's time to focus on our mind's positive capabilities—to tap into that miraculous power and channel it toward physical and emotional wellness.

From the vantage point of recovery, it can be fascinating and useful to objectively observe our mind's messages to us during the course of each day. We can discover what negative beliefs we're still holding and see how they continue to influence our health and self-image.

Once we've learned to do that on a regular basis, it's only a small step—albeit a hugely rewarding one—to control the power of our mind rather than helplessly allow it to control us.

THOUGHT FOR TODAY: God designed my mind to serve rather than savage me.

March 25

Reckon the days in which you have not been angry. I used to be angry every day; then every other day; then every third and fourth day; and if you miss it so long as thirty days, offer a sacrifice of thanksgiving to God.

—Epictetus

I used to explain the roiling rage I so often felt by telling people that I was "born angry." In reality the anger within me built steadily over years and years. Along the way, my explosive behavior caused considerable damage.

It was all too obvious how my anger harmed the people around me. I could see it in their faces—in the expressions of fear, disappointment, and embarrassment. The toll was also evident in destroyed relationships and lost jobs.

What was not obvious was the degree to which my anger damaged me physically. Only in recent years have I learned that unbridled anger is the epitome of inner stress. As such, it disrupted and depressed my immune system, increasing my vulnerability to chronic and even life-threatening illnesses.

As my anger receded in recovery, it left room within me for the gestation and eventual birth of faith. It gave way also to the possibilities of understanding, caring, loving, and giving. As these qualities grew, my anger continued to subside—to the point where I suffer from it only rarely in my life today.

THOUGHT FOR TODAY: Thank you, God, for making recovery possible.

He walks with nature, and her paths are peace.
—Edward Young

When it comes to emotional and spiritual revitalization, there's nothing quite like being outdoors. Indoor activities are fine, and frequently our only choice, but when we create or take the opportunity to work out in a natural setting, something very special takes place.

If we are fortunate enough to be able to walk or run on a beach, for example, we are treated to the sight of pelicans skimming the waves. We may spot a school of dolphins, a wayward seal, or come upon an interesting shell or bit of driftwood. We can smell and taste damp salt air.

On higher ground, riding a mountain bike in the hills, we may spot a coyote, a roadrunner, or a deer. We capture the sound and feel of wind as we speed down an incline. We witness and savor the seasons, from the first blur of green in spring to the crunch of fallen leaves in autumn.

Exercising in a city park offers a different sort of kaleidoscope. Apart from shifting sights, sounds, and colors, there is always the fun of people-watching. After being confined indoors, it's comforting and renewing to be warmed by the sun and caressed by the breeze.

THOUGHT FOR TODAY: Outdoor activities can add a new dimension to my fitness program.

March 27

Facing it—always facing it—that's the way to get through. Face it!

—Joseph Conrad

When we were little and fearsome shadows loomed on the bedroom wall, we pulled the covers over our head and pretended the images weren't there. Most of us have long since outgrown our childhood fears and fantasies; all too often, however, we hide from the realities of adulthood that generate fear and stress.

For example, we avoid confronting a person who is causing us emotional pain—a boorish neighbor, a nasty co-worker, a hurtful parent. We cancel doctors' appointments and reschedule lab tests for fear of what we might find out about our physical condition. When we are having financial problems, we hide overdue bills in a drawer and pretend we never received them.

Like the shadows of childhood, the longer we deny or hide from such problems, the larger and more frightening they become.

As challenging as it may be, the only way out of these dilemmas is to face and deal with the difficulties causing our distress. In most cases, there are actions we can take, either on our own or with the help of others and God, that will not only resolve the problem, but also alleviate our inner turmoil.

THOUGHT FOR TODAY: Fears that are faced increase my sense of control and inner strength.

Let every man's hope be in himself.

—Virgil

I can still hear my mother urging, "Straighten up—stop slouching!" For years she kept after me to improve my posture, but the message never got through. Well into adulthood, my body had a decided forward tilt. I slouched when I sat and slumped when I stood or walked.

There are, of course, many reasons for poor posture. In my own case, it was an outgrowth of extremely low self-worth. I didn't want to be observed, or even noticed, so I rounded my shoulders and averted my eyes. Had it been possible, I would have rendered myself invisible.

I certainly didn't know it, but from childhood I paid a physical price for my poor posture. I suffered muscle tension, back pain, and headaches. Undoubtedly my digestion, breathing capability, and even my eyesight also suffered to a degree.

It sounds simplistic, but the truth is that over the years my posture has improved along with my self-esteem. The better I feel about myself, the taller and straighter I carry myself. I feel better physically, and more and more these days I have a satisfying sense of ease and even grace as I move about.

THOUGHT FOR TODAY: The way I present myself reflects the feelings I have about myself.

It is well that there is no one without a fault, for he would not have a friend in the world. He would seem to belong to a different species.

—William Hazlitt

It may not be obvious at first, but the pursuit of perfection is a major cause of stress. Paradoxically, we insist on perfection in the belief that we will benefit, but in truth its pursuit drags us down mentally, emotionally, and physically.

We return to college for a degree and, because nothing less than perfect grades will do, cause ourselves such anxiety that we can't concentrate. We undertake an important project for our employer with the goal of matchless perfection. While working on the project, we're so stressed out we can't sleep.

In the same vein, we approach special occasions—Christmas, Thanksgiving, vacations—feeling responsible for creating perfect experiences for everyone involved. Needless to say, the resulting pressure is enormous and debilitating.

If we see ourselves in any of these examples, perhaps, in the interest of our health, it's time to reaffirm the reality that there are enough stressors in life without adding more. Perhaps it's time to lower our overblown expectations, accept our limitations, trust our capabilities, and let the best we can do be enough.

THOUGHT FOR TODAY: There are far more important things in life than trying to be perfect.

Today, whatever may annoy,
The word for me is Joy, just simple Joy.
　　　　　　　　　—John Kendrick Bangs

Inner joy is my Divine birthright, my spiritual heritage. The joy I feel within is an expression of the real me, the natural me, the true me. It is also a reflection of God's will that I be lighthearted and free.

Because of life's ebb and flow, there are times when I may not feel joyful. Unforeseen events and unwanted responsibilities may darken my mood. Mistreatment or thoughtlessness by others may fill me with anxiety or anger. Adversity or tragedy may threaten my faith and serenity.

Yet even in the midst of such challenges, I can still choose my reaction to what is going on in my life. Indeed, at such times it is critical that I make a choice concerning my attitude and subsequent actions. Hopefully, that choice will be to return to my true self, and the sources of my inner joy.

I am joyful to be surrounded by loving family and friends. I am joyful in the reality of God's presence and power. I am joyful because of the way I am able to handle life's challenges, and because I can freely share my inner joy with others.

THOUGHT FOR TODAY: Am I drawing upon my reservoir of inner joy?

March 31

The most exhausting thing in life, I have discovered, is to be insincere.

—Anne Morrow Lindbergh

It's easy to get carried away when we move out in a new and exciting direction, especially in areas related to personal or spiritual expansion. We can't help being motivated when we are surrounded by like-minded people with similar aspirations.

It's a lot more difficult, however, to "walk like we talk" when we're on our own, or after the first flush of enthusiasm fades. In any new, constructive pursuit, the challenge is to remain disciplined and consistent, matching our words with actual deeds on a day by day basis.

For example, it's not only dishonest, it's also harmful to our inner being, when we extol the virtues of love while continuing to be inattentive or even emotionally abusive to our own family members. Similarly, we do damage to ourselves and others when we preach environmental restraint but fail to set an example in our personal actions.

As we progress along a new path, we often gain awareness of contradictions in our lives. We may then feel a need to bring about greater harmony between our beliefs and deeds—to become living rather than verbal examples for others.

THOUGHT FOR TODAY: Self-respect flows not from one's preachings, but from one's practices.

The life of an adventurer is the practice of the art of the impossible.

—William Bolitho

It was my first white water rafting trip down a river with Class IV and V rapids. Because of my apprehension, I had trouble fastening the zippers, buckles, and belts on my wet suit, helmet, and life jacket. When the guide gave his no-holds-barred safety talk, I thought seriously of backing out.

Once we maneuvered successfully through that first drenching rapid—it was called Black Hole—I settled down and started to relish the challenge. It turned out to be one of the most exhilarating experiences of my life.

In years past it would have been unimaginable for me to participate in such an adventure. I led a sedentary life and didn't associate with active, outdoor people. I was too overweight and out of shape to meet the physical demands of such a trip. And I couldn't have walked through the fear—not only of the adventure itself, but of any kind of failure on my part.

The most remarkable thing about it all was not the rafting trip *per se,* but how it helped change my perception of myself. It showed me, clearly and dramatically, that I am capable of far more than I'd ever thought possible.

THOUGHT FOR TODAY: How will I know unless I try?

April 2

It is a consolation to the wretched to have companions in misery.

—Publilius Syrus

We don't need "before and after" pictures to remind us of what it used to be like in the old days. Memory alone serves that purpose well. We gravitated toward lower companions, people we considered worse off than we were, so that by comparison we could sometimes feel better about ourselves.

We were bonded together by misery and despair; we commiserated with each other and fed on our mutual lack of hope. We were partners—drinking partners, overeating partners, partners in poor health and negativity.

Somehow, miraculously, our attitude and outlook on life changed for the better. We chose new goals, and as we progressed toward them, we grew apart from our old friends and began to surround ourselves with new ones.

Today our close relationships are rooted in trust, mutual respect, and common aspirations. We are attracted to people whose love of life is reflected in the way they care for their bodies, minds, and spirits. We are companions in gratitude, and our fondest wish is to help each other grow emotionally and spiritually.

THOUGHT FOR TODAY: My new friends reflect the health, joy, and freedom of my new life.

Tears are blessings, let them flow.

—Harry Hunter

In our pursuit of wellness, it is crucial to acknowledge and express our feelings. It has been a major challenge for many of us to become aware of our hidden emotions, as well as to accept them and reveal them to others.

Learning to cry has been an important benchmark of progress. Although we used to avoid crying at all costs, we've discovered it can be the ultimate expression of what we're feeling—of not only sadness, fear, anger, and pain, but also joy, love, and relief.

It was hard to believe that crying could ever be anything but awkward and embarrassing. But we've come to realize that it's a natural tension reliever. It's also a clear and articulate way of letting others know the depth of our feelings and what our needs are.

When we cry in the presence of another person, it's an expression of trust. We are willing to be vulnerable and to let others know us intimately. From that standpoint, our ability and willingness to cry these days reflects growing self-worth and emotional wholeness. It's our way of saying, "It's all right to have this feeling; it's an acceptable part of me."

THOUGHT FOR TODAY: I'm grateful that I'm no longer a bottled-up, closed-off person.

April 4

The choicest pleasures of life lie within the ring of moderation.

—Martin Farquhar Tupper

I used to gain weight every time I went on vacation. During my hard-earned time off, I rationalized, I deserved to treat myself well. So I sampled new and different foods to my heart's content, snacked at all hours, and ate twice as much as usual.

As one can imagine, I returned home feeling stuffed, unhealthy, and regretful. While struggling to lose the weight, I vowed I would never do that again. But I did, over and over.

These days I still enjoy new and unusually prepared foods while traveling. Like so many people, however, I've learned to bring my dietary guidelines along with me and not use traveling as an excuse to overeat.

I also establish a special mindset before leaving on vacation. Here are a few of the things I tell myself: What does "treating myself well" mean, if not to respect my body and protect my health? I don't have to sample everything in one sitting; the food will be there later.

If I overeat, I'll feel lethargic; all I'll want to do is sit around. If I eat wisely, on the other hand, I'll have plenty of energy for all the other enjoyable activities, besides eating, that vacations offer.

THOUGHT FOR TODAY: Care*free* doesn't mean care*less*.

*Change means the unknown. . . . It means, too
many people cry, insecurity. Nonsense! No one from
the beginning of time has had security.*
— Eleanor Roosevelt

Anyone who has been on this planet for an hour or
more knows that change causes stress. It matters little
whether the change is expected or unexpected, or
"good" or "bad." Illness, financial difficulties, the
breakup of a relationship—we've all been through
such stress-producing experiences.

Paradoxically, even change that we initiate ourselves in order to *reduce* stress in our lives—such as
changing jobs, moving, or traveling—can be highly
stressful. In short, our common experience is that
change of almost any kind seems to be synonymous
with stress.

Why is this so? For one thing, change usually
requires physical, emotional, and even spiritual adjustments on our part—and human nature favors the
status quo. Beyond that, change generates fear of all
kinds: fear of the unknown, fear that we won't measure up, fear that things will get worse rather than
better.

However, the stress caused by change need not
always be prolonged and harmful. We frequently
have more of a choice in the matter than we realize.
Half the battle is learning to accept the reality that
change is an inevitable part of life and the growth
process, and that nothing would exist without it.

THOUGHT FOR TODAY: I will move forward with
the flow of change.

April 6

*All things change, creeds and philosophies and out-
ward system—but God remains!*
                                                —Mary Augusta Ward

Change—we are all familiar with the many aphorisms
on the subject, such as "Nothing is permanent except
change." We've thought about it often, and there is no
doubt in our minds that we will always face and be
involved with change of one kind or another.

   Yet despite our philosophical and intellectual
understanding, the reality of change in our life almost
always throws us off balance. It can cause us to act
immaturely and at times even irrationally.

   When we find ourselves negatively affected by
change, it can be helpful to recognize that our stress
has more to do with our attitude and reaction toward
events than the actual events themselves.

   We can reduce stress by choosing to look at
change as a challenge or opportunity rather than a
threat. We can reduce stress by approaching change
with a sense of curiosity and open-mindedness rather
than bewilderment and fear.

   During periods of change, many of us find reas-
surance and serenity by placing our faith and trust in
God. We've come to believe that change is an integral
component of His plan for good in our lives.

THOUGHT FOR TODAY: God is with me at all
times, in all places, under all circumstances.

We cheat ourselves in order to enjoy a quiet con-
science, without possessing virtue.
—Madame de Lambert

Early in recovery, it became necessary to reshape our
attitudes concerning health and sickness. Because our
view of the world had long been distorted and out of
synch with reality, many of us tended to see sickness
as more "useful" and even more desirable than health.

Looking back, it was easy to see that we got a lot
out of our illnesses and injuries. We received more
than our share of sympathy, but that was the least of
it.

We "worked" our poor health in ways that lowered other people's expectations and allowed us to
avoid responsibility. We had a built-in excuse for
behavior—such as laziness or abusiveness—that otherwise would have been unacceptable. In some cases
our illness became our identity; it was our primary
way of relating to the world and other people.

In our new life, we don't need to carry on like
that. Because we've taken actions to change our
thinking and get rid of our character defects, we no
longer require excuses or rationalizations. We've
learned to stand on our own. We're developing a new
self-image based on physical, emotional, and spiritual
growth that reflects wellness.

THOUGHT FOR TODAY: I no longer have to punish or compromise myself to get what I need.

April 8

If in the last few years you haven't discarded a major opinion or acquired a new one, check your pulse. You may be dead.

—Frank Gelett Burgess

More than twenty years ago I met a man who was destined to have a major impact on my life. He guided me through the pain and confusion of early sobriety, helped smooth the way toward my eventual belief in a Higher Power, and in general has remained a stabilizing and inspirational force.

What impresses me most about my friend is that he has continued to change and grow throughout the years. Today he is a far different person than when I first met him. For all his wisdom and success, he remains open-minded, teachable, and adventurous.

Although he is hardly a young man, he travels often, enjoys new sports and physical activities, and stays in good shape. He also keeps himself mentally stimulated by reading extensively and by listening attentively to the ideas and experiences of others.

His spiritual life, in particular, seems to be in constant flux. He frequently comes to me with new ideas, philosophies, and interpretations; he talks enthusiastically about spiritual principles and how they affect his life in positive ways.

One of my fondest hopes is to follow his example—to be as aware, interested, and vital as he is in the years ahead.

THOUGHT FOR TODAY: Life is change; living is changing.

Freedom is re-created year by year,
In hearts wide open on the Godward side.
> —James Russell Lowell

Personal freedom is something we all long for. Far too often, though, we passively stand by and hope that someone or something will take an action that will set us free. We wait for a situation to change or an event to occur that will bring more freedom into our life.

In other words, we tend to see our personal boundaries in external things: financial status, a demanding long-term project, a domineering or unrelenting parent, gender- or race-related societal restrictions. We limit ourselves, usually unwittingly, with the message, "If such-and-such happens, then I'll be free!"

Moreover, many of us settle for limited objectives and aspirations because we are still bound to the past, to our old ideas, and to an outdated self-image.

Past limitations notwithstanding, the reality is that we have far more choice in self-liberation than we may realize. Personal freedom comes not from outer things or external events falling into place, but entirely from our own beliefs, attitudes, choices, and actions.

Each of us is a freeborn child of God. Personal freedom is our Divine birthright; it rises from our hearts, minds, and souls.

THOUGHT FOR TODAY: The key to personal freedom can be found within myself.

April 10

Blot out vain pomp; check impulse; quench appetite; keep reason under its own control.

—Marcus Aurelius

Some time has passed since we made that first critical decision to improve the quality of our lives. We made major commitments in the areas of diet, exercise, and stress control, and once we were able to follow through with consistency, we began to take pleasure and pride in the changes that were taking place.

The process continues. Now we find that we can improve our overall well-being to an even greater degree by focusing on our "insides"—the feelings, attitudes, and hidden motives that influence and often determine our day-to-day behavior.

We're becoming more aware and accepting of our true selves, and as the result are no longer driven to appear "better than" or "less than" other people. We're learning to keep our egos in check, and that has made it possible to live comfortably with others instead of always being on the offensive or defensive.

Where once we were at the mercy of our obsessions and negative thinking, we no longer are compelled to act on every impulse. We're learning how to separate fact from fiction in our thoughts and feelings.

THOUGHT FOR TODAY: Am I changing on the inside as well as on the outside?

It is the mind that maketh good or ill,
That maketh wretch or happy, rich or poor.
—Edmund Spenser

At a small gathering of close friends, a woman described what her life had been like prior to recovery. She had been so tormented by her mind's incessant outpourings that she had a recurring fantasy of actually performing a lobotomy on herself. As shocking as her admission was, it struck a responsive chord within me. I identified completely.

I too had long been tyrannized by my thoughts, mental images, and dreams. For years I tried in vain to silence my mind. When willpower failed, I tried to numb my brain with alcohol and other drugs. But in the end my mind's onslaughts almost always propelled me into self-destructive attitudes and actions.

Over a period of years in recovery, I've learned various techniques that allow me to focus and control my thoughts. Meditation and prayer, in particular, help quiet and redirect my mind. I also try to use relaxation exercises such as deep breathing and visualization. In its own special way, physical exercise brings me mental tranquility. As the gratifying result of these activities, most of the time my mind now serves rather than rules me.

THOUGHT FOR TODAY: Do I control my thoughts, or do they control me?

April 12

This world belongs to the energetic.
                                        —Ralph Waldo Emerson

One of the hidden yet altogether magical benefits of regular workouts is that they boost our energy level. Instead of feeling tired and lethargic, as we did so often when we led a sedentary life, it now seems that the more energetic we are the more energy we have.

One rewarding result, in addition to feeling strong and fit, is that our overall lifestyle has become more active than ever. Day by day, just about everywhere we are and in everything we do, we choose physical exertion over physical inertia. At first it was a matter of consciously changing our habits, but now it has become second nature.

If we are early for an appointment, we take a walk. We wash our own car instead of paying someone else to do it. We take the stairs instead of the escalator. Instead of circling the parking lot looking for the closest space, we don't mind parking some distance away from our destination.

In short, we keep our bodies in motion whenever possible. We do so not out of a sense of obligation, but simply for the joy of feeling good about ourselves.

THOUGHT FOR TODAY: I'm proud and grateful for my active lifestyle.

It is not the answer that enlightens, but the question.
—Eugène Ionesco

We never questioned the precept that personal and spiritual growth is a continuum, and would be a life-long mission. After a while, however, some of us become complacent.

We were, after all, more comfortable with ourselves and in the world than ever before. Our relationship with others had become more service- than self-oriented. People admired and respected us. We thought we had all the answers.

Then, suddenly, the bottom dropped out of our life. We felt alienated, empty, spiritually bereft. In some cases the crisis was precipitated by a particular event; more often, it had been building for some time—but we had ignored the warning signs of inner disquiet.

Looking back, it's clear that we stopped growing soon after we stopped searching, stopped asking questions. We began to regress when we rested on our "spiritual laurels." In short, our lack of humility set the stage for our downfall.

We've since given up the notion that we will ever know "enough." We've learned that the way to continue growing, and achieve ever-greater peace of mind, is to remain open-minded and teachable.

THOUGHT FOR TODAY: The spiritual path is endless and ever-fulfilling.

April 14

To improve the golden moment of opportunity and catch the good that is in our reach, is the great art of life.

—Samuel Johnson

After being confined for more than two decades in a prison of my own making, I finally found freedom. Recovery opened wide the door to the world and, in time, the door to my inner self.

During recent years, I've had the opportunity to take on challenges that have helped me discover personal resources I didn't know I had. One year I learned how to scuba dive. The next, I experimented with high-altitude hiking. Not long after that, I started taking white water rafting trips down rivers with Class IV and V rapids.

Each challenge revealed something new about myself. I discovered, for example, that I had always set personal limits far below my capabilities; it's good to know how tough I really am. I learned to trust myself and others at deeper levels; on more than one occasion, my life depended on it.

I also found out that fear need not be a barrier, but can be an exciting motivational force. Yes, it's an achievement to get safely through the rapids or to the top of the mountain, but the greater achievement is facing and overcoming the fear.

THOUGHT FOR TODAY: Each new adventure is self-discovery; each self-discovery is a new adventure.

We should do everything both cautiously and confidently at the same time.

—Epictetus

The transition from passivity to assertiveness is a reflection of growing self-respect, and for many people represents a significant milestone of personal growth. One difficulty, however, is that assertiveness can bring on considerable stress.

How can one stay calm while "taking on" a hospital's computerized bookkeeping department over a major foul-up? How can one remain stress-free and self-assured when meeting with the boss to insist on a long-overdue raise or promotion?

We often walk a fine line between self-assertion and high anxiety when we feel strongly about something, or when we respond to unfair treatment. But there are guidelines that can help us stay balanced and on course.

First, it's essential to have the right motive for "standing up" to a person or institution. Our goal is not revenge, but to retain self-respect and build self-esteem. Second, it's important to mentally walk through the confrontation in advance. That way we're less likely to be caught off guard.

Finally, if things get out of hand despite our best efforts, we can temporarily leave the scene to meditate, practice a stress-reduction technique, or use the Serenity Prayer.

THOUGHT FOR TODAY: Stress need not be a by-product of assertiveness.

April 16

To some will come a time when change
Itself is beauty, if not heaven.
> —Edwin Arlington Robinson

There was a time when we dreaded facing the challenges of each new day. We feared that we couldn't meet our responsibilities, achieve our goals, follow through with our commitments. But now we find our days exciting, for they are filled with opportunities to enhance our physical, emotional, and spiritual well-being. Some of these opportunities are put in front of us and, consequently, are clearly evident; others are created by our own willingness, enthusiasm, and imagination.

There was a time when we saw each less-than-perfect attempt—each faltering step—as an enormous failure. We berated ourselves fiercely. Today, as we work toward constructive change in our lives, we take special care to give ourselves messages of encouragement and approval. Next to God, we are our own strongest allies, our greatest source of strength.

There was a time when we struggled and fought to change our lifestyle, to become different within. These days, thank God, our efforts are Divinely guided. We flow smoothly toward our new objectives.

THOUGHT FOR TODAY: I am open to whatever the day brings forth.

The little reed, bending to the force of the wind, soon stood upright again when the storm had passed over.
—Aesop

Once, while waiting for a department store purchase to be rung up, I watched a middle-aged woman throw a fifteen-minute tantrum. She had phoned ahead to be sure the store carried a particular item; when she arrived she discovered that the salesperson had been mistaken. Her rage and the stress it generated (not only in herself, but in everyone within earshot) was at once shocking and embarrassing.

Later, I thought about the new friends I've made in recovery. It occurred to me that few if any of them would react so inflexibly under similar circumstances. That's one of the ways we benefit as we gradually become less self-centered: We learn to go with the flow of life, to take things as they come, to see ourselves and our needs and desires in perspective.

These days when we start to get upset, we pause and ask ourselves, "How important is it?" How important is it that our train or plane is fifteen minutes late, that the department store's skirt was chambray rather than denim as promised? Is any of it worth the stress of getting angry and upset? Speaking for myself, I'd rather bend than break.

THOUGHT FOR TODAY: How important is it?

April 18

I will hew great windows for my soul.
—Angela Morgan

Each and every time we take a run, go on a bike ride, or play a set of tennis, we benefit in major ways. We burn calories; we gain muscle tone and self-esteem. Doing what we do gives us an edge.

Quite often, additionally, we receive a benefit that's difficult to describe—one we hadn't counted on or expected. It takes place when we are concentrating on the tennis ball floating toward us and are poised to swing, when we are racing down a steep hill on our bicycle, when we are fully energized during an aerobics class.

During these special times, we are so totally absorbed and in tune with the present that we are unaware of all else. There are no distractions, neither external nor internal. Momentarily, it is as if we have entered a new dimension.

The three centers of our being—physical, mental, and spiritual—are synchronized and focused on a single goal. We are in harmony with ourselves and our surroundings.

When we come to know this transcendence, we realize that it is the hidden reason for doing what we do, the secret goal behind our efforts, the heart of the athletic experience.

THOUGHT FOR TODAY: Athletics can be soul-stirring.

The art of being wise is the art of knowing what to overlook.

—William James

What is it that compels us to look at ourselves and our lives through the wrong end of a telescope? The answer may not be readily apparent, but the fact is that many of us do tend to focus on the small, unimportant things.

In our relationships, for example, we frequently get hung up on a partner's idiosyncrasies or distracting habits. We overreact to such trivialities as an almost-empty gas tank or an unmade bed, while ignoring the compatibility and warmth we share.

At work, similarly, we zero in on an associate's lateness, or that someone failed to add paper to the copy machine, rather than taking pride in our achievements as a team.

We often take just as limited a view of ourselves, dwelling on an imperfect haircut or a couple of extra pounds, rather than being pleased with our overall appearance and fitness.

Apart from the emotional energy we waste on such pettiness, and the damaging stress such reactions cause, we miss out on the big, important, and truly meaningful parts of life. It's simply not worth it.

THOUGHT FOR TODAY: My point of view shapes my perspective.

April 20

There is a destiny which makes us brothers; None goes his way alone.

—Edwin Markham

It took me several years of seeking to fully understand that spirituality is far more than simply believing in God. Spirituality has since become a concrete and dynamic force in my life, affecting many of my thoughts, attitudes, and actions.

I try, for example, to show my respect for the gift of life by taking the best possible care of my body, mind, and spirit. I try to live by spiritual principles. I try to expand my spiritual consciousness and deepen the relationship with my Higher Power.

At the beginning, as the desire for progress along these lines became an important new priority in my life, I had to disassociate myself from people who made light of my spiritual quest. It was also necessary to distance myself from those whose attitudes and behavior were perpetually negative and destructive.

I chose instead to seek out and surround myself with people who are following the same path. Over the years, I've tried to develop and nurture relationships with like-minded souls, who themselves are dedicated to spiritual growth.

THOUGHT FOR TODAY: Supportive company, traveling in the same direction, can speed my progress.

Accusing the times is but excusing ourselves.
— Thomas Fuller

Anyone who has ever been dependent on alcohol, drugs, tobacco, or food knows how vitally important it is to guard against "slips." Even while we are recovering, our addictions can be cunningly seductive.

When we look back, we find that the most artfully set traps—the ones that snared us most quickly and most disastrously—were often baited not with an actual substance or overt craving, but with our interactions with other people.

When we fought with a family member and didn't get our way, for example, it was always tempting to eat, drink, or smoke "at them." If someone rejected or disappointed us, we went out on a binge. If we felt we were being unfairly criticized at work, we retaliated by going back to our addiction.

Now that we have a solid foundation in our new lives, we don't use the actions of others as excuses or rationalizations to return to our dependencies. Even when we are actually harmed by another person, and our anger or emotional upset seems justified, we try to keep the event in perspective and our priorities in order. It's certainly not worth ruining our health—or losing our life—over hurt feelings.

THOUGHT FOR TODAY: It's not what "they" do to me; it's what I do to myself.

April 22

Whatever is unknown is magnified.

—Tacitus

We stifled and hid many feelings during our past life. But the one emotion we disguised more diligently and buried more deeply than any other was fear. When our fear masqueraded as something else— anger, jealousy, and anxiety—we weren't even aware of it. Yet even when we knew without question that we were afraid, we wouldn't admit it to anyone.

Why were we so unwilling to own up to our fears? More than anything, we thought it would make us appear weak and ineffectual. Many of us had been taught from childhood to put on a good front, no matter what. Our role models were fearless macho men or fearless independent women.

Over time we've learned that certain emotions are highly corrosive, and that fear is among the worst. Even as we worked hard to hide our fear from others and ourselves, it ate away at us relentlessly.

How freeing it is to air and share our fears with others! How constructive it is to discuss our fears with someone we trust. What a relief to discover that virtually all of our fears—of the past, present, or future—diminish when they are brought to light.

THOUGHT FOR TODAY: Fear can't be contained; it corrodes or explodes.

Surmounted difficulties not only teach, but hearten us in our future struggles.

—James Sharp

I once worked on a business writing project which required close daily contact with the company's public relations executive. I found it almost impossible to put up with his know-it-all attitude, his supercilious treatment of me, and even his personal habits.

The three months I spent working with him were unbearable; I dreaded each day. Somehow, I got through it, and when it was over I felt as if I had been released from prison.

From today's vantage point, it's clear that the emotional pain was of my own making. If a similar situation were to arise now, I'd certainly try to handle it in a way that would be less stressful and harmful to me.

First and foremost, I would try to practice the spiritual principle of acceptance, acknowledging my powerlessness over the man's personality and behavior.

I would try to be less judgmental and more understanding of him. Instead of focusing only on his behavior toward me, I would concentrate on my own actions and reactions. Finally, I would fortify myself by remembering that, with God's help, I can transcend just about anything a day at a time.

THOUGHT FOR TODAY: Difficult people need not cause me difficulty.

April 24

Do not craze yourself with thinking, but go about your business. . . .

—Ralph Waldo Emerson

No one can dispute the miraculous power of the mind. Our mental capabilities enable us to acquire knowledge and skills of infinite variety; to create soul-stirring music, art, and literature; to invent life-enhancing technologies.

Yet for all the value and splendor of our thought processes, *too much* thinking can sometimes be our undoing. Let's say, for example, that we've made a major mistake at work, financially, or in a relationship. Unrelenting deliberation on our part can literally paralyze us, forestalling whatever remedies may be called for.

By remaining stuck in our own mind, so to speak, we remain stuck in the problem. In such cases, the more analysis we do—the more we cogitate, speculate, and ruminate—the more we distort reality and the more upset we become.

If we want to move forward following a major mistake or similar mishap, a far better course than "thinking it to death" is to discuss it with another person or write about it. That way, we can gain objectivity and clarity and find solutions. Action is the next step. Then, with God's help, we can let it all go and get on with our life.

THOUGHT FOR TODAY: Thinking points the way, but only footwork gets us there.

Of all knowledge the wise and good seek most to know themselves.

—William Shakespeare

For several days now I've been upset and off the beam. I've been haunted by nameless fears and have had a growing sense of inner disquiet. It's time to find out what's going on, and to do something about it.

So today, I plan to carefully observe myself and make changes in my attitude and behavior whenever it seems necessary. As I drive to work, I will be conscious of my feelings and actions in traffic and toward other drivers. Am I aggressive and impatient? Or am I tolerant and relaxed?

On the job, I will periodically check my disposition. Am I making it harder on myself by approaching everything I do with dread or disdain? Am I being a people pleaser just to get by? Or am I doing the best work I can, no matter what the circumstances?

Today I will closely watch the way I interact with others. Am I preoccupied with myself? Or am I listening attentively, communicating carefully, and being patient and understanding?

My self-observation will also include the way I treat myself. Am I being self-critical and self-abusive? Or am I being kind and loving?

THOUGHT FOR TODAY: I can't break free and move forward until I know what's holding me back.

April 26

Nothing is ever done beautifully which is done in rivalship, nor nobly which is done in pride.
—John Ruskin

In gyms or on playing fields, it's easy to spot the aggressive, do-or-die competitors, those men and women for whom exercise and sports activities are extensions of their workaday worlds. Intense, hard-driven competitors on the job, they bring that same thrust to the court.

Some of us are like that ourselves. Needless to say, our competitive approach to workouts does little to release stress and help us wind down.

Exercise can and should be fun and relaxing. That's how we soothe our souls while toning up and staying healthy. If we're the least bit creative, we can find various ways to transform workouts from chores or competitive battles into positive and enjoyable experiences.

Cross-training—switching between different activities every few days—not only helps avoid burnout, but reduces the risk of injury. We can also keep workouts fresh and interesting by varying our routine. Runners and cyclists, for example, can alter routes as well as the times of day when they set forth.

One of the best ways to have fun while exercising is to join others—a few friends or an entire group—with the goal of conviviality rather than competition.

THOUGHT FOR TODAY: If I must compete, let my adversary be stress.

How little do they see what really is, who frame their hasty judgment on that which seems.
—Robert Southey

Like so many people, I was culturally conditioned from childhood to judge and value others primarily by their appearance. The basic criterion was "attractiveness," which in my frame of reference was strictly limited to age, height, weight, facial structure, hair and eye color, and so on.

Well into adulthood, I also judged and valued myself according to those same superficial and arbitrary standards. Needless to say, I always came up wanting, which served to reinforce my feelings of low self-worth while adding to my self-consciousness in social situations.

It took a gradual spiritual awakening to open my mind, change my perspective, and make it possible for me to look beyond people's surfaces. I learned to value others based on their inner selves, their individuality, and special character traits.

More and more these days, what draws me to people is their spirit. As far as I'm concerned, attractiveness has nothing to do with looks, and everything to do with such qualities as warmth, depth, compassion, exuberance, and the joy of living.

THOUGHT FOR TODAY: I will try to value and accept myself and others in the same way that God values and accepts us all.

April 28

Never let us be discouraged with ourselves.
—François de S. Fénelon

We often hear, especially in our support groups, "Be good to yourself!" And we are learning to do just that. We're taking care of our physical beings as never before, by eating right and exercising.

But when it comes to taking care of our psyches, we may not do as well. Many of us are still in the habit of being harshly self-critical. In practically every area of our life—work, sports, even routine daily activities—we tend to automatically chastise rather than gently correct ourselves for minor errors or missteps.

We miss an easy tennis shot and exclaim, "I can't play worth a damn!"—instead of silently saying, "Bend your knees a little more on the next one." At other times our self-criticism may be more subtle, taking the form of impatience, disappointment, or discouragement with ourselves.

When we treat ourselves unkindly, it's sure to be hurtful. Beyond that, *destructive* rather than *constructive* self-criticism is wholly counterproductive; it does nothing to help us progress.

Being good to ourselves need not be limited to eating the right foods, taking warm baths, and the like. It should also include being gentle, emotionally supportive, and patient in everything we do.

THOUGHT FOR TODAY: I will treat myself as I would a dearly loved friend.

The true art of memory is the art of attention.
— Samuel Johnson

We finish shopping and can't remember where we parked the car. We get an overdue notice in the mail and suddenly realize we've forgotten to pay the mortgage. We run into an old friend and, for the life of us, can't think of his name.

Most of us react with embarrassment and even mortification when we experience incidents of forgetfulness. We make fun of ourselves ("I must be getting senile!"); we get angry at ourselves ("I'm such an idiot!").

When we respond to forgetfulness by attacking ourselves in these ways, obviously we don't do a whole lot for our self-esteem. And we do absolutely nothing about the problem itself.

In most cases, there are simple reasons for the mild memory lapses we all experience periodically. Certainly when we are preoccupied with something, and inattentive, we can become forgetful. When we are tired, fearful, or self-obsessed, our memory also suffers.

More than anything, *stress* blocks the channel of memory. Physical and emotional tensions have powerfully negative effects on our thought and memory processes. If we recognize and address such tensions, chances are we'll soon become mentally sharper and less forgetful.

THOUGHT FOR TODAY: I'll attack the problem, not myself.

April 30

The surest method of arriving at a knowledge of God's eternal purposes for us is to be found in the right use of the present moment.

—Frederick William Faber

Through prayer and meditation, I will seek knowledge of God's will for me and the power to carry it out. I will try not to let any uncertainty on my part keep me from following this course.

Experience has taught me that in God's time I will know what He would have me do. My inner voice or intuition may speak to me; I may be guided by the words or actions of another person; I may be led by the way events unfold or circumstances fall into place.

All too often in the past, I turned to God as a last resort. I sought His will only after I had exerted my own will to no avail, bringing about neither relief nor a desired result. From now on, I will try to turn to God first.

I am convinced that I can't go wrong by seeking God's will. When I take that action, I gain not only guidance and strength, but also the fruits of His love for me. I have no doubt that God's will for me is to enjoy His blessings, and to live happily, joyously, and freely.

THOUGHT FOR TODAY: God in my life is good in my life.

*Try to be happy in this very present moment; and put
not off being so to a time to come.*

—Thomas Fuller

When I went for a haircut not long ago, the barber
told me it was his sixtieth birthday. Then, shrugging
aside my congratulations, he confided that he wasn't
at all happy about reaching that milestone. To the
contrary, all he could think about were friends who
had died, longevity statistics, and the probability that
he had, in his words, "maybe fifteen more years if I'm
lucky."

It was hard not to be swept along by the barber's
fearful projections. As he clipped my hair, we en-
gaged in a serious discussion about the importance of
making the most of our remaining years. We agreed
that it was essential to make the right advance
decisions concerning our families and careers. We
went on and on about sound investments, retirement
plans, and the like.

Driving home, it dawned on me that we had
overlooked the most important reality of all. By
focusing on the years to come—on future-oriented
safeguards and scenarios—we had failed to consider
the present. Longevity charts and milestone birthdays notwithstanding, the only thing that really
counts is putting the most into, and getting the most
out of *this day*.

THOUGHT FOR TODAY: The future is in God's
hands.

May 2

To be trusted is a greater compliment than to be loved.

—George MacDonald

Because of past experiences, especially when we were children, some of us have a deep and lingering distrust of close relationships. We may feel that if we are free and open with someone, we are likely to be hurt or betrayed. We may feel that if we permit ourselves to be intimate (and we are not speaking necessarily of sex), it is almost certain we will be rejected or abandoned.

So long as we allow yesterday's painful experiences to dictate present expectations, that's how long we will limit our ability to love and be loved.

That's why it is so important to recognize and accept these new realities: Today is not yesterday; everything has changed. Whereas in the past we operated from the perspective of a child, with a child's resources, today we have the perspective and resources of an adult.

As the result, we have choices regarding each and every intimate relationship. We can move quickly or slowly; we can stay or we can leave; we can be as independent or as dependent as we wish.

THOUGHT FOR TODAY: Do I still believe that if I care too much, I'll be harmed?

If you are losing your leisure, look out! You may be losing your soul.

—Logan Pearsall Smith

It usually happens at certain times of the year—spring break, summer vacation, Christmas. Relatives or dear friends come to visit, and the challenge is to show them the best possible time.

For several days in a row, life is a whirl of fun. We spend a whole day and half the night at an amusement park, checking out every ride and attraction. We go to a ballgame and a concert, and no group of fans was ever more enthusiastic. We pack a picnic and hike down to the beach or lake, and the air never smelled sweeter.

After we've said our good-byes, we reflect on what an incredibly good time we had. We're inspired and rejuvenated, and feel as though we've been on vacation ourselves. We vow not to wait so long until next time; we can do the same sort of thing on our own, without waiting for special occasions.

Weeks and months pass, and we're caught up in the same old routine. Has it been almost a year since we've been to an amusement park, a concert, a ballgame? Isn't it time to make some plans and have some fun? What about this weekend? What about *tonight*?

THOUGHT FOR TODAY: Recreation is a priority, not an option.

May 4

We deceive and flatter no one by such delicate artifices as we do our own selves.
—Arthur Schopenhauer

Sometimes an unexpected experience reminds us of how ill and deeply troubled we once were, and fills us with gratitude for our life today. That's what happened when a new business associate and I traveled together.

It became clear the first day that the man was a compulsive overeater. Not only did he consume excessive amounts of food, he was also preoccupied with eating.

Most significantly, he constantly tried to delude himself concerning his obsessive relationship with food. He ordered extra helpings because it was "outstanding." He finished food I had left on the pretext of sampling it. He initiated lengthy discussions with waiters about the preparation of foods in order to support his view of himself as a gourmet rather than an overeater.

I know all about denial. For years it was the primary symptom of my alcoholism. No matter how damaging my addictive behavior, I did all I could to rationalize, alibi, or otherwise deny it.

As I watched my friend during that trip, I could only pray that one day he too would be graced with a moment of clarity, come to terms with his denial, and get a start on the road to recovery.

THOUGHT FOR TODAY: Am I grateful for the way it is, compared with the way it used to be?

To choose time is to save time.

—Francis Bacon

The boss asks us if we can possibly work on the weekend, and we can't afford to say no. By the same token, we can't afford to give up our spare time. We were going to spend a day with the kids, catch up with unpaid bills, return phone calls, and so on. Now, the things we had planned to do just won't get done.

That's the way life is. Traffic backs up, cars break down, people get sick, there are emergencies at work. Lack of time is a problem for most of us.

An even greater problem, however, is the way we frequently react to these unavoidable situations. We do a lot of negative projecting. We become resentful toward the people, places, and things that take away our time. We become unraveled.

If we want to break out of this vicious cycle, the first thing we must do is ask ourselves what's most important in our lives. Work? Spiritual growth? The relationships with our family members? Sobriety?

Once we're sure of our priorities and their necessary order, we're better able to make the right choices concerning the time that's available to us.

THOUGHT FOR TODAY: Do I need to take some time to better manage my time?

Measure, time, and number are nothing but modes of thought or rather of imagination.
—Benedict Spinoza

Since we can't beg, borrow, or steal more time, and can only spend what's available, the challenge is to use that time as effectively as possible. The process usually begins when we determine our priorities in life, and then try to fulfill them each day with carefully made choices.

If, following that, we still experience time-related stress, perhaps we're fighting this reality: We can only do so much with the hours we have. Once we become more accepting of this unalterable fact, it will be a lot easier to face time restraints objectively, and to make whatever adjustments we can.

Perhaps, for example, we can find a new, time-saving route to work; or we can try a different form of commuting that allows us to combine travel with reading. It may be possible to delegate some of our responsibilities at work and at home.

In order to create a few extra hours to get caught up, we may be tempted to forego exercise, meditation, sleep, or support-group meetings. But that's not usually a wise choice. When we give short shrift to our wellness needs, we can't be at our best physically, emotionally, and spiritually.

THOUGHT FOR TODAY: Time may be limited, but it's mine to fill as I choose.

It is the false shame of fools which tries to cover unhealed sores.

—Horace

A number of years ago I was referred to a gastroenterologist because of chronic digestive problems—upset stomach, indigestion, and the like. He ran me through a series of diagnostic tests which, to my relief, turned out to be completely normal.

Following that, the doctor questioned me at length about my job, my family life and other relationships, and even my attitudes about various things. He then suggested strongly that stress and stress alone might be responsible for the physical problems I was experiencing.

I remember feeling offended; I shook my head in vehement denial. In my view, stress couldn't possibly be the problem. To admit otherwise would mean that I was weak and couldn't handle all that life had to dish out. For many months thereafter, I continued to pay a painful price for my denial.

Today when I don't feel quite right, physically or emotionally, stress is the very first thing I consider. And if it turns out that stress is indeed the culprit, I'm not the least bit embarrassed or unwilling to acknowledge that reality. Because only then can I move from the problem into the solution.

THOUGHT FOR TODAY: To acknowledge stress need not be shameful; it affects us all.

May 8

The absence of alternatives clears the mind marvelously.

—Henry Kissinger

Some of us had to go to the end of the line, so to speak, before we could make a turnaround concerning critical health matters. It was only after we hit rock bottom that we finally surrendered and sought help for our chronic overeating, smoking, or drinking.

In the case of overeating, perhaps we had lost much of our physical mobility, or had begun to suffer heart problems. Perhaps a physician warned us that years of heavy drinking had resulted in liver damage. Or perhaps our nicotine addiction had made it impossible to climb even one flight of stairs without becoming short of breath.

For all the pain and suffering we went through, we were able to recover. And for that we are grateful beyond words. One way we express our gratitude is by making wise health choices today. When we become ill, as but one example, we don't deny that fact. We're open-minded and accepting of whatever help is available.

We also express our gratitude by helping others—by showing those who are still actively addicted that they need not ride to the end of the line, but can get off the train at any stop.

THOUGHT FOR TODAY: I need not wait for my pain to become unbearable before getting help.

Faith is the force of life.

—Leo Tolstoy

Every once in a while, someone we haven't seen in a long time compliments us on the way we look, on the sense of well-being we exude. "What's your secret?" they ask teasingly.

For a moment, we're tempted to tell them what the secret of our serenity actually is: *We have come to believe and trust that God will guide us, support us, and care for our every need.*

But we restrain ourselves in anticipation of a skeptical reaction. It wasn't all that long ago that we, too, might have had a similar reaction: How can you put so much faith in something you can't see or hear—in something that may not even exist? How can you trust in a Power that few people can explain and no one really understands?

If we had gone ahead and shared the secret with our acquaintance, at that point we'd explain, "That's the other part of the secret. True, we'll never be able to understand God, but we don't have to try. All we really have to do is make a leap of faith from the restrictions of our own minds to the freedom of God's infinite wisdom, power, and love."

THOUGHT FOR TODAY: Cross over the bridge.

May 10

Pain is no longer pain when it is past.
> —Margaret Junkin Preston

Sometimes I feel like apologizing to my body for what I've put it through. Sometimes I want to berate my body for not responding quickly enough to the demands I impose on it. But most of the time, I want to thank my body for its incredible flexibility, its innate healing power, and its amazing capacity for change.

During the last two decades, I became sober after years of alcoholic drinking; I kicked a two-pack-a-day cigarette addiction; I radically altered my diet; I lost a substantial amount of weight; I made regular exercise an important part of my life.

In each case, the surrender and transformation was accompanied by considerable physical and emotional discomfort, lasting from several days to several weeks. The symptoms ranged from withdrawal in the case of alcohol and nicotine; to hunger pangs, cravings, and self-pity in the case of food; to muscle soreness and mental resistance in the case of becoming physically fit.

Because I gave my mind and body enough time, they adjusted and stabilized. The old patterns and lifestyle gave way to the new. In the long run, patience, persistence, and a strong commitment paid off. Life has never been better.

THOUGHT FOR TODAY: The joy will soon replace the discomfort.

Divine Providence has granted this gift to man, that those things which are honest are also the most advantageous.

—Quintilian

An overriding priority in our new life is to be completely honest and aboveboard at all times and in all situations—to the best of our ability. Initially, we chose this path because we were tired of paying the price for our "white lies" and deceptive behavior. But as time passed, a dedication to honesty began bringing rewards far greater than the simple peace of mind we had originally sought.

We view our honesty today as a commitment to emotional and spiritual growth. When we truthfully and openly share our feelings, reveal our secrets, and relate our experiences, we are brought closer to ourselves, others, and God.

Our friends and loved ones know we can be trusted; in turn, we ourselves feel trustworthy. As the result, our self-esteem grows and our relationships improve. Our honesty and trustworthiness, and the respect those qualities generate, make a huge difference in the way people treat us these days.

We've also found that the practice of rigorous honesty puts us in touch with—and helps us fully appreciate—our inner resources of courage and strength.

THOUGHT FOR TODAY: Complete honesty in word and deed is the keystone of emotional and spiritual well-being.

May 12

Meditation is the life of the soul; action is the soul of meditation.

—Francis Quarles

When we first experiment with meditation, many of us get caught up in the fear that we are not doing it right. Because of our anxiety, it's difficult to focus our minds, let alone get in the proper spirit of meditation. Even though we persist, our efforts are overlaid with frustration and self-doubt.

Some of us don't even get that far. Our concern that we won't be able to meditate properly (perhaps we feel we are not "spiritual" enough) keeps us from getting started even though we are interested.

If we fall into either of these categories, it can be helpful to consider certain basics about the practice of meditation. The important thing is not how we do it, but that we have the willingness to initiate the process and follow through. In other words, the act itself is the objective; there is no right or wrong way to meditate.

Of course, progress will come with regular practice. As with anything else, repetition will make the experience less awkward and more natural. Along these lines, it helps to meditate during those times when we are most relaxed—upon awakening, following exercise, or even while taking a bath.

THOUGHT FOR TODAY: Meditation can be anything I want it to be.

Water washes everything.

—Portuguese proverb

Now that I have become a regular swimmer, it's hard to imagine ever giving it up. The aerobic advantages are of course well known; swimming provides exercise for the entire body without putting undue stress on bones, joints, and muscles.

Then, too, there's nothing quite like the silky feel of water on one's skin. When I'm finished with my swimming workout, I feel clean and invigorated. All muscular tension has dissolved; I'm completely relaxed and supple.

Physical benefits aside, swimming almost always calms my mind. When I'm in a pool, lake, or ocean, it's easy to put my thoughts on hold as I watch the interplay of light and shadow and listen to the sound of my body moving through the water.

During the forty minutes of swimming, it's as if I've been transported to another plane. I am far from the workaday sounds of voices, traffic, radios, telephones. This sense of positive isolation often leads me into a meditative state. My swim can bring about spiritual experiences, ranging from a simple state of tranquility to an active interface with my Higher Power.

THOUGHT FOR TODAY: There's a lot more to working out than strengthening muscles and burning calories.

May 14

The promises of this world are for the most part vain phantoms, and to confide in one's self, and become something of worth and value, is the best and safest course.

—Michelangelo

When we first set out to change our lifestyle, we did so largely because we wanted to improve our self-worth. We expected we'd make progress along these lines, but we never dreamed there could be such a dramatically positive alteration in the way we felt about ourselves.

In the past, before we started taking actions to improve our health and well-being, our behavior around other people all too clearly reflected our low opinion of ourselves. We tended to mumble our words, avert our eyes, and even camouflage ourselves with drab, nondescript clothing. Without being truly aware of it, some of us behaved in ways designed to repel rather than attract others.

Today, thankfully, our growing self-worth allows us to feel and act increasingly self-confident and poised. Because we are more relaxed and accepting of ourselves, our true personalities are at long last emerging.

We are becoming more open and outgoing, with nothing to hide. We feel more attractive on the inside and, as the result, are becoming more appealing to other people.

THOUGHT FOR TODAY: The better I feel about myself, the more attractive I am.

The Wright brothers flew right through the smoke screen of impossibility.
—Charles Franklin Kettering

We've all had people in our lives who have been nonsupportive, skeptical, and even vehemently critical of our goals and aspirations. The motivation for such behavior may range from envy to a desire to keep us confined within someone's long-standing image of us.

There is the teacher or close friend who insists our career choice is unrealistic or overly ambitious. There is the spouse who is certain we will never be able to quit smoking because our past efforts have been unsuccessful. And there are the parents who react with horror when we announce we are learning to ski—because, they say, we've always been accident-prone.

If we remain passive in the face of such negative influences, they can have a deadening effect—not only on our personal self-confidence, but on our ability to perform and progress in certain areas.

One of the hallmarks of maturity is a willingness to periodically assess our ideas and attitudes. If we find that they are not working or are based on false information, we must do what's necessary to let them go or transcend them. What is possible or impossible in our lives is entirely up to us.

THOUGHT FOR TODAY: Am I being limited by my old ideas—or someone else's old ideas?

May 16

I shall not hold my little peace; for me
There is no peace but one.

—Alice Meynell

Finding ways to reduce stress in my life is an ongoing challenge. I've always been a high-strung, driven person. When I'm willing to use it, the one tool that unfailingly alleviates stress for me is surrender—*giving up, letting go, letting God.*

Typically, I'm on my way to an appointment. Traffic is inching along because of roadwork, and I know I'll be very late. I'm getting more and more upset, to the point of physical symptoms. My fists are clenched, my stomach is churning, I have a pounding headache. When I finally realize the absurdity of my reaction, I take a deep breath and surrender. I tell myself, "I'm in traffic. There's a car in front of me and one behind me. There's nothing I can do." I accept my powerlessness and soon become composed.

Or perhaps I'm swimming laps in the local college pool. Halfway through my workout, two new swimmers start crowding my lane, occasionally bumping me. I lose my cool and end up gulping water. I begin to feel exhausted. Eventually I see the irony: I'm swimming to reduce stress and enjoy myself, but the opposite is occurring. I surrender, relax, and regain my rhythm.

THOUGHT FOR TODAY: When there's nothing I can do, there's always one thing I can do: Surrender.

*You can never have a greater or a lesser dominion
than that over yourself.*

—Leonardo da Vinci

It's up to me to make my life more meaningful and
fulfilling. It's up to me to take the initiative in
exploring new and diverse intellectual, physical, and
spiritual activities.

There are so many opportunities each day to get
out of myself and enrich my life. I can strike up
conversations with people whose points of view or
backgrounds are unlike my own. I can experiment
with and learn new physical skills, from water sports
to the martial arts. I can stimulate my senses by
listening to new forms of music, by trying new foods,
by attending art, cinema, and theater events outside
of my usual pattern.

I can approach my life as an oil painter would a
canvas. I have a choice as to colors and composition,
style and texture. Even after I have begun, I have the
ability to change my palette and reshape the work.

If I follow the same routine day after day and
month after month—if my life is weighed down with
sameness to the point of boredom—where does the
responsibility lie?

THOUGHT FOR TODAY: If there are limiting
boundaries to my life, it is likely that I've structured
them myself.

May 18

The strongest principle of growth lies in human choice.

—George Eliot

That special occasion is just around the corner. This time, hopefully, we're going to experience it differently. Because frankly, we're sick and tired of the Holiday Blues.

Year after year we've trudged through the same bog of self-pity and poor-me-ism. On our birthdays we've bemoaned the fact that we are one year older and haven't accomplished more. On Independence Days we've enviously whined that other people are having real picnics, with real friends and real family. During year-end holidays we've wallowed in nostalgic sadness for good companions and good cheer long gone.

From now on we're going to follow a different path. One thing that can help us is to remember that the holiday or anniversary—beyond its personal meaning—is simply another day. Depending on what makes us comfortable, we can invest as much or as little emotion as we choose.

We can also choose how we approach the special occasion—with self-pity and sadness, or with gratitude for the health, good friends, and good times that we have today.

THOUGHT FOR TODAY: Special days can bring stress or satisfaction. The choice is mine.

Almost all absurdity of conduct arises from the imitation of those whom we cannot resemble.
—Samuel Johnson

There's that TV ad again, the sleek and smiling couple honing their bodies on the newest machines, wearing the latest workout clothes, pitching the perfect diet food.

Those flashing images might inspire and motivate some of us into action. But if we're considerably overweight, seriously out of shape, or many dollars away from being able to join a health club, those perfect people could make us feel more depressed than ever. We might rationalize, "I'll never look like that. So why even try?"

If we believe that fitness and good health are important objectives, we should beware of trying to remake ourselves into a marketer's idea of perfection. It's a sure setup for failure and discouragement. However, that doesn't mean we have to choose the alternative of resignation and the same old unhealthful lifestyle. There's an in-between place for each of us.

We can find it by shifting our mind-set from those advertising images into the reality of our own lives, our own bodies, our own needs and capabilities. We can set our own personally unique goals. We can think and act realistically as we work toward good health.

THOUGHT FOR TODAY: Someone else's vision of perfection has no relevance to what's right for me.

May 20

Men suffer from thinking more than anything else.
—Leo Tolstoy

I was telling a longtime friend about the trouble I was having with negative thinking. "I know what you mean," she interrupted excitedly. "This is going to sound corny, but hear me out."

She went on to tell me about being barraged with a volley of negative thoughts each morning before her feet even hit the floor. They ranged far and wide, from her finances to her looks to her relationship with an older sister.

As in my own case, some of the thoughts involved events that had already occurred, some related to future possibilities, and some floated into her head without apparent rhyme or reason.

"Here's the corny part," she continued. "I read about a man who went on what he called a 'negative thought diet.' The way it works, you imagine that each negative thought is the worst possible food for your body and soul. And you avoid it.

"Nothing else was working, so out of desperation I tried the diet for a week. It's been going so well that I'm still on it six weeks later. I can't tell you how good I feel! It's like I've been set free."

THOUGHT FOR TODAY: Negativity is hazardous to my health.

*Love doesn't just sit there, like a stone; it has to be
made, like bread; remade all the time, made new.*
— Ursula K. Le Guin

Faded romance is not only the stuff of novels and
movies, but all too frequently a part of life itself. Most
of us have been in relationships which began passion-
ately, but after a time lost their magic—even though
love was still shared.

It's one thing to love someone, but it's quite
another to keep that love fresh and alive. So through
words and actions, we try to express our loving
feelings, not just once in a while, but often.

We show love by being supportive and encouraging, refusing to "give up" on friends and family
members even when they are tempted to give up on
themselves. We are good listeners, generous with our
time and attention; but we also know when to back
off, letting our loved ones learn from their own
experience.

Sometimes, though, love involves teaching another person what we've already learned. We try to
do so with patience and gentleness. We respect the
quality and pace of our loved ones' personal growth
without getting in the way or comparing their
progress to our own.

THOUGHT FOR TODAY: I value the love in my
life, and am unwilling to let it drift away.

Humility, like darkness, reveals the heavenly lights.
—Henry David Thoreau

Now that we're following a spiritual path, there are moments, hours, and even entire days during which we enjoy real peace of mind. This newfound serenity is a priceless gift. Indeed, it seems nothing short of miraculous, considering that our emotions in the past were usually limited to excitement, anxiety, or anger.

To bring about this inner tranquility, many changes have had to take place in our lives. We've had to uncover our true selves and come to grips with the self-centeredness which to this day can put us on an emotional rollercoaster. We've had to alter our attitudes, modify our behavior, and learn new and more realistic ways of getting along with ourselves and the people around us.

Of greatest significance, we've come to believe in a Power greater than ourselves. A basic thrust of our life today is seeking God's will for us, and doing our best to carry it out. The more we are able to put aside our own limited desires and to align our thinking and actions with God's plan, the more humility we gain. And this, above all else, is the key to our serenity today.

THOUGHT FOR TODAY: Serenity can be found on the road from self-centeredness to humility.

What lies behind us and what lies before us are small matters compared to what lies within us.
> —Ralph Waldo Emerson

Four days had passed since my heart surgery. It was two A.M., but I couldn't sleep. As I stared at the instrument which monitored and displayed my heart functions, I wondered if I could somehow influence my pulse rate.

I vaguely remembered reading about biofeedback experiments—people who actually lowered their skin temperature by imagining themselves in a freezing environment; yogis who used the power of their minds to almost instantaneously slow their blood flow.

I decided to try it. I visualized my heart and "willed" it to pump less rapidly. I focused all my thoughts toward that end. To my amazement, my pulse rate began to decrease incrementally—from 72 to 69 to 67. Over a period of several minutes it dropped all the way down to 64. Then, using the same technique, I was able to bring the digital readout up to 90.

At the time, my little experiment simply helped get me through a restless night. Since learning more about biofeedback techniques, I've come to strongly believe that I can use my mind not only to influence my body's workings, but to improve my health. This belief, and its practical application, gives me encouragement, hope, and peace of mind.

THOUGHT FOR TODAY: Am I truly open-minded about the healing power within?

May 24

It is a grievous illness to preserve one's health by a regimen too strict.

—Duc de La Rochefoucauld

For time immemorial, overweight people have fallen prey to hucksters offering quick fixes. Each year in the U.S. alone, billions of dollars are spent on liquids, powders, and pills promising to take weight off quickly and effortlessly.

Chances are, those of us with a weight problem have tried one or more of these products in the past, and will be sorely tempted to do so again.

Promises and overblown expectations aside, researchers have proven that crash and fad diets not only fail as a rule, but also can cause serious harm to the dieter. In the first place, the pounds lost through extremely low-calorie diets are usually water or muscle tissue. As a result, the weight we lose is easily regained.

More seriously, consistent or repeated crash dieting deprives us of essential nutrients. This nutritional deficit not only adversely affects metabolic function, but also physical appearance. When we don't consume enough nutrients, our bodies turn muscle tissue into energy; we tend to look peaked and to become flabby.

Beyond all of that, crash diets don't bring about a change in eating habits, which, as we all know, is a prerequisite to achieving and maintaining long-term weight loss.

THOUGHT FOR TODAY: I will take care of my health needs sensibly and safely.

Powerful indeed is the empire of habit.
                                    —Publilius Syrus

When I congratulated a friend for quitting smoking, he responded, "I'm not out of the woods yet. But almost." He told me it had been three weeks since his last cigarette, and he felt confident that he could stay stopped a day at a time. However, he was still having troublesome cravings at certain times.

"I want a cigarette first thing in the morning, before I'm fully awake," he said. "Every time I talk on the phone I automatically reach for one. At work, I set a pace that builds to a crescendo, and that used to be the time for a cigarette break. And of course, after meals."

When I nodded understandingly, my friend said he had already found ways to break away from some of his habit patterns. He brushes his teeth as soon as he awakens, forestalling the day's first cigarette. At work he has set a new rhythm, avoiding peaks which make him feel deserving of a cigarette "reward."

"The next thing"—he smiled confidently—"is to move my phone to the other side of the desk. That way I'll have to hold the receiver with my smoking hand. It's worth a try, wouldn't you say?"

THOUGHT FOR TODAY: Can I find ways to alter my destructive habits, or do I see them as unchangeable, destined to forever rule my life?

May 26

I am not now That which I have been.
— George Gordon Byron

We knew hardly anything about ourselves. The awareness we did have was limited to the emotional turmoil of our lives—our constant anxiety, irritability, moodiness, and depression. Certain substances— alcohol, drugs, food—would temporarily relieve our inner disquiet, but the symptoms always returned. Eventually the "cure" became worse than the problem.

In recovery, we began at long last to gain an understanding of what was going on inside of us. By looking carefully at our feelings and behavior patterns over the years, we were able to identify the character flaws responsible for most of our emotional difficulties.

We could see how our greed and envy, for example, kept us in a state of dissatisfaction and eroded our self-worth. We could see the futility of our resentments and how they harmed no one but ourselves.

In the same way, we could see how our impatience caused tension in relationships and triggered many of our disastrously impulsive actions.

Once a clear picture emerged, we realized it would actually be possible to finally change our self-destructive ways. And we resolved to move forward in that direction.

THOUGHT FOR TODAY: Self-awareness sets the stage for change.

Tomorrow to fresh woods, and pastures new.
                                            —John Milton

It was truly revelationary to discover that our character defects had been causing a lifetime of anxiety, anguish, and self-destructive behavior. Even more revelationary was the solution presented to us by other recovering people who had been in the same boat.

The first step toward change, we were told, was to become entirely willing to have our character flaws removed. We were encouraged to look deep into our hearts and ask ourselves, for example, if we were truly ready to be rid of the pride that for so long had alienated us from our fellows. Were we also willing to be rid of the self-centered fear that had been such a powerful motivating force in our lives?

We *were* willing to let go of our flaws, unquestionably, but we had little faith in our ability to bring about those changes. Indeed, the prospect was overwhelming; we'd been trying to change our behavior for years with little success.

That's the point, we were told. We don't have to do it on our own, nor can we. God alone has the power. If we ask Him with faith and humility to remove our character defects, we were promised, He will assuredly do so.

THOUGHT FOR TODAY: When I am willing to change, God will help me do so.

By suffering comes wisdom.

—Aeschylus

I can't count the times I've heard or read the expression, "No pain, no gain." It's long been a credo of sports coaching, and in recent years it has become an advertising cliché. Personally, I don't believe that pain is a prerequisite for growth. Moreover, in my experience, pain in and of itself doesn't necessarily result in progress of any kind.

There were any number of periods in my life when I went through intense emotional and physical pain and learned absolutely nothing from the ordeals. Indeed, on some occasions I welcomed pain because of my extremely low self-worth, or used it as an excuse to avoid responsibility.

This is not to say that one can *not* grow through pain. In my own case, the possibility of such growth depends on my willingness to honestly look at myself in relationship to the experience—to be self-searching and self-aware.

I also believe that personal and spiritual growth can come about as the result of pain*less* choices and actions, as well as from pleasurable life experiences that can teach us valuable lessons. These days, I tend to learn as much from joy and serenity as from pain and adversity.

THOUGHT FOR TODAY: I can grow from pain or pleasure, but only if I'm willing to change.

To teach is to learn twice.

—Joseph Joubert

One of the greatest joys of our new life is the ability and desire to teach others what we have worked so hard to learn ourselves.

When a friend asks us to share our spiritual ideas and beliefs, and we are able to explain how spirituality enhances our life, we appreciate that reality all the more.

By passing along our experience, hope, and joy to others who want to quit smoking or overeating, we benefit in several ways. We are reminded of the desperation that finally brought about our own surrender. We also feel renewed gratitude for our recovery, and the freedom and health we enjoy today.

When we have the opportunity to introduce someone to a new sport, craft, or art form, we can't help but feel pleasure. The teaching process automatically rekindles our own love for that special activity. It restores our enthusiasm and reminds us of the joys we may have been taking for granted.

When we give of ourselves at any level—whether teaching a child to read or helping someone understand the nature of nicotine withdrawal—we are bound to experience a solid sense of purpose and well-being.

THOUGHT FOR TODAY: By passing along what I have received, I receive even more.

May 30

The wealth of rich feelings—the deep—the pure;
With strength to meet sorrow, and faith to endure.
—Frances S. Osgood

We don't usually think of food as a drug, but that's how some of us used it. Food soothed us when we were overwrought, subdued us when we were angry, numbed us when we felt guilty, and even filled our time when we were bored. In short, overeating blocked out our painful feelings and allowed us to cope with our problems.

When we sought help and began to recover from our food addiction, we were inundated by the same feelings we had buried or sidestepped for years. As painful as some of those feelings were, this time around we toughed them out and gradually found ways to work through them.

In the case of anger, for example, we learned to express it appropriately and constructively, instead of keeping it inside. As for fear, the underlying thread and activator of most of our unpleasant emotions, we found relief by putting ourselves in God's hands—turning to faith rather than food.

Boredom, in turn, seemed to take care of itself. The world opened up for us and we set out to enjoy it.

THOUGHT FOR TODAY: Is my eating problem really a living problem?

But still I dream that somewhere there must be
The spirit of a child that waits for me.
                                        —Bayard Taylor

For almost a month I had ridden my new mountain bike on asphalt streets and level dirt roads. Now it was time for my first real off-road experience.

I rode with an avid cyclist, the woman who had inspired me to take up the sport. We traversed meadows and stream beds, and as usual she was encouraging and helpful. At first, everything went smoothly. Then, as we began a steep descent, fear gripped me. I visualized myself with a shattered leg and a serious case of road rash.

I told my friend to stop. Trying to keep the panic out of my voice, I asked, "What do I do if the bike slides out from under me?" Her response was quick and reassuring. "Stay loose and just let yourself fall. That way you won't get hurt."

Later, I thought about what natural athletes we are as children, and how quickly we learn before fears, self-consciousness, and other inhibitions cause physical tension. I realized that I would have to regain that childhood birthright in order to eliminate my fear. I would have to learn again to "stay loose" mentally and emotionally, and to let my natural abilities reassert themselves.

THOUGHT FOR TODAY: I have natural grace and skill; I won't let my mind trip me up.

June 1

Character building begins in our infancy and continues until death.

—Eleanor Roosevelt

Even in recovery, our character flaws never seem to disappear entirely. Thankfully, however, they do change in intensity and frequency as we strive to become less self-centered. We still get angry from time to time, but these days our anger rarely develops into out-of-control rage or smoldering resentment.

In some cases, our character defects actually evolve into character *assets*. For example, where once our compulsiveness resulted in single-minded, irresponsible behavior, we are now able to harness its energy in constructive ways. Our compulsiveness can be transformed into determination, drive, and discipline—the traits we need to complete challenging projects and reach ambitious goals.

In the same way, the perfectionism which once led us into a vicious cycle of failure and frustration, now can express itself in organizational skills, as well as care and pride in our realistic objectives and accomplishments.

At one time, we were tormented people-pleasers, eagerly seeking approval no matter what the cost. That negative adaptability now manifests itself as an asset; we are able to get along with others as never before, without compromising our values and individuality.

THOUGHT FOR TODAY: I am a work in progress.

More important than learning how to recall things is finding ways to forget things that are cluttering the mind.

—Eric Butterworth

We've never been especially fond of competition, yet we'll soon be up against half a dozen other candidates in a job interview. The pressure has been mounting; right now we feel fragmented, unfocused, and fearful.

We can't help remembering similar situations in the past, when we "blew it" because of our disordered mental state. And we can't help remembering how we berated ourselves for not being better prepared emotionally.

It goes without saying that competition is sometimes unavoidable, and that we're going to be more successful in some competitive situations than others. But if we prepare ourselves mentally and emotionally for the opportunities that are available, we will certainly have a much better chance of holding our own.

Meditation is an excellent way to become prepared. Sometimes just a few minutes can be enough to bring relaxation—to free our bodies of tension and our minds of the clutter and self-doubt that can trip us up.

The process of meditation helps us let go of fear and find self-confidence. All else being equal—that is, if we are qualified in other respects—calm faith in ourselves may just give us the edge.

THOUGHT FOR TODAY: Meditation can bring me to my clear-minded best.

June 3

Nature is the art of God.

—Dante Alighieri

The ocean waters near my home have recently turned inexplicably warmer, as much as five to ten degrees. For the first time in memory, numerous species of marine life normally found south of the equator have turned up in our northern waters.

In a newspaper article describing the phenomenon, a group of marine biologists expressed amazement, admitting they had no real idea of what was causing the temperature change. My first reaction was one of concern. It was unsettling to learn that after decades of study and billions spent on research, scientists couldn't explain potentially critical changes in our environment.

What would happen to the weather, I wondered. What about surf and ocean currents? What about marine life and the food chain?

But I was soon able to put my concerns aside. Actually, I find it intriguing that there are powerful and mysterious forces in nature over which we still haven't the least bit of control, let alone understanding. I find it comforting to remember that a Power greater than us all regulates and orchestrates not only the unpredictable patterns of nature, but the individual destiny of each of us.

THOUGHT FOR TODAY: There is always the certainty of God.

Life is to be fortified by many friendships. To love and to be loved is the greatest happiness of existence.
—Sydney Smith

We all know what it feels like to be alone. At one time or another, each of us has experienced sadness, self-pity, and even depression because of our isolation from others.

Now we've become aware that unwanted alone-ness also can have weighty physical consequences. We believe it can even change healthy people into sick ones. When we're alone, for example, some of us are less inclined to care for ourselves properly. Similarly, when illness strikes we seem to have less incentive to do what it takes to get well.

That's why, these days, we value our friendships and other close relationships in a new and very special way. The sense of belonging and actual companionship we get from them is as important to our physical health as it is to our emotional well-being.

Taking it further, we've begun to see that the *quality* of our relationships also is significant in this regard. Relationships based on love, understanding, patience, and open communication tend to enhance our overall well-being. In turn, relationships fraught with hostility, resentment, and dishonesty invariably have the opposite effect.

THOUGHT FOR TODAY: Loving relationships in my life contribute to my wellness.

June 5

It's not what you were, it's what you are today.
—David Marion

We all occasionally compromise ourselves in order to avoid confrontation. For some of us, such behavior was a constant in our lives. Passivity and acquiescence became a protective cloak that helped us make our way through the world.

In our new life, we've come to realize that continuing passivity damages us in many ways. When we sidestep real-life issues and eventualities so as not to "make waves," we end up feeling helpless, humiliated, and resentful. We are constantly disappointed in ourselves. All of these feelings add up to a sizable burden of stress.

It's been a major challenge to become more assertive, but we're succeeding. We're finally learning to stand up for ourselves, instead of continuing to live according to other people's priorities. Day by day, we are walking through the fear of confrontation and rejection and finding ways to express our feelings and opinions.

The more assertive we're able to be, the better we feel about ourselves. We have more self-respect, as well as more time and energy for our own priorities. The stress that used to overwhelm us continues to diminish.

THOUGHT FOR TODAY: The path of least resistance can lead to an emotional dead end.

The mouth that lies slays the soul.

—John Ray

I learned early on that I could get a lot of attention by dramatizing events and problems in my life. It was my habit to make mountains out of molehills, and I became a master at drawing other people into my high-drama world. I always had a story to tell.

Yes, I blew everything out of proportion to feed my need for self-importance and to elicit sympathy. But the truth is that I didn't know any other way to live. Because of the way I was raised, I rarely experienced peace of mind. I never learned the value of calmness and serenity.

I paid a big price for those years of living from one crisis to the next. Over time, I suffered a number of serious health problems that were either caused or exacerbated by the constant stress. Eventually it became clear that if I didn't change, my lifestyle would be my undoing.

Slowly but surely, I became aware of my tendency to overdramatize and act impulsively. Gradually I was able to change. These days, I try to evaluate situations as they arise and not give them one iota more attention or emotion than they deserve.

THOUGHT FOR TODAY: Do I still have a need to overdramatize events—and my role in them?

*The very word "God" suggests care, kindness, good-
ness; and the idea of God in His infinity, is infinite
care, infinite kindness, infinite goodness. We give
God the name of good: it is only by shortening it that
it becomes God.*

—Henry Ward Beecher

Today I will visualize the abundance with which God
has blessed me. He provides me with everything I
need, sometimes in answer to a heartfelt prayer, but
always in accordance with His Divine plan for good in
my life.

I visualize the genuine enthusiasm with which I
now approach each new day. My positive outlook and
energy lead me toward rich and satisfying feelings and
experiences.

More often than not, I feel a deep sense of inner
strength, security, and serenity. I have a wellspring of
God-given resources and capabilities that can safely
see me through every life experience.

I will visualize the life-enhancing power of my
mind. There are no limits to my creativity and
imagination, nor to the flow of positive thoughts and
ideas with which I can shape my existence.

I am grateful for the special traits that have
begun to flourish within me. My growing understanding, compassion, and ability to express love and hope
enrich my relationships with others and myself in
ways I never dreamed possible.

THOUGHT FOR TODAY: Am I taking full advantage of my God-given abundance?

*Seize now and here the hour that is, nor trust some
later day!*

—Horace

It's amazing how creative we can be when it comes to
finding excuses for putting things off. Some of us not
only regularly fall into the trap of procrastination, but
have turned it into an art form.

We definitely intend to stop overeating and lose
weight. But we'll be going on vacation in a few weeks.
Then, a month after that will be Thanksgiving, and
Christmas. So we might as well wait until after the
first of the year. . . .

Our health problems would be helped significantly with regular exercise, no question about that.
But there's no point in taking up walking if we're
going to buy an exercise bike. Besides, it will be a lot
easier to work out after we've quit smoking. . . .

We're absolutely going to write a personal inventory to become more self-aware; we know how much
our friends have benefited from that. But let's see,
this weekend we're supposed to wax the car and bathe
the dog, then there's our anniversary the following
week. . . .

If we could divert even half the energy that we
spend on procrastinating toward positive, life-
affirming actions, we'd be well on our way to good
health and well-being.

THOUGHT FOR TODAY: Haven't I put it off long
enough?

June 9

*A man should never be ashamed to own he is in the
wrong, which is but saying, in other words, that he is
wiser today than he was yesterday.*

—Alexander Pope

Recently a friend and his eight-year-old son came to
visit me. The boy watched television in another room
while his father and I talked. We soon heard a crash,
and found the boy standing over the fragments of a
porcelain egg. His face was red and he was on the
verge of tears, but he adamantly denied touching the
souvenir.

The scene reminded me so much of my own
behavior—not only as a child, but also as an adult—
that it was hard to keep from smiling. No matter what
damage I caused, no matter how obvious my culpa-
bility, I almost never admitted my wrongs. Pride and
fear kept me silent.

When I looked at the little boy's face that day, I
clearly remembered the inner turmoil I felt when
I refused to admit I was wrong. I knew; they knew; I
knew that they knew. Yet I stubbornly held my
ground.

It's so much easier to promptly admit it when I'm
wrong. It's always a relief to apologize and clear the
air. It's such a freeing experience to swallow my
pride, own up to my mistakes, and go back to feeling
serene again.

THOUGHT FOR TODAY: When I am wrong, I will
promptly admit it.

It is not who is right, but what is right, that is important.

—Thomas Huxley

Whenever there is a disagreement or conflict of some kind in our personal or work relationships, many of us tend to approach it in absolute terms: Who is right? Who is wrong? Where does the fault lie? Frequently, our main concern is to prove that we are blameless.

Such a reaction only serves to prolong and deepen a disagreement. We learn nothing about ourselves and are unable to solve or resolve anything. If there is any resolution at all, it takes the form of one person or "side" feeling smug and self-righteous while the other feels hurt, defeated, and resentful.

It is a spiritual axiom that whenever we are emotionally upset, we need to look within ourselves to search out the character flaws that may be contributing to our distress. The same principle has great relevance to our interactions with others.

If we are to achieve harmonious and stress-free relationships, we need always look first at our part in any quarrel or dispute. No matter what another person has done or said, we're always better off focusing on how *we* might have contributed to the problem through action, word, or attitude.

THOUGHT FOR TODAY: In the interest of harmony and spiritual growth, am I willing to look at my role in the conflict?

June 11

All our actions take their hue from the complexion of the heart, as landscapes do their variety from light.
—William Thompson Bacon

As my reservoir of guilt and dread gradually drained in early recovery, I began to experience periods of well-being and serenity. At the time, I associated those positive emotions solely with being happy, doing something pleasurable, or simply feeling good.

Ultimately, well-being took on new meanings and dimensions. It could result from varied experiences, not only such obviously pleasurable ones as being on a winning softball team or spending an enjoyable day at the beach.

More and more these days, my sense of well-being—or the lack of it—relates directly to my motives, behavior, ability to be disciplined, and self-respect.

When I've kept my priorities in order, even in the face of temptation, frustration, or similar pressures, I have a sense of well-being.

Even though I am mentally exhausted after a long day of work, I'm rewarded with a sense of well-being if I've given my all.

When I see an easy chance to gain something by being dishonest—and choose not to—I feel a sense of well-being.

When I stand up for my beliefs, despite argument, contempt, or even animosity from others, I gain a sense of well-being.

THOUGHT FOR TODAY: It's not where I go or what I do, but how I act and who I am.

The positive emotions are no less a physiological factor on the upside than are the negative emotions on the downside.

—Norman Cousins

When people asked us how we were doing, we almost always said "fine"—even when we weren't doing well or feeling well. We were used to repressing our feelings, especially painful ones; besides, we rationalized, we were private people and didn't want to burden anyone.

These days, however, we are not so quick to internalize our true feelings and concerns. We've learned that when we do, we harm ourselves. We've come to believe that there is a very powerful connection between the mind and body, which together comprise an amazing self-healing system.

We find that the system works to our best advantage when our mind sends our body truthful and self-affirming messages. And the opposite takes place when we input negative messages by repressing our feelings or deprecating ourselves. Then the system can work against us.

In essence, our self-healing system is at its best when we have inner peace. That's why we try to communicate—to ourselves as well as to others—openly, honestly, and fearlessly. When we get angry, we let it out. When we feel like crying, we do. And if we need to ask for help, we do that too.

THOUGHT FOR TODAY: I will strengthen my mind-body alliance.

June 13

Defined in psychological terms, a fanatic is a man who consciously overcompensates a secret doubt.
—Aldous Huxley

We step on the bathroom scale in the morning and discover to our horror that we weigh two pounds more than we did yesterday. From that moment on, the day is ruined. Our preoccupation with those two pounds impinges on and influences everything we do.

We approach our fitness and sports workouts, for example, solely in terms of "calorie burning," so that they become remedies for a problem rather than the enjoyable life activities they are meant to be.

Those of us who get caught up in this obsessive approach to weight loss know that it can sabotage our health and fitness programs and turn us into emotional wrecks. At such times, we need to focus on some basic realities. Our primary goal is to enhance our overall well-being; losing excess body fat is but one means to that end. Moreover, because weight consists not only of fat, but also muscle, bone, and, in particular, water, it changes hour by hour.

For these reasons, it's better to approach the morning scale-reading not with dread but with objectivity. Let's not forget that our scale is meant to be an indicator, not a tyrant or guilt-giver.

THOUGHT FOR TODAY: An obsessive pursuit of well-being will cause me more harm than good.

The fire you kindle for your enemy often burns yourself more than him.

—Chinese proverb

No one will disagree that anger creates stress. When **we** get angry our adrenaline flows, our heart races, our breathing becomes rapid and shallow.

If we quickly and constructively deal with our anger, the stress can be as short-lived as the emotion. If on the other hand we allow anger to develop into resentment, we will reexperience the stress each time we mentally rehash the event that made us angry in the first place.

It follows that as long as we carry resentment, we will have stress simmering along with it. And as we well know, this long-term stress can cause physical symptoms ranging from muscle tension to a weakening of the body's immune system.

Many of us have allowed resentments to accumulate and burden us for years. We've never fully gotten over the hurtful experiences—such as parental abuse, lack of love, or rejection—that we suffered long ago. Our feelings may have been justified when those experiences first occurred; however, we pay a tremendous emotional and physical price by continuing to re-create them in our minds.

THOUGHT FOR TODAY: Locked-in resentment causes locked-in stress.

Man is free at the moment he wishes to be.

—Voltaire

We're finally making progress in dealing with a lifetime of resentments and the long-term stress they've been causing us. We've acknowledged at a gut level that our resentments hurt no one but ourselves.

But where do we go from here? It's one thing to sincerely want to release resentments in the interest of self-preservation, but knowing how to effectively go about it is quite another matter.

There are a number of steps we can take to become free of our resentments. A good way to start is by making a list of them—including our recollections of the event, the people or institutions involved, and how we were harmed at the time. Seeing a long-ago occurrence against the backdrop of today's realities can help us recognize the futility and childishness of hanging on to resentments.

We can also unburden ourselves by practicing the spiritual principle of forgiveness. Looking back, we can try to be understanding of our "adversary" and consider how we might have contributed to the discord.

Above all, we can rely on faith by turning to God and asking Him to remove our resentments.

THOUGHT FOR TODAY: Am I doing all I can to defuse the destructive power of my resentments?

Who would not give a trifle to prevent what he would give a thousand worlds to cure?

—Edward Young

For many of us with nagging but relatively minor health problems, there comes a time when we finally shift our focus from treatment to prevention. The change may be the result of a doctor's admonition, a gradual dawning, or a moment of clarity.

A friend of mine had such a sudden realization one day while cleaning out his medicine cabinet. "By the time I was through I had filled a shopping bag with expired prescriptions and over-the-counter medicines," he said. "I couldn't remember what half the stuff was for.

"Whenever I got sick, which was often—with colds, indigestion, muscle soreness, you name it—I'd make a beeline to the drugstore. I'd load up on medicine, rest up, get well, then go out and run myself into the ground all over again.

"So now I've been concentrating on prevention rather than treatment, and it's been over a year since I've been sick," he told me proudly. "It's all pretty basic stuff—there's nothing magical about it. You know, balanced diet, plenty of rest, exercise, less stress. It's made a world of difference. I've never been healthier or felt better."

THOUGHT FOR TODAY: I have more control over my health than I may realize.

June 17

Accept my thoughts for thanks; I have no words.
                                        —Hannah More

There was a time, for many of us, when one or another special desire loomed large and often. After the daydream had run its course, we dismissed it from our minds. It was, after all, only a daydream.

Our desires and aspirations were not the stuff of fairy tales. They didn't involve living on a tropical isle with a perfect mate or coming into a fortune. To the contrary, they were quite practical and down to earth.

They involved things like becoming comfortable enough with ourselves to spend a quiet day alone; sleeping the night through without being tormented by our own mind-chatter; climbing a flight of stairs, or carrying a suitcase across an airport terminal, without becoming winded and exhausted; having a loving and supportive network of friends; becoming free of our addictions and obsessions—free to live our lives as they were meant to be lived.

When we glance backward and then forward again to the present moment, it's amazing how many of these dreams have turned into reality. Even more amazing, however, is how often we take them for granted.

THOUGHT FOR TODAY: Now that my dreams are reality, have I remained grateful?

Life is a quarry, out of which we are to mold and chisel and complete a character.
—Johann Wolfgang von Goethe

Spiritual fitness has become a major new priority in our lives. When we are spiritually fit, we have a solid sense of God's presence and love. It is easier to accept whatever comes our way. We possess inner poise, strength, and serenity. We have a desire to serve others.

As with other forms of fitness, spiritual fitness is something we work for on a continuing basis. Just as we can lose muscle tone and endurance when we stop exercising, so too can we lose the sense of purpose and well-being that comes from regular spiritual activity.

Of course, spirituality's focus is uniquely personal for each of us. Here are just some of the ways we nourish our spiritual selves. . . .

We seek closeness with our Higher Power through prayer and meditation. We regularly participate in those activities which we find spiritually fulfilling—such as seeking oneness with nature, helping others, interacting with other spiritually aware people. We try each day to be conscious of our blessings and to sincerely express our gratitude to God.

THOUGHT FOR TODAY: Am I enriching my spiritual self?

June 19

The spectacles of experience; through them you will see clearly a second time.

—Henrik Ibsen

It's not something we would proudly include on a psychological résumé, but most of us tend to blame other people for making us feel a certain way.

Various actions or even innuendos by others—what we call "button pushing"—bring predictable responses from us. We complain, "He made me angry," or "They got me really depressed." We may go so far as to say, "She took all the joy out of my life."

When we blame others for our emotions, we set ourselves up as helpless, hapless victims. What we fail to realize is that it's possible to *choose our response* to anything that happens in life.

We may be limited in our ability to change the external stimulus—whether it's a parent's unkind remark or a supervisor's unfair criticism—but we have unlimited ability to control our own reactions and determine how we actually experience events.

Once we start taking responsibility in this way, it becomes satisfyingly clear that we create our own emotions—not just anger and sadness, but also excitement, fulfillment, and joy.

THOUGHT FOR TODAY: For better or for worse, I alone am responsible for my reactions.

A moment's insight is sometimes worth a life's experience.

—Oliver Wendell Holmes

Thinking back over my life, I can recall numerous disastrous mistakes and missteps which could have been avoided or prevented had I listened to the warnings of my inner voice. In each instance I allowed the louder, more strident voice of ego and self-will to drown out the intuition which would have served me so much better.

It has taken a lot of willingness and practice to be able to differentiate between the conflicting voices within, and that remains an important goal. Another goal is to develop greater trust in my caring, protective inner voice. There is no question that it is the truest source of guidance available to me.

My inner voice has been strongest and most persuasive during the times in my life when I have been closest to God. Bearing that in mind, I try through prayer to ask Him for guidance and through meditation to listen for His response.

It may come in the form of a sharp emotional reaction, a physical sensation sweeping through me, an image, or an actual verbal admonition. Regardless of how the message ultimately expresses itself, it will be there.

THOUGHT FOR TODAY: More often than not, the answer can be found within.

June 21

Second thoughts are even wiser.

—Euripides

I went to an electronics show not long ago where the latest high-tech video equipment was displayed. Some of the gadgetry was remarkable in capability, and I fantasized about what might be available five or ten years into the future.

I imagined an electronic device that would capture my thoughts as quickly as they formed in my mind, then print them out on a screen. I then began to reflect on the nature of my moment-to-moment thoughts. For the most part, they consist of fragments— old ideas and memories, future-oriented speculations and fears—which speed through my consciousness like shooting stars.

The revelationary and somewhat frightening part of my fantasy was realizing how often I *act* on these incomplete "mind bursts." More often than not, such random thoughts, and the feelings and actions they precipitate, influence and actually shape my life.

The device that I envisioned could certainly save me a lot of grief by allowing me to review each thought fragment before automatically acting on it. But why do I need such a device? Why can't I do my own reviews to determine the soundness of my thoughts—starting right now?

THOUGHT FOR TODAY: I will weigh the thought before taking the action.

In delay we waste our lights in vain; like lamps by day.

—William Shakespeare

We fully understand that the past is behind us, the future hasn't yet arrived, and all that exists is the present moment. The concept of *living in the now* has become an important part of our philosophy. Sometimes, however, we forget about the word "living"— that part of the phrase indicating energy, incentive, and action.

All too often we get stuck where we are, waiting for some outside person or outside influence to get things moving so that our lives can improve. We become captives of contingency, so to speak.

We may decide to revitalize our life by moving from the city to the country. But because the whole project is *contingent* on selling the house, our personal and spiritual progress grinds to a halt. There are things we want to do and places we want to go, but we put our aspirations and goals on hold "until the kids grow up," or until we find someone special to share the adventure.

We can always find excuses to keep us from taking risks and getting on with our lives. Yet if we keep waiting for every piece of the puzzle to fall perfectly into place, life will pass us by.

THOUGHT FOR TODAY: It's one thing to appreciate the here and now, but it's quite another to actively and energetically *live* in it.

June 23

What we need more than anything else is more facts about feelings.

—Don Robinson

We usually know when we are under stress; our body tells us—with a stiff neck, a gnawing stomach, a throbbing headache. We also usually know the source of the stress. However, we tend to characterize it in general terms—the job, the marriage, the money situation—and that's as far as we go.

If we take the time to go further, we're likely to find that our stressful feelings are as much the result of our reactions to life's events as the events themselves.

That's why some of us write out a "stress inventory" during trying times. This practice helps us pinpoint the particular aspect of our job or relationship, for example, that's upsetting us. More important, it can reveal how we may be contributing to the stress. Here are the kinds of questions we might ask. . . .

What sort of occurrences usually cause my strongest negative reactions? Are there certain people to whom I almost always react negatively? Is the way I react based on present reality, or is it tied to memories of painful past experiences?

Of course, each of us can develop our own list of questions. If we are honest with our answers, the inventory can show us exactly where to focus our attention.

THOUGHT FOR TODAY: Do I know enough about my stressful feelings?

To desire the same things and to reject the same things, constitute true friendship.

—Sallust

In addition to their well-known physical and emotional benefits, fitness programs and sports activities provide the opportunity to meet other people and enrich our social lives. Exercise and sports offer a natural and easy way to get involved and make friends, especially for those of us who have difficulty getting to know others, either because of shyness or a history of isolation.

Without a doubt, the love of a particular sport—such as tennis, volleyball, surfing, or skiing—brings people together in very special ways. People who train together and enjoy a particular activity form a unique bond; almost automatically they have a feeling of camaraderie and a basis for mutual understanding.

Team sports offer still another kind of fellowship. Team membership gives us a feeling of being needed and a sense of belonging. Team spirit, in turn, can be a great morale booster.

Having one or more sports "buddies" can do wonders in helping us stay committed. We can cheer each other on, provide encouragement, and objectively assess each other in an affirmative and noncompetitive way.

THOUGHT FOR TODAY: Sports can help me out of my shell.

June 25

Nothing under the sun is accidental.
—Gotthold Ephraim Lessing

Well into my thirties, I reacted with total predictability when adversity of any kind came my way. "Why is this happening to me?" I'd cry. Soon thereafter I would be awash in self-pity. I fully believed that I was a perennial victim. Conversely, when something fortuitous occurred, I considered it a lucky break—the exception that proved the rule.

Over a period of years, I've developed a dramatically changed view of life's ebb and flow. I've become convinced that all occurrences in the lives of others as well as my own—the seemingly good and seemingly bad—come to pass for a definite reason.

This is not to say that I'll ever fully understand some of the events that have taken place in my lifetime, nor does it guarantee that I can ever fully accept the fairness or rightness of certain occurrences.

On the broader scale, however, I have come to believe without reservation that God has a plan for ultimate good in my life. All that has taken place, all that is taking place at this moment, and all that will take place in the future, is in accord with His destiny for me.

THOUGHT FOR TODAY: Each day and each year of my life, God's plan for good prevails.

Fill the unforgiving minute with sixty seconds' worth of distance run.

—Rudyard Kipling

As we pursue our physical, emotional, and spiritual goals, it can be rewarding to think of fitness in these areas as *readiness*. When we are fit, we are ready to take advantage of the special opportunities that come our way, and we are truly able to live life to its fullest.

Because we take actions each day to maintain our emotional fitness, we are well equipped to participate positively in new relationships, work challenges, or family involvements. We can be there for others, healthy and whole.

Because we work diligently to stay physically fit, we are ready to make the most of the ski season when it arrives, for example, or to spend long hours hiking through the hills when spring flowers are in bloom. We have a special edge while traveling; we can explore remote areas and enjoy demanding physical adventures.

Because we strive for ever greater spiritual strength, we're better prepared to face adversity, to apply time-proven solutions to problems as they arise, to accept life on life's terms, and to enjoy God's grace in and around us.

THOUGHT FOR TODAY: Fitness is readiness.

June 27

He that respects himself is safe from others. He wears a coat of mail that none can pierce.
—Henry Wadsworth Longfellow

It seems like ages ago, but there was a time when our low self-esteem and fear of people caused us to feel and act like social misfits. Because we became easily flustered, we frequently were tactless and clumsy. We rarely entered or departed rooms and situations, but instead barged in or fled.

Our feelings and behavior have changed dramatically because we have changed on the inside. Over months and years, we've gained self-awareness and have worked hard to grow and mature. We have developed faith and trust in God and, as the result, have a new source of inner strength.

Today, we are usually poised and confident in social situations. Because we've come to know ourselves, it's easier to express ourselves. Because we have learned to value ourselves, we are better able to recognize and appreciate the value of others. Almost always, we remain composed and tactful.

Where once our lack of confidence in social situations burdened us with stress, and caused us to feel inept and unacceptable, our inner poise now brings a deep sense of self-assurance and well-being.

THOUGHT FOR TODAY: Now that I've become comfortable in my own skin, it's so much easier to be comfortable with other people.

Enthusiasm is that secret and harmonious spirit which hovers over the production of genius. . . .
—Isaac D'Israeli

I will approach this day with enthusiasm, eager to recognize and claim all the good that is in store for me. I am determined to find joy today and to share it freely with others.

From my own past experience, I know that when I am enthusiastic, there is always something new to spark my interest and appreciation. When I am enthusiastic, I am sensitive and alert to shadings and facets of life that I might otherwise overlook or ignore. There is the richness of music and art in infinite variety, as well as the constantly changing landscapes of the natural world. There are the pleasures of insights and ideas, humor, laughter, and warm fellowship.

By approaching today's routine activities and responsibilities willingly and enthusiastically, they will be so much easier to handle, and I will get so much more out of them.

Because of my enthusiasm, I'll have a far better chance of achieving my objectives and of taking full advantage of opportunities that are put before me. My hours will be filled with accomplishment and growth, with good feelings and right actions.

THOUGHT FOR TODAY: Enthusiasm is inspirational—and contagious.

June 29

The preservation of health is a duty. Few seem conscious that there is such a thing as physical morality.
—Herbert Spencer

During the first several months after I quit drinking, the next obvious priority was to get my emotional house in order. There was a lot to deal with— becoming self-aware, coming to terms with the past, learning to let go and let God.

Once I began to feel more stable and comfortable in the world, I started thinking about getting healthy in other ways. Even after a substantial period of sobriety, I was still an overweight, out of shape, two-pack-a-day smoker.

No sooner than I vowed to quit smoking and lose weight, an insistent thought began to reverberate in my mind. "It's too late for you," it said. "You've already ruined your health. You might as well just forget it."

And that's exactly what I did for the next few years. I forgot it. But then, a couple of things turned me around. First, my health deteriorated. Second, I realized that my stubborn attitudes about smoking, eating, and exercise were pure rationalization and thoroughly self-defeating.

Finally, and most important, life was becoming increasingly precious to me as I progressed in recovery. More than anything, I wanted to prolong it—and live it to the fullest.

THOUGHT FOR TODAY: It's never too late to start taking better care of myself.
180

The secret of making one's self tiresome, is, not to know when to stop.

—Voltaire

As we pursue our health and fitness objectives, it is important to receive support from those with similar goals, and to be supportive of them. Such interaction helps us to stay committed, allows us to learn from the experience of others, and provides encouragement and hope when we need it.

There is a big difference, however, between constructively discussing one's fitness and diet programs, and obsessively talking them to death. We all know what it's like to become the captive audience of friends or family members who insist on telling us far more about their bodies or diets than we ever care to know.

Come to think of it, at one time or another most of us have victimized others in the same way. It's easy to become so caught up in what we are trying to accomplish that we unthinkingly bore others to tears. Our unbridled enthusiasm can even cause us to pressure others to follow our example.

The point is, as the saying goes, that action speaks louder than words. We have a far better chance of succeeding in our endeavors if we consider them somewhat personal in nature, and save our energies for the action rather than the announcement.

THOUGHT FOR TODAY: When someone expresses interest, do I spring the trap?

July 1

Nature forms us for ourselves, not for others; to be, not to seem.

—Michel Eyquem de Montaigne

At a shopping mall, a friend and I overheard a mother and her young son arguing over a hundred-dollar pair of sneakers. He had to have them because all his friends had them; she wasn't about to put that kind of dent in the family budget.

We were inclined to side with the mother, even though we identified with the pressures on the boy. We acknowledged that most of us, to one degree or another, are motivated by the desire to appear a certain way, to receive certain kinds of reactions, to either blend in or stand out.

If we fall too deeply into that trap, my friend and I agreed, we end up forsaking our true selves. Then, virtually every choice we make is motivated by how it makes us seem, rather than who we actually are and what we actually need.

On the way home, we decided that it might be a good idea for both of us to look at our own behavior in that regard. If it turns out we're slipping into the trap, we promised each other, we would honestly and humbly try to get back to our true selves.

THOUGHT FOR TODAY: Check the motive before you make the move.

There is nothing so easy but that it becomes difficult when you do it with reluctance.

—Terence

From time to time a professional association invites me to speak at their monthly meeting. I usually agree; it's easier to say yes than to come up with a logical or even legitimate reason to say no. I've always dreaded public speaking, but that's beside the point. The real problem is not my fifteen-minute talk, but the days of anguish I put myself through beforehand.

In the same way, for years I would begin torturing myself a full month before income tax time actually arrived. Even early in my career, when the paperwork was limited to three or four uncomplicated items, and no further tax was due, my reluctance and procrastination turned a simple chore into an ordeal.

Looking back, the same sort of approach has tainted social obligations, diminished my job performance, and made any number of experiences more stressful—not just for me, but for everyone around me.

I'm learning, albeit slowly, that whenever I resist a task or responsibility, it becomes twice as difficult and takes twice as long. I have to remind myself that challenges need not become chores, that opportunities need not become obstacles, and that my attitude makes all the difference.

THOUGHT FOR TODAY: Willingness smooths the way.

Happiness is neither within us only, or without us; it is the union of ourselves with God.

—Blaise Pascal

We've always been highly pragmatic people, culturally conditioned to gauge our standing in the world—and with ourselves—by measurable accomplishments and tangible assets.

For a good part of our lives, our sense of well-being increased commensurately when we received a promotion and a pay raise, when we traded in our old car for a new one, or when we bought a house of our own after years of living in a rented apartment.

We couldn't have imagined back then that one day well-being would come more from such seeming abstractions as faith, trust, and gratitude than from the material world.

Yet that is exactly what has occurred. While it's true that money, property, and prestige still can make us feel good about ourselves, today's deeper sense of rightness and joy comes from our relationship with God.

We have abiding faith that He has a plan for good in our lives. We have growing trust that He is always there for us, especially when we turn to Him for guidance and courage. We have strong feelings of gratitude for His presence in our lives and for the blessings He has bestowed upon us.

THOUGHT FOR TODAY: I'm at my best when I'm aware of God's presence.

Observe always that everything is the result of a change, and get used to thinking that there is nothing Nature loves so well as to change existing forms and to make new ones like them.

—Marcus Aurelius

With all our hearts we want to live healthier, more inspired lives. We want to embrace new ways of living. Yet something inside of us resists change.

What's keeping us from taking the actions that will improve our well-being? Why aren't we pursuing the goals we've longed for? What's preventing us from turning our will and life over to the care of a loving God?

For most of us, the answer, in a word, is fear. We're fearful of the transition between the familiar and the unknown. We're afraid of the learning process as well as the discipline and effort that will be required. One of our greatest concerns is that we'll fail.

As we all know, there is no easy way around such deep-rooted and multilayered feelings. Yet just as we may have fear within us, we also have innate courage to do what it takes to fulfill our dreams.

Even the most monumental changes can be accomplished a day at a time. We can move forward at our own pace. Most important, we can replace fear with faith by relying on God and by accepting the guidance and support of those who have gone before us.

THOUGHT FOR TODAY: Life is change.

July 5

No man is free who is not master of himself.
—Epictetus

I once heard a young man describe how his various obsessions caused him unremitting torment and how he was trying to become free of them. "When I wake up in the morning, I ask myself what the *obsession du jour* is, and I proceed from there," he said, only half jokingly.

I laughed heartily at the phrase, for I identified completely. While my obsessiveness no longer leaves me battered and bloody, periodic obsessions can still wreak more emotional havoc than I'm willing to endure.

When I'm obsessed with something—whether it's an unanswered phone call, several unwanted pounds, or something considerably more serious—the price I pay is painful and predictable. I experience life in limited and extremely distorted ways. I become preoccupied, anxious, and angry, and find myself excluding others from my narrowing world.

When I'm able to stop a rising obsession dead in its tracks, or overcome one that has already begun to take hold, I'm always delighted and sometimes amazed with the mental freedom I gain. Instead of wasting my time and emotional energy on a single irrelevant or irremediable issue, my mind is fully available for creative, interesting, and life-enhancing pursuits of all kinds.

THOUGHT FOR TODAY: Set me free and keep me free, God, from obsessiveness.

Thought, busy thought! Too busy for my peace!
—Edward Young

During meditation, a common problem—or what some of us perceive as a problem—is the inability to quiet our minds long enough to get the process started. And even if we can get started, thoughts and images—random memories and forgotten fears—filter into our consciousness. We can't help thinking of tasks waiting to be completed; we can't help feeling self-conscious or self-critical.

The truth is that very few people are able to quiet their minds completely for more than short periods at a time. Remembering this, we shouldn't be discouraged when we temporarily lose the focus of our meditation. It will return.

When free-floating and unexpected thoughts break our calm, it is better not to resist, but to let them flow through without influencing us. Indeed, resistance is what can turn random thoughts into longer-lasting distractions. We can "observe" such thoughts without judging them.

It can also be helpful during meditation to visualize extraneous thoughts as something nonthreatening and pleasurable, such as the wind rustling leaves, or a bubbling stream bringing sound to the forest. Each of us can choose our own image, just as we each choose our own form of meditation.

THOUGHT FOR TODAY: My goal in meditation is spiritual consciousness, not mental unconsciousness.

July 7

I have the greatest riches of all: that of not desiring them.

—Eleonora Duse

In sports, as in all activities, there's no such thing as being perfect. While competitive athletes occasionally receive top-of-the-scale scores for their performances, world champions themselves would be the first to scoff at the idea of athletic perfection.

Yet some people still set their sights on this unattainable goal while participating in sports and fitness programs. Each time they step out on a court, run in a race, or tee off, they expect a perfect performance from themselves. They are intent on serving only "aces," leaving other runners in their dust, or shooting under par.

Those of us who have traveled this frustrating road know that such single-mindedness takes all the pleasure out of what ought to be a deeply satisfying experience. Moreover, the undue pressure we put on ourselves inhibits performance and leads to discouragement.

Certainly there's nothing wrong with expecting and working toward steady improvement in a physical fitness program. In fact, that's what helps us stay interested and motivated. When we stop trying to achieve perfection, that's when we perform at our best and enjoy ourselves to the utmost.

THOUGHT FOR TODAY: Less than perfect is fine with me.

It is not by the gray of the hair that one knows the age of the heart.

—Edward George Bulwer-Lytton

A friend and I attended a play one night. During the intermission, she pointed out two couples chatting at the refreshment bar. "I've been watching them," she said. "Just out of curiosity, how old would you say they are?"

"I'd guess early sixties," I answered.

"You mean my age?" she said with a surprised laugh. "They seem so much older!"

As we waited for the curtain to rise, we agreed that people who reach a certain age are expected to feel and act a certain way. We'd seen it among our friends, some of whom had already gloomily conceded, "It's time to slow down." Sadly, most were in good health and hadn't even reached a so-called advanced age. They were in their sixties, fifties, and even their forties.

My friend and I thankfully concurred that neither of us had fallen into the trap of "acting our age." Nor had we allowed our respective ages to set us apart from other generations, younger or older. This helped us avoid cultural pressures and remain young in spirit. We concluded with satisfaction that we do what we feel like doing, and are as young or old as we want to be.

THOUGHT FOR TODAY: My spirit is ageless.

July 9

It is a great thing to know the season for speech and the season for silence.

—Seneca

It wasn't all that long ago when we had no real idea of what we wanted or needed. And when we did know, many of us lacked the self-confidence and sense of worthiness that would allow us to speak up on our own behalf. Even when we absolutely had to have something—whether it was a schedule change at work, or more physical attention in a relationship—we tended to remain passive and silent.

Our newfound ability to express ourselves is a direct reflection of rising self-esteem. In our relationships, especially, it's becoming easier to tell our partners, friends, and co-workers what we desire and require.

We are learning that our wants and needs are far more likely to be met when we verbalize them. It's also beneficial, we've discovered, to be assertive and specific when we privately visualize and affirm our aspirations and intentions.

In either case, whether we speak outwardly or inwardly, we know the difference between a request and a demand. And we know better than to make our happiness contingent on getting exactly what we ask for.

THOUGHT FOR TODAY: Speaking up for myself speaks well of myself.

If you judge people, you have no time to love them.
—Mother Teresa

I don't remember the details, but I know that even in grade school I was already judgmental. I constantly placed others above or below me on my own imaginary scale. By the time I was a teenager I was alienated from everyone.

When I reflect today on my history of judgmentalism, I begin to understand the mental mechanics that take place when I am in that frame of mind.

All the little negative cogs and gears of my brain—*disdain, cynicism, disrespect, arrogance, anger*—become activated. They mesh and propel my thoughts antagonistically outward, preventing any genuine, sincere interaction with anyone. In no time, this process completely blocks out the possibility of being loving or of receiving love.

For a long time, the lack of love that my judgmentalism helped cause was of no conscious concern to me. But love has since become the epitome of all things that are valuable and desirable in my life. Compared to love, all other emotions and experiences tend to pale. Given a choice between judgmentalism and love, there is no choice.

THOUGHT FOR TODAY: Judgmentalism limits me, poisons me, defeats me.

July 11

The bow too tensely strung is easily broken.
—Publilius Syrus

Whether we are children taking our first steps or adults learning brand-new skills, it's hard to imagine making progress without trying. Indeed, "trying" is usually a necessary ingredient in achievement of any kind. But sometimes trying can work against us, making it more difficult to be natural and relaxed in our actions.

With most things we do that involve effort—getting in and out of a car, raking leaves, reading a book—it never occurs to us to "try." Yet when we confront something new that we think may be difficult—something that we perceive as a challenge and perhaps beyond our capability—then we begin to *try*. The harder we try, the more stress we create for ourselves and, of course, the harder it becomes to achieve our goal.

When we are learning a new sports activity, for example, trying too hard causes us to tense up and lose flexibility. Similarly, if we put too much pressure on ourselves to lose weight, we may feel that we are punishing rather than benefiting ourselves.

In such spiritual activities as prayer and meditation, moreover, trying too hard can inhibit the natural flow of our communication with God.

THOUGHT FOR TODAY: Trying too hard can be trying.

Joy is like restless day; but peace divine
  Like quiet night;
Lead me, O Lord, till perfect day shall shine
  Through Peace to Light.

—Adelaide Anne Procter

Today I will visualize myself as a spiritually centered individual. I am filled with God's strength and surrounded by His protecting presence.

When change comes into my life, I will acknowledge and accept it rather than deny or resist it. Change is inevitable, yes, but more important change is God's way of providing me with new and more abundant opportunities, of leading me toward personal and spiritual growth.

If unexpected or seemingly calamitous events occur, I will return to my spiritual core. I know from experience that I can trust God to help me transform adversity into advantage.

I see myself as adaptable and resilient, able to maintain my equilibrium at all times. When I turn to the Divine source of stability within, I can undergo any experience and undertake any challenge with calm and composure.

I will visualize my connection with God as unbreakable. He is a constant source of security and serenity. I pray that with His Divine guidance I can become a source of stability and comfort for those around me.

THOUGHT FOR TODAY: When I am God-centered, I am poised and serene.

July 13

The final mystery is oneself.

—Oscar Wilde

As a youngster I saved up to buy a telegraph kit and tried to learn Morse code, but I didn't get much beyond the international distress signal S.O.S. I tapped out those letters constantly. Although I didn't realize it at the time, they symbolized my own personal distress growing up.

Since I wasn't the least bit self-aware for many years, it was impossible for me to recognize the numerous physical and emotional S.O.S.'s of my life. Repeatedly I'd find myself in deep trouble, and would then feel stupid because I hadn't seen it coming.

Now that I'm getting to know myself, I'm far more sensitive to my own emotional and physical calls for help. More often than not, I've discovered, the distress signals of my mind, body, and spirit are closely interrelated.

When I'm feeling irritable or fearful, for example, those are usually signals to rest and pay more attention to my spiritual priorities. Similarly, a sleepless night may indicate that I've neglected to keep a commitment or failed to admit a wrong. By responding quickly at the first sign of an S.O.S., I can usually come to my own rescue before any real harm has occurred.

THOUGHT FOR TODAY: Have I learned to decode and act upon my personal distress signals?

It is good to rub and polish our brain against others.
— Michel Eyquem de Montaigne

Of all the myths about health, fitness, and aging, none is more pervasive than the notion that our minds stop developing at a certain point and begin deteriorating after that. Nothing could be further from the truth. The reality is that our intellectual growth can continue throughout our life.

However, such growth does not occur automatically. Like many other parts of our bodies, our minds have to be exercised in order to remain healthy, agile, and alert. In the same way, the maintenance of intellectual fitness requires not only desire, but commitment and disciplined effort.

Our choices in this regard are virtually unlimited; the entire world is our gymnasium. Social interaction, for example, is an ideal way to achieve mental fitness, especially if we become involved with people who challenge us intellectually.

We can keep our minds sharp by attempting to solve our own problems rather than relying on others to think for us. We can also further our intellectual growth and enhance mental agility by remaining curious—by our eagerness for new ideas and experiences. Among other activities, we can travel, take courses, read, and, in general, do our best to stay current with the times.

THOUGHT FOR TODAY: Am I challenging myself mentally?

July 15

Self-preservation is the first law of nature.
— Samuel Butler

"I'd been training for my first marathon—you know how much I like to run," a friend told me. "After a while I noticed that I was getting too thin. On top of that, I was experiencing a lot of muscle soreness. So I went to see a nutritionist.

"She mainly asked questions about my diet and level of physical activity, and she took a body-fat measurement with ultrasound. She told me that my body had no stored fat left to use as fuel for the heavy running. I had burned it all off.

"She said my body was actually trying to force me to slow down—by making me tired and by secreting lactic acid to make my muscles sore. The message, which I'd been ignoring, was eat *more* or run *less*.

"Later, I realized my body was trying to communicate with me in other ways too. I was getting minor injuries for no apparent reason—that, plus the fatigue.

"I never did run the marathon," my friend added, "but I did put the weight back on. Now that I've learned to listen to my body, I'm running better than ever. And I'm also feeling better."

THOUGHT FOR TODAY: When my body gives me a prescription, I will try to fill it promptly.

*Mishaps are like knives that either serve or cut us as
we grasp them by the blade or the handle.*
— James Russell Lowell

Who among us has not backed out of a parking space
and caused a fender bender? Sliced into a finger while
preparing food? Lost a wallet or purse? And who
among us has not compounded the trauma by heaping
guilt and self-recrimination on himself or herself?

It's difficult and inconvenient enough to experience and try to rectify a mistake or mishap when it
actually occurs. But many of us make it worse and
punish ourselves further by becoming angry and self-
critical. We tend to relive the incident over and over,
each time reactivating the stress it originally caused.

As someone once said, "Life is in session."
Almost every day, we must face and deal with unpleasant realities, most of them unforeseen. Once
we've made a mistake or have been involved in a
mishap, all we can really control is our reaction.

Depending on our attitude, our mistakes and
mishaps can either demoralize or serve us. They
serve us when we choose to learn and benefit from
them.

THOUGHT FOR TODAY: Now that it's over, what
can I learn from it?

197

July 17

Reason saw not, till Faith sprung the light.
—John Dryden

God is in charge—that is a vital reality in my life. I have faith that He has the absolute wisdom, the perfect plan, and the unlimited power to bring all things together for ultimate good.

Yet periodically, more often than I care to admit, I forget about God and start trying to run the show myself. I forget about seeking His will and try to make things happen my way and in my time. I forget about availing myself of His wisdom and power and try to figure things out entirely on my own. When I slip into this willful state, I invariably end up frustrated and overwhelmed.

How comforting it is at those times to be reminded that God is in charge. I may have lingering concerns and reservations about my own abilities, but when I reaffirm my trust in Him, courage and a sense of security return.

God is in charge! By acknowledging that truth, I am able to let go of the problems that have arisen, as well as those I have created myself, and again turn my will and life over to His loving care.

THOUGHT FOR TODAY: With God all things are possible.

Life is a series of surprises, and would not be worth taking or keeping if it were not.
—Ralph Waldo Emerson

No one ever promised that our ship would always sail along on an even keel or make port exactly as planned. There are bound to be days when storms blow in, or when we float motionlessly in a dead calm sea.

Nevertheless, many of us find it difficult to accept the stops and starts and ups and downs that occur on our journey toward personal fulfillment. Those of us recovering from chemical or behavioral dependencies, for example, sometimes become impatient and even panic when our emotional barometer plummets for no obvious reason.

Similarly, when we experience a "down" day in our exercise or weight loss program, we become frustrated and disappointed in ourselves. We may also feel overly responsible and depressed when we temporarily lose our special feeling of connectedness with God.

On those occasions, we might remind ourselves that there is a natural balance to each of our lives. For every up cycle, there is a compensating down cycle; for every high-energy day, there is one that is less so. Once we embrace this principle of natural balance, we will be more accepting of the ups and downs that are an inevitable part of personal growth.

THOUGHT FOR TODAY: I will flow along with the natural fluctuations of my life.

He that is afraid of every starting grass may not walk in a meadow.

—Gabriel Harvey

Every person who has ever wanted to try a new sport or exercise knows how inhibiting ego-generated fear can be. It has the power to stop us dead in our tracks before we ever get started.

We visualize ourselves in aerobics class, stuffed into Spandex tights, huffing and puffing to keep up. We imagine people snickering as we attempt to jog.

When we let such fears keep us from getting out there and trying, we're obviously giving ourselves the wrong messages.

We are accepting a childish message when we decide that if we can't be good at something right away, we don't want to do it at all.

We are accepting a self-centered message when we think that everyone on the court or in the gym will stop what they are doing and watch us.

We are accepting a self-defeating message when we are afraid that we will get in the way, that people will be annoyed at us for taking up court space.

The next time ego-generated fear threatens to sideline us, let's remember that everyone—even champions—started at the beginning and went through a learning process.

THOUGHT FOR TODAY: I will disregard negative messages and give myself a chance.

Much unhappiness results from an inability to re-member the nice things that happen to us.
—W. N. Rieger

The feeling comes over us more often on Mondays than on Fridays, and when we're overtired rather than rested. It's nothing major, and certainly falls far short of depression; it's more of a gray malaise tinged with a little self-pity. We say we're "in a funk."

We all occasionally have these emotional sinking spells. Fortunately, however, it's not that difficult to lift ourselves out of them. Usually, all it takes to raise our spirits is to mentally revisit places we've been, things we've done, and feelings we've shared that have been joyous and exhilarating. Every one of us has such memories—of a special vacation, a great concert, an outstanding achievement.

When we review past pleasures in this way, we can't help feeling grateful for the personal miracles that have taken place in our lives. As we all know, experiencing and expressing gratitude almost always revitalizes our sense of well-being.

Mental reviews of this sort don't have to be limited to past pleasures and blessings. We can also give ourselves an emotional boost by reflecting on the good things that are part of our lives at this very moment.

THOUGHT FOR TODAY: Does my occasional self-pity obscure the joys in my life?

The time to win a fight is before it starts.
—Frederick W. Lewis

Those of us who put high priority on peace of mind and emotional well-being live far differently today than we used to. Admittedly, it hasn't been easy to become less contentious in our actions and reactions, but the increasingly high price we were paying gave us little choice.

In the past, for example, we rarely were content to stand on the sidelines when family arguments erupted. We jumped in with full force and fury, even if the dispute had nothing to do with us.

At work, similarly, we tended to be opinionated and combative. We reacted to even mild criticism with vengefulness. In social situations and close relationships, we were frequently antagonistic. We were unwilling to compromise and, in fact, sometimes went out of our way to provoke further discord.

Most of our interactions today are a source of joy rather than stress. As our sense of inner security has increased, we're better able to live in harmony with those around us. When we sometimes find ourselves in volatile situations, we no longer automatically throw fuel on the fire, but instead try to play a conciliatory role.

THOUGHT FOR TODAY: Blessed are the peacemakers.

It matters not how long you live, but how well.
—Publilius Syrus

"The good life"—for most people the phrase evokes images of sunny beaches, epicurean meals, and endless vacations. When we seriously think about it, however, we realize that such activities and delights have only superficial relevance to truly living well.

What are the basic ingredients of a quality life? Certainly emotional well-being ranks high. The more self-aware we are, the more choices we have concerning our behavior, reactions, and attitudes.

Friendship and fellowship, too, help us live well by giving us a sense of belonging. Our interactions with others provide opportunities to share beliefs and common goals, as well as love and understanding.

Service to others also brings fulfillment—by allowing us to look beyond our own problems and actively express our gratitude for the blessings we've received.

Our efforts to achieve and maintain physical well-being also contribute to a quality life. Taking the best possible care of our physical selves enables us to explore and participate in life to the fullest.

The underlying ingredient, which brings all else together in the most meaningful way, is our belief and faith in a Higher Power and the practice of spiritual principles.

THOUGHT FOR TODAY: I am grateful for the inner changes that allow me to enjoy a quality life.

July 23

Rule your mind, which, if it is not your servant, is your master.

—Horace

Every once in a while my mind zeroes in on a minor pain and sets out to convince me that I am close to full cardiac arrest. My heart rate increases, and as my fear escalates, other symptoms surface in rapid succession—cold sweat, light-headedness, shortness of breath.

Following one particularly frightening false alarm, I sat quietly and thought about the awesome power of my mind. I was fascinated by its ability to produce symptoms forceful enough to send me to an emergency room.

It then occurred to me that I might be able to channel that very same power toward healing and wellness. I thought: Perhaps I can use my mind to slow my heart rate when I am fearful, to steady me when I am overwrought, or to cool me down when I am overheated.

I have since begun to move somewhat successfully in that direction. When I'm in a situation with the potential to catapult me into crisis, I try to consciously differentiate between true and false thoughts, and to respond accordingly. I am learning to control my mind, instead of letting it control me.

THOUGHT FOR TODAY: I can stop myself from being swept away by my mind's negative urgings.

Every life is a profession of faith, and exercises an inevitable and silent influence.

—Henri-Frédéric Amiel

It is particularly painful to watch a loved one suffer from health problems that are the result of overeating. Those of us with a spouse, partner, or family member in this situation know what it's like to suffer along with them out of sheer frustration.

We've tried everything we can think of to get him (or her) to lose weight. We've bought them diet books and trial memberships to health clubs, and passed along Twelve-Step program literature. We've shopped for and prepared healthful and nutritious meals. For months and in some cases years we've pleaded, cajoled, and even threatened.

But so far all our efforts have been for naught. We're worried sick, angry, and fed up all at the same time. We are at an emotional crossroads and don't know which way to turn.

In order to maintain our own health and stability, we must first accept, *without reservation*, this fact: We are not responsible for another person's eating habits, weight, or health. In fact, we are completely powerless in this regard. All we can do is lovingly express concern, and then offer support if and when the person becomes willing to take positive action.

THOUGHT FOR TODAY: I will gladly share my experience, strength, and hope, but I cannot assume responsibility for another person's health.

July 25

They that will not be counseled, cannot be helped. If you do not hear reason, she will rap you on the knuckles.

—Benjamin Franklin

It had been strongly suggested by several people that I join a support group to get help for my dependency. Yet I was still reluctant to make the initial telephone call and reach out, even though I knew they were right. I rationalized my fears in various ways: "I don't have time." "It will be too depressing to be around those kinds of people." "I don't want to be brainwashed." "I'm not a joiner, and besides, what can you learn from lay people?"

Eventually I became open-minded enough to give the support group a try. And like so many other people, I received benefits beyond measure.

These days, providentially, there is a support group network for virtually every dependency, illness, and health objective. There are Twelve-Step programs modeled after Alcoholics Anonymous with a broad variety of focuses. There are support groups for people with illnesses of almost every kind, including heart disease, diabetes, AIDS, and cancer. There are groups for people who suffer from depression, who want to improve their relationships, who want to stop smoking, who want to strengthen their faith.

In most cases, help is just a phone call away. One need only be open-minded and willing.

THOUGHT FOR TODAY: I don't have to do it alone.

To live is not to live for one's self alone; let us help one another.

—Menander

For people with physical, emotional, or spiritual problems, the proliferation of support groups in recent years is no less significant than dramatic advances in medical technology. Unquestionably, support groups have become one of our most valuable resources as we strive to better our lives. These are some of the benefits we receive. . . .

Because we share a common problem, our new friends can understand and empathize at the deepest levels;

We have a unique opportunity to learn from the experiences of others, to dispel myths about our condition, and to acquire new tools for living;

We find new resolve and hope when we see others getting well and reaching their goals;

We receive encouragement and support from others who recognize our progress when we are unable to do so;

Because we have new friends to turn to, there is less pressure on our families and partners. Moreover, our group-mates can usually be more objective than those with whom we've had long emotional attachments;

We're encouraged to help others—especially newcomers to the group—and when we do, our problems seem to fade away.

THOUGHT FOR TODAY: My support group offers not only fellowship and understanding, but also **real** solutions to our common problem.

July 27

What a fool an injury may make of a staid man.
—John Keats

Like most people, I don't know very much about the physiology or psychology of pain. I know even less about the communication process that takes place in my body when I injure myself. The one thing I do know, however, is that when pain strikes, the attitude I take toward it can greatly influence its intensity and duration.

Some years ago, for example, I tripped over a tree root while hiking and seriously sprained my ankle. The pain was intense for weeks. What compounded it and kept it alive were the negative attitudes and mental resistance I added.

I was angry at myself for being clumsy. I was afraid that my ankle wouldn't heal properly. I was impatient because I had to use crutches. I felt sorry for myself for all sorts of related reasons.

These days I know better. When pain occasionally comes my way I try to approach it with as positive an attitude as I can muster. I try to accept the pain rather than react like a victim. I try to relax around it rather than allow myself to become physically and emotionally tense. I do everything possible to free myself of anxiety.

THOUGHT FOR TODAY: My negative attitudes can prolong pain and make it worse.

*Refrain tonight, And that shall lend a kind of easiness
to the next abstinence: the next more easy; For use
almost can change the stamp of nature.*
—William Shakespeare

Even though we have the willingness and determination to abstain from overeating, smoking, or drinking, sometimes we can be caught off-guard by the offer of a drink, cigarette, or high-calorie treat. If the person presses, we may become flustered; we're not sure whether to make an excuse, explain ourselves, become defensive, or what.

That's why it's important to plan out in advance what we are going to say in such situations. In most cases, a simple but firm "No, thank you," will do the job and make us feel good about ourselves.

Each time we are able to say, "No, thank you" to a well-meaning friend proffering a snack or newly opened box of candy, we strengthen our defense against overeating.

Each time we are able to say, "Thank you, but no" to the offer of spiked eggnog or a glass of champagne at a party, we are able to fortify ourselves against a disastrous relapse.

Indeed, each time we are able to calmly and authoritatively turn down any harmful substance or activity, it's enough to make us feel wonderful, self-protected, and grateful all day long.

THOUGHT FOR TODAY: I love hearing myself say, "No, thank you."

To see a world in a grain of sand,
and heaven in a wild flower,
hold infinity in the palm of your hand,
and eternity in an hour.

—William Blake

There are times in all of our lives when we feel bored and restless. All our activities and involvements seem static and stale. Everything appears to be overly familiar and unchanging.

But of course, the way things sometimes seem to be has little to do with the way they really are. Our feelings and attitudes, more than anything, shape our perceptions.

When we make the effort to notice just some of the myriad subtleties around us, one fact becomes startlingly clear: The world and our lives are constantly changing.

From moment to moment, the sky grows ever lighter and ever darker. The complexion of city streets glows and fades hour by hour—crowded, empty; glistening, dusty; echoing, still. Clouds billow and stretch, inviting us to see a dragon, a butterfly, a ship.

The old becomes new again. Our imagination and inner spirit leads us to new experiences and new excitement. Our power of choice revitalizes our activities and relationships. We find new expressions of ourselves in what once seemed familiar. Each moment becomes a new starting point.

THOUGHT FOR TODAY: I can seize and shape this day so it is like no other.

A man commends himself in praising that which he loves.

—Publilius Syrus

To a large extent, the foundations of emotional well-being are formed in childhood. Those of us in recovery from dysfunctional backgrounds have become well aware of that truth; we know what it feels like to always be filled with self-doubt. How we yearned to win approval, to be appreciated, to be praised!

In my own case, that appreciation and praise never came. I still remember proudly bringing home exemplary report cards, only to be ignored by my mother and father. A basic thrust of my recovery has been to come to terms with my upbringing. I've had to accept the reality that approval from my parents will be forever unavailable.

I have learned that it's far more important to appreciate and approve of *myself*. The more progress I make in this area, and the more emotional stability I gain, the more easily I can express my appreciation and approval of others.

And the opposite is also true. When I make an effort to pass along a compliment, to give credit, or to express appreciation for someone's presence in my life, I unfailingly feel good about the kind of person I am becoming.

THOUGHT FOR TODAY: My feelings about myself are the ones that count the most.

July 31

By losing present time, we lose all time.
> —W. Gurney Benham

The pressure of time is something we all experience daily. Our bedrooms, kitchens, offices, cars, and bodies are cluttered with clocks and watches of all shapes, sizes, and capabilities. Our desks, walls, and wallets are laden with hourly, daily, weekly, and monthly calendars of every style.

We accumulate these timepieces and scheduling aids to make our lives simpler and more manageable. In reality, however, many of us compartmentalize and fragment our existence. We become tyrannized by time; instead of being free to enjoy the present, we mortgage ourselves to some nonexistent future period.

If it's easy to relate to this scenario, we might want to rethink our concept of time. Most of us see time as an onrushing steamroller that will crush us unless we outrun it or at least take the wheel. But in truth, time doesn't move at all; it is always *right now*. From that standpoint, time is an illusion.

That being so, let's do our best to stop pressuring ourselves about *time wasted, time misspent, lack of time, time yet to be*. Instead, let's focus our emotional energy on the here and now.

THOUGHT FOR TODAY: *Now* is the time.

August 1

Wonders are many, and none is more wonderful than man.

—Sophocles

I was sitting in a doctor's waiting room, feeling sorry for myself because of a sprained knee. A young father and his nine-month-old son entered the room. I quickly became fascinated with the baby, who was blossoming in nine different ways at once: He was on the verge of walking, he was making his first attempts at speech, and he was grasping for things with the beginning of true coordination.

As I watched, I underwent a major shift in attitude. For weeks I had been focusing myopically on minor aches and pains—on things not quite right—rather than on the major miracles of my body.

The baby's actions reminded me that each of us is a marvel of interrelated chemical and electronic systems—self-contained, self-propelled, self-adjusting, and self-healing.

I thought then about our amazing inborn capacity for unlimited learning. The mind teaches the body; reactions and counterreactions are initiated and coordinated at a deeply subconscious level. At that moment, my renewed awareness of all those God-given capabilities filled me with awe and gratitude.

THOUGHT FOR TODAY: I will be grateful for my many physical and intellectual blessings and not take them for granted.

August 2

Forewarned, forearmed; to be prepared is half the victory.

—Cervantes

No matter what our goals, there are always obstacles that can prevent us from reaching them. Some, such as physical or financial limitations, are actual. Others, such as unfounded fears or distorted perceptions, are creations of our minds.

Before taking on a new challenge, some of us find it helpful to first draw up a list of all the things, real or imagined, that can keep us from achieving our goal. This technique prepares us mentally and emotionally before we set out. We will know what to expect, what should be avoided, and what needs to be changed in order for us to succeed.

Let's say that our goal is to get in shape for a ten-day bicycle tour. Our list of potential obstacles might include: lack of time for training; a tendency to start out enthusiastically, then become quickly bored; concern that others on the tour might be much younger (older) than we are; and fear of physical or psychological incapability.

Once we have completed our list, we can review each item, decide whether it is real or imagined, and then look for possible solutions.

THOUGHT FOR TODAY: If I know what to expect, I'm more apt to succeed.

What we hope ever to do with ease, we must learn first to do with diligence.

—Samuel Johnson

Several years ago I joined a club which enabled me to use the swimming pool at the local college. I committed myself to swimming four days a week and building up to a one-mile workout.

It didn't take long for me to become discouraged. I had difficulty maintaining sufficient momentum to receive cardiovascular benefits. I tired easily and was distracted by swimmers in adjacent lanes. The biggest distraction was my own mind, which constantly tried to persuade me to quit halfway through the swim.

Another club member suggested that I use a mantra while swimming. He then explained that repetition of a particular phrase anchored his mind in the present, focused his energy on swimming, and transformed his workouts from drudgery into pleasurable experiences.

The mantra I decided on was "I love my life, thank you, God." When I began using it, splitting the two phrases between strokes, I couldn't believe what a difference it made in my performance.

I no longer have a problem with distractions or my own negativity. The mantra has helped me improve my technique and stamina. The words I've chosen also give spiritual overtones to my workout by allowing me to keep God in my thoughts.

THOUGHT FOR TODAY: A focused mind leads to a focused, more fulfilling workout.

August 4

Fields are won by those who believe in the winning.
—Thomas Wentworth Higginson

We know about self-fulfilling prophecies and how they can influence our lives positively or negatively. We've learned that if we expect a slow recovery from an illness, it's likely that the illness will drag on. We've learned that when we approach a job interview with the belief that we will do poorly, that's probably what will happen.

We've made considerable progress in sidestepping or reversing our negative expectations. But we sometimes still run into trouble when a negative expectation combines with a self-effacing belief. In a typical scenario, we enter a new relationship not only with the usual apprehension, but with such beliefs as: "I'm impossible to get along with. . . . He (she) won't like me once he (she) gets to know me."

If we expect the relationship to fail for these reasons, chances are we'll be less motivated to make it work, and may even subconsciously go about sabotaging it.

In order to give the new relationship a chance, we have to try to overcome our apprehension and, more important, disavow any negative beliefs about ourselves. We have to try to leave old ideas behind and let things develop and flow as they are meant to.

THOUGHT FOR TODAY: Today is a clean slate.

*More things are wrought by prayer
Than this world dreams of.*

—Alfred Tennyson

Just about everything we undertake in life requires a learning process. As young children we learn to walk and eat with utensils. Later, we may learn to speak a second language, to dance, to use a computer. In each case we start from scratch, usually awkwardly, and continue practicing until we are proficient.

When we set out to learn something new, most of the time we do so because it is important and necessary to our lives. We practice because we want to become more and more accomplished at the activity.

The same is true of our spiritual pursuits, and in particular the way we build our relationship with God through prayer and meditation. When we first seriously try to communicate with our Higher Power, many of us feel awkward and unsure of ourselves. Either we've never attempted to pray before, or we've done so by rote because we were "supposed to."

Like any other uplifting activity, prayer takes practice. We can't expect to be comfortable and assured from the start. But if we set aside the time to regularly pray, it will surely become more natural—and we will surely develop a deep and loving relationship with God.

THOUGHT FOR TODAY: Like everything else, prayer gets easier with practice.

August 6

A true friend is the greatest of all blessings, and the one which we take least thought to acquire.
                                        —Duc de La Rochefoucauld

Of all the stress in my past life, none came on more quickly or caused more pain than that resulting from interactions with other people. Because I had a low degree of self-esteem, and a high degree of self-consciousness, I frequently isolated myself to avoid those stressful feelings.

I shunned family get-togethers and social affairs and went out of my way to avoid contact with people I knew. I usually chose solitary forms of entertainment and recreation.

Paradoxically, just the opposite is true today; relationships with others have become essential in achieving peace of mind. I rely on my friends to help me gain and maintain a clear perspective. I turn to them to defuse my anger, to clarify my confusion, and to share my joys.

It took me a long time to come out of my shell and learn to be at ease with people, but the accomplishment has brought a special richness to my life. Where interaction with others once caused me untold stress and anguish, today my overall sense of well-being and continuing spiritual growth is due in large measure to my friendships.

THOUGHT FOR TODAY: Now that I am welcoming others into my life, I'm enjoying a new sense of security.

There's a time for all things.

—William Shakespeare

We know how important it is to take time out to quiet our minds, to become centered. We also know that it's vital to stay physically relaxed, to keep our bodies supple.

But it seems that on most days we're just too busy. In the morning it's all we can do to get ready for work and arrive on time. Once there, we're barraged with endless problems; there are fires to put out, deadlines to meet, mistakes to remedy. On the really bad days we work overtime and consider ourselves lucky to have a sit-down dinner before bedtime. If anyone were to suggest taking a short relaxation or fitness break, our likely response would be, "Dream on, dreamer!"

In reality, however, the time is available to us *if we're willing to take it*. Can we find five minutes before lunch? Because that's all it takes to quietly meditate or to use other techniques that will help us relax and regain our composure. Can we find three, four, or even ten minutes in the afternoon? Because that's all it takes to do some stretching exercises, to go for a short walk, or to give ourselves a nutritional boost with a snack.

THOUGHT FOR TODAY: There are 1440 minutes in each day. How many do I allot for spirit, mind, and body?

August 8

He that does good for good's sake, seeks neither praise nor reward, but he is sure of both in the end.
—William Penn

Just about every one of us who has ever tried to lose weight is familiar with the "yo-yo syndrome." We tried, we failed; we started, we stopped; we lost, we gained. *Ad infinitum.*

We didn't know it at the time, but probably the most important reason for our continued lack of success is that we were dieting with the wrong motives.

We cut down on calories to become more attractive to a spouse or partner. We avoided rich desserts to gain the approval of friends and loved ones. We went on crash diets to get ready for vacations or to prepare for bathing-suit weather. We skipped meals because a doctor had warned us about the health consequences of excess weight, or because we felt a slimmed-down look might further our career.

We've since learned that if we are going to make meaningful progress in any area of self-revitalization— physical, emotional, or spiritual—we can't do it for others, but must do it only for ourselves. Outside pressures or temptations may provide temporary incentive, but long-term accomplishment can only come from a deep personal commitment.

THOUGHT FOR TODAY: My goals are sound, but what about my motives?

We employ the mind to rule, the body to serve.
—Sallust

Some years ago following a surgical procedure, I went through a period of considerable physical pain and emotional stress. A friend urged me to listen to a "directed visualization" tape that he used almost daily. I accepted his offer out of politeness.

The next day, when I switched on the cassette player, I was immediately captivated. The tape had been developed by a physician who had obviously "been there" insofar as physical and emotional pain was concerned. He had prepared a simple yet highly creative series of mental exercises to help the listener become relaxed, and to stimulate the immune system and focus the body's healing power.

I listened to that directed visualization tape several times a day during the weeks that I was bedridden. It relieved much of the pain and virtually all of the stress I had been feeling.

By following the tape's suggested imagery—visualizing, for example, the surgical site bathed in a healing light—I became an active participant in my own recovery, rather than a passive and helpless victim. I'm convinced that my participation went a long way toward speeding up the healing process.

THOUGHT FOR TODAY: Am I open-minded about healing techniques that are adjunctive to medicine?

Say you are well, or all is well with you, and God shall hear your words and make them true.
                                        —Ella Wheeler Wilcox

When I told my friend how much I had benefited from the directed visualization tape he had given me, he suggested that I create my own tape. Follow the basic outline of the professionally produced tape, he suggested, but personalize it in terms of your own illness and particular objectives.

I gave it a try. After several days of experimentation, I completed a fifteen-minute script incorporating these goals: relaxation and stress relief, pain reduction, healing of the surgical site.

In order to put myself into a deeply relaxed state, I talked softly for five minutes or so about pleasant and soothing personal memories. For the next five minutes I talked about the painful area; in calm but confident terms I visualized the wound becoming healed, supple, and whole. I described "arrows" of pain floating away from my body.

Finally, I concentrated all my body's healing power—and all the positive spiritual energy in the universe—toward the site.

It was relatively easy and actually quite enjoyable to create a personal tape. And it did what it was supposed to do. The technique really worked.

THOUGHT FOR TODAY: When illness or injury strikes, directed visualization can help restore a sense of control.

The more we know, the better we forgive.
Whoe'er feels deeply, feels for all that live.
                    —Anne Louise Germaine de Staël

The steps toward progress we have taken in recent months, and in some cases recent years, have allowed us to come to terms with the past and move forward in our new life. But one or more painful memories, and the painful emotions they evoke, simply refuse to go away. Perhaps it's time for forgiveness.

Many of us tend to view forgiveness in rather narrow terms—letting someone off the hook for having wronged us in some way. But forgiveness is much more than that. It allows us to literally disconnect ourselves from a past act or situation that continues to cause us emotional distress. Moreover, we can grow spiritually through forgiveness because the process allows us to practice tolerance, understanding, acceptance, and compassion.

Some of us find it helpful to draw up a list of all the individuals and institutions we are now willing and able to forgive. We forgive them one by one, and in each case, we imagine the emotional cord that has bound us so tightly finally becoming untied and setting us free.

THOUGHT FOR TODAY: I practice forgiveness for my own sake.

August 12

The beginning is the most important part of the work.
—Plato

For many of us, life used to be mostly about endings of one kind or another. Today, providentially, it is mostly about beginnings. Whether these beginnings have to do with fitness programs, spiritual pursuits, or recovery from addiction, one of the most difficult but ultimately invaluable lessons we've learned is that a strong foundation is essential to ongoing progress.

We used to start new endeavors unprepared and end up in a frustrating start-stop-start-stop cycle. Now, because we first take the time to build a solid foundation, we have a base of knowledge and experience from which we can draw for years to come.

We used to take on too much, too soon; as the result of our zealousness, we often became discouraged before we gave ourselves a real chance. By beginning again, this time gradually and carefully, we structure a foundation that helps us remain consistent yet flexible.

We used to approach new challenges with a weighty sense of obligation. But now, because we start out sensibly, we develop respect, appreciation, and even love for what we are doing.

THOUGHT FOR TODAY: If I am grounded on a solid foundation, I have made a good start.

There is no season such delight can bring as summer, autumn, winter, and the spring.

—William Browne

Every so often I find myself overreacting to changes in the weather. Hot and dry Santa Ana winds can make me nervous and irritable. When it is foggy for more than several days in a row, I sometimes become sad and even depressed.

I've been known to react in the same negative and self-defeating ways toward seasonal changes. In the summer there are "too many tourists"; in the winter there is either too much or too little rain.

The irony is that I live in a part of the world noted for its almost ideal climate. Obviously, then, I can hardly blame the weather for my periodic mood swings and foot-stamping attitudes. And even when a shift in weather or change in seasons triggers a black mood, I still have a choice concerning the intensity and duration of that mood.

In all fairness, these bouts of negativity have been occurring less frequently. I'm learning to adjust my attitude and set myself straight in anticipation of weather and seasonal inevitabilities. Just because the Santa Ana winds are wild and hot tempered, that doesn't mean I have to act the same way.

THOUGHT FOR TODAY: When I have an "attitude," who can I blame but myself?

August 14

God be praised, who, to believing souls, gives light in darkness, comfort in despair.

—William Shakespeare

We tried every method we could think of or had heard about to quit smoking. We went cold turkey, then tried tapering off. We used special filters, chewing gums, hypnosis, and aversion therapy. We stopped buying cigarettes, but ended up filching them from other people. Nothing worked.

When we saw friends succeeding where we had failed—using some of those same methods—we became even more discouraged. Those were bleak and desperate days. We totally lost faith in ourselves and in our ability to *ever* overcome our addiction to nicotine.

As tragic as it seemed at the time, that loss of faith was a blessing in disguise, for it led us directly to putting our faith in a Power greater than ourselves. And that's what worked for us when we tried one last time to quit smoking.

During the first several days of confusion and anxiety, we continuously turned our thoughts to God. We relied on His strength when the smell of tobacco smoke rekindled the craving, when we were tempted to buy a pack of cigarettes, when we were envious of smokers and felt sorry for ourselves. In every instance, He came through for us. And He continues to do so.

THOUGHT FOR TODAY: I need not become desperate before seeking God's help.

Man's mind is larger than his crown of tears.
                              —William Ellery Leonard

We can never have too many weapons in our arsenal to combat resentments and their devastating effect on our physical, emotional, and spiritual well-being. Mental imagery, the same process we've used to help us relax, to achieve our goals, and to enhance our immune system, can also be effective in overcoming resentments and the stress they cause.

In a quiet and comfortable setting, become as relaxed as possible and visualize clearly the person you resent. Imagine good fortune coming to him or her. Picture the person receiving love and approval, wealth, peace of mind—whatever you think he or she would want and value. If you find this difficult, don't be concerned. The more you repeat the process, the easier it will become.

Put yourself in the other person's place—coming from the same background and experiencing the same pressures. Imagine how the situation might appear from that perspective. Then, think about how your behavior might have contributed to the original problem. Try to see the event and the other person's actions in a new and different light.

Finally, picture your resentment leaving you. Be aware of how much better you feel. Commit yourself to your new understanding.

THOUGHT FOR TODAY: Mental imagery is a valuable, multipurpose tool.

August 16

The wise for cure on exercise depend.

—John Dryden

It's been a long, hard, stressful day. As the hours have passed, our bodies have responded by becoming increasingly tense. Our neck, shoulder, and back muscles are so tight they hurt. Our chest feels constricted because we haven't been breathing properly. We have a bad headache.

When we leave work, we have several choices. We can do nothing and pay for it with a miserable, sleepless night. We can turn to alcohol or other sedatives and pay an even greater price. Or we can use exercise to help us relax.

Granted, when we are tired and tense, the last thing we usually feel like doing is taking a swim, a jog, or even stretching out our muscles. Once we are able to get past that initial reluctance, however, we are rewarded in several ways.

Exercise releases the muscle tension and tightness that has accumulated in response to stress during the day. Exercise encourages us to breathe deeply and evenly while calming our minds. Exercise can also divert our attention from our problems and dramatically alter our perspective and mood.

THOUGHT FOR TODAY: Exercise is the medicine that requires no prescription.

Worry is interest paid on trouble before it comes due.
—William Ralph Inge

It's been a long time since I've carried a good-luck charm. But for almost twenty years, when I emptied my pockets at night there was bound to be a plastic-encased four-leaf clover, a special coin, or some other talisman.

It's not that I was hoping for good luck; rather, I was trying to avoid bad luck. I was a world-class worrier. For the most part I worried about big things such as sickness, financial ruin, or being forsaken. But I could worry just as intensely and suffer just as much over such trivialities as the neighbor's noisy cat, an oil spot on the driveway, or tulip bulbs that had never bloomed.

I can't say exactly what caused me to give up my good-luck charms and become less of a worrier. Perhaps I finally realized that most of my worries are not based on present reality, but are past or future oriented.

Perhaps, too, I was able to see that worry spins me into a vicious cycle: Worry generates stress and physical problems, which generate still more worry. Most important, perhaps I understood that no matter how much I worry about something, it never helps. It always hurts.

THOUGHT FOR TODAY: Why worry?

August 18

The most difficult thing in life is to know yourself.
—Thales

It can be interesting and useful to think about the way we define ourselves as individuals. We tend to focus on particular facets—our size, gender, vocation, material possessions.

Some of us perceive and define ourselves solely in negative terms—our incapability, unworthiness, faults, past behavior, and in comparison to other people or unrealistic ideals. If we're still defining ourselves in these limited or deprecatory terms, aren't we a long way from true self-acceptance?

In my own case, what brings me closer to self-acceptance is trying to recognize and acknowledge the *whole* me. That includes the sum of all my experiences, good and bad. It concerns the present reality of me—not the me I want to be or hope to be, nor the me I think others see.

Going further, when I work toward realistic self-definition and self-acceptance, I try to start with a clean mental slate. When I rely on erroneous information by falling back on old ideas, distorted perceptions, and an outdated self-image, I'm bound to be unsuccessful in seeing and valuing my true self.

THOUGHT FOR TODAY: Am I defining and valuing myself realistically?

God is an unutterable sigh, planted in the depths of the soul.

—Jean Paul Richter

On a day off not long ago, I drove to a nearby lake and rented a small fishing boat. I rowed out to my favorite spot, dropped the anchor, and began casting. The fish weren't biting, but that was all right. It was a crisp, cloudless day and I felt completely relaxed.

Some time later, I realized that the boat was drifting close to the rocky shore. I rowed out a hundred yards or so and this time made sure the boat was securely anchored. The wind came up, and as I watched the anchor rope strain, I remembered the insecurity of my old life. For years I drifted, aimless and out of control.

Then I began thinking about some of the things that keep me anchored and stable today. My faith in God, certainly, is the most powerful force. The knowledge that He is always with me provides a sense of security like nothing else. Loving friendships, too, are a source of stability and constancy.

The routine of my work and life also keeps me grounded. And so long as I anchor myself securely in the present moment, it's unlikely that I'll drift out of reality and into fear.

THOUGHT FOR TODAY: Faith is the anchor of my existence.

August 20

*There is no distance on this earth as far away as
yesterday.*

—Robert Nathan

The phone call came at 9:30 yesterday morning. It
wasn't unexpected, but the news was far from what
we had hoped for. That was almost twenty-four hours
ago, but we're still re-creating the event. We're
rehashing the phone call, the caller's tone of voice,
the disappointment, our response. To a large extent,
we've given up today for yesterday.

After all this time, one would think that trying to
center ourselves in the present moment would be one
of our highest priorities. One would think it unnecessary to remind ourselves that the here and now is
worthy of our undivided attention and energy. Yet if
we regularly spend precious hours reliving and re-
gretting events that took place a day, a week, or years
in the past, we obviously do need to remind ourselves.

When we squander our mind and spirit on
occurrences that are over and done with, that doesn't
leave much for right now. And right now is all we
have; right now is what life is all about. So let's try to
put aside preoccupations with the past. Let's choose
to live today.

THOUGHT FOR TODAY: Why relive yesterday,
when today is brand new?

It is a bad plan that admits of no modification.
—Publilius Syrus

Since childhood, most of us stuffed ourselves with snack foods and fast foods—we ate far too much sugar, salt, and fat. When we finally decided to work toward a future of better health, we concluded that changing our eating habits was among the most important and simplest actions we could take.

But simple doesn't necessarily mean easy. We encountered many traps along the way, most of them baited with old ideas and understandable resistance on our part.

Initially, we felt deprived. We felt sorry for ourselves because we had to give up certain foods we'd enjoyed for a long time. It was pointed out that we could find equally enjoyable substitutes and that we would eventually develop new food preferences. And, of course, that's what happened.

We believed that the new foods in our diet were probably too expensive and hard to prepare. But when we shopped and discovered that fresh foods cost far less than processed foods, we saw through our own rationalizations.

Some of us expected too much, too soon, and became discouraged. We felt it would be impossible to ever change our eating habits. But by easing off, and making *gradual* changes, we ultimately became successful.

THOUGHT FOR TODAY: I can shape my future for good health.

August 22

The Present is the living sum-total of the whole Past.
—Thomas Carlyle

Several years ago I came across an old photograph of myself. It was clearly evident that I had not yet stopped drinking or started to take care of myself. I was overweight, my skin had an unhealthy pallor, my eyes were downcast.

A wave of unexpected guilt and remorse swept over me as I remembered the way I had lived in the past. So many missed opportunities, so many wasted years. For a moment I felt like crying.

I put the photo back where I found it and forced myself into a different frame of mind. Isn't it true, I asked myself, that the sum of all my experiences add up to the person I am today? Don't I feel good about that person? So in reality, those years had not been wasted.

I've since come to believe that it was somehow necessary for me to go through those years of self-destructive behavior and poor health. According to a Divine plan, I was exactly where I was supposed to be back then, just as I am exactly where I'm supposed to be today.

THOUGHT FOR TODAY: Remembering the past can make my life and health today all the more meaningful and precious.

Lynx-eyed toward our neighbors, and moles to our-selves.

—Jean de La Fontaine

We'd be reluctant to admit it, but many of us put a great deal of emotional energy into judging others. Sometimes, during the course of an afternoon or evening, we negatively snipe at everything and everyone: "Look at what she's wearing! . . . I hate this city. . . . My God, how can they stand each other?"

When we refuse to see anything positive, but instead concentrate and comment on only what we perceive as negative, *we're* the ones who suffer. There's a price for judgmentalism, and it's a heavy price indeed. Constant negativity of this sort floods us with stress, sends our immune system deadening messages, and literally poisons our outlook on life.

Of course, there is a solution. We can gradually train our minds to be more tolerant and less cynical. We can learn to notice and appreciate the goodness of others. We can begin to focus on the positive qualities of our world and the people in it.

This new approach to life may be simple, but it is not necessarily easy. It requires willingness, a major change of attitude, and discipline on our part. However, the beneficial impact on our lives will be more than worth the effort.

THOUGHT FOR TODAY: Just for today, I will temper my thoughts, restrain my tongue, and put judgmentalism aside.

Nothing in life is more wondrous than faith—the one great moving force which we can neither weigh in the balance nor test in the crucible.

—William Osler

Faith is impossible to measure, difficult to comprehend, and by its very nature indefinable and even mysterious. However, we need not concern ourselves with what faith is or is not. All we need to know is that it works, and that it is a powerful force capable of bringing about changes that otherwise might well be beyond the realm of possibility.

In my own case, after years of repeatedly taking one step forward and several steps backward, faith allowed me to finally make major, steady progress in the right direction.

Heaven knows I had the need, desire, and willingness to change. But I lacked confidence in my ability to bring change about. Faith was the missing piece of the puzzle. When I finally was able to believe in God and put my faith in His unlimited power, that's when the impossible became possible.

Along the way, I've learned not to compare my faith with that of others. Faith is personal and individual. It is a reflection of the unique relationship each of us has with the God of our own understanding.

THOUGHT FOR TODAY: I am faith-filled and change-oriented.

A friend is a present you give yourself.
—Robert Louis Stevenson

As we travel farther along the road to spiritual well-being, our values, behavior, and attitudes change ever more dramatically. These changes are evident in every area of our lives, and especially so in our friendships.

Where once our friendships tended to be superficial "arrangements"—based on obligation and exchanges of favors—today we reach out sincerely and unconditionally, without expectation of receiving anything in return.

In the past our friendships often were overlaid with tension. Our interactions, while not overtly malicious, were proving grounds for competition and rivalry. Now, in sharp contrast, our friendships are based on love and mutual support.

We used to be reluctant to let our friends know us, to see who we really were; we always held something back. These days we are honest and open, willing to share our feelings. We have become trusting and trust*worthy*, and as the result our friendships are deep and meaningful.

The friends we have today, and the very special quality of these friendships, are a significant blessing in our new, spiritually centered lives.

THOUGHT FOR TODAY: Now that I've become a friend to myself, it's so much easier to be a friend to others.

Nothing requires a rarer intellectual heroism than willingness to see one's equation written out.
—George Santayana

Journal writing is a powerful tool that can help us heal emotionally and even physically. When we write about distressing experiences, in particular, the benefits can be substantial and almost immediate.

In the first place, describing events and our reactions to them leads to objectivity and a more accurate perspective. Then, reviewing what we have written allows us to rethink the event. Even though the occurrence itself doesn't change, it usually loses its power to harm us emotionally.

Taking it a step further, scientific studies have shown that people who explore traumatic experiences or bring repressed emotions out in a journal can actually benefit physically. Among the results are improved immune system function and fewer stress-related illnesses.

On a day-to-day basis, journal writing offers other valuable, albeit less dramatic benefits. The blank page need not be intimidating. When we keep daily records of our exercise or weight-control programs, for example, it is easier to measure progress and see where we need to strengthen our efforts. Journal writing can also provide us with an outlet for creative expression while allowing us to highlight and relive our joys.

THOUGHT FOR TODAY: Journal writing can be fulfilling and healing.

Love grants in a moment
What toil can hardly achieve in an age.
> —Johann Wolfgang von Goethe

After I had been through a major illness and surgery, friends in a support group told me about new and continuing studies linking emotions to physical well-being. Scientists have proven that negative emotions have a negative impact on the body's immune system, that positive emotions enhance it, and that love is probably the most potent "enhancer" of all.

I thought about the concept as it related to my own life. I certainly had strong feelings of love for my family and close friends. From the very first day in my support group, moreover, I had begun to experience a new kind of love, based on fellow sufferers helping one another overcome a common enemy.

On the other hand, to be perfectly honest, there had always been a dark side to my nature. I had a predilection for cynicism, judgmentalism, sarcasm, and general negativity.

Clearly, I had a lot of work to do in this area. In the interest of my health and peace of mind, it has become an ongoing challenge to find ways of increasing positive feelings—toward the people I encounter, the places I go, and the events that unfold in my life day by day.

THOUGHT FOR TODAY: Love has the power to heal.

August 28

To love is to choose.

—Joseph Roux

My loving feelings may not make the world go 'round, as the song suggests, but they certainly go a long way toward improving my physical and emotional well-being. I know this to be true from personal experience, and that's why I try to find ways of turning negative emotions into positive ones.

When I dislike someone or something—either because I've been rubbed the wrong way, or I'm simply feeling surly—I try to act "as if" I like the person or thing. In other words, I don't give my negativity a voice or even a chance to breathe. If I can't be loving, at least I can be neutral.

If I find myself looking down on someone, I try to explore my feelings. It usually turns out that my negative reaction is based on something insignificant. If I'm being judgmental, it always helps to recognize that I'm probably focusing on the same qualities in another person that I dislike in myself.

When my negative feelings occasionally overshadow my loving feelings, I ask a simple question: Are the "rewards" I may be getting from my negativity worth the stress I'm causing myself?

THOUGHT FOR TODAY: It's not up to someone else to bring out my loving feelings.

Sing away sorrow, cast away care.

—Cervantes

Self-pity is a soul-sickness that can blind us to our blessings. Depending on our attitude, just about anything can cause us to feel sorry for ourselves: dissatisfaction with our appearance, performance, or relationships; health problems; criticism from others; plans that fall through.

Many people can roll with these kinds of eventualities. However, some of us find it quite difficult to get over bouts of self-pity. It seems to take longer and longer to get ourselves back on an even keel.

"Instant bookkeeping," as it is sometimes called, can speed up the process. For every debit entry (complaint) that leads to feelings of self-pity, we force ourselves to enter a credit (blessing).

For example, when we are unhappy about our looks, we might recognize—on the credit side of the ledger—the friends and family members who love and accept us exactly as we are. When we become impatient because we've been sidelined by an injury, we might make note of our overall good health.

Similarly, when we begin to feel sorry for ourselves because something hasn't gone our way, we might make a positive ledger entry regarding the way our life is today compared with how it used to be.

THOUGHT FOR TODAY: My true credits far outweigh my imagined debits.

Happiness is a by-product of an effort to make someone else happy.

—Gretta Brooker Palmer

You would think we'd know by now that self-centeredness brings nothing but frustration and unhappiness. Yet periodically we return to our old ways, convinced that if we can get what we want we'll be satisfied and happy.

The thing is, when we insist on having our way, it's all too easy to rely on manipulation, deceit, and dishonesty to bring others around. Inevitably, we pay a big emotional and spiritual price for such behavior.

Thankfully, we are making progress in this area. Over the months and years, we have become considerably less self-centered and far more thoughtful of others. It's becoming almost second nature to take the initiative in helping friends and loved ones; to inconvenience ourselves for the sake of someone else; to let go and let others have their way.

These days, nothing gives us greater satisfaction than being of service to others. The payoff is rich and immediate. It's not that we receive anything material for our efforts. Rather, we are rewarded with good feelings that well up inside of us whenever we put others above ourselves.

THOUGHT FOR TODAY: Today and every day, my goal is to become less self-centered.

Our chief wisdom consists in knowing our follies and faults, that we may correct them.

—John Tillotson

I knew my name, I knew my date of birth and where I lived. But for a long time I had no real idea of why I felt and behaved as I did, or what I wanted out of life.

My lack of self-awareness kept me locked in an unchanging pattern of self-destructiveness, boredom, and despair. It was only in recovery, when I was urged to take specific steps toward gaining self-awareness, that there arose the possibility of change and growth.

I have since come to believe that self-awareness is an essential ingredient for learning and change. It can transform any positive or negative experience into a lesson and, eventually, into life-enchancing wisdom.

As I continued to work on my character flaws in recovery, I went through several periods where it seemed that I was moving backward rather than forward. I eventually realized that I was actually making considerable progress, and was simply becoming ever more sensitive to and aware of the subtleties of my feelings, motives, and resulting behavior.

THOUGHT FOR TODAY: Awareness of my character flaws leads me to the next step—taking responsibility to correct them.

September 1

The mind ought sometimes to be diverted that it may return to better thinking.

—Phaedrus

"A penny for your thoughts." We've all heard the expression, and chances are we've had trouble responding to it. How can we possibly sum up what we've just been thinking? Haven't we been thinking of *nothing*, and *everything*?

It can be startling to tune in to what's actually going on in our minds at any given moment. An endless inner dialogue is always taking place, replete with memories, speculations, and concerns: how we're feeling, what we want; judgments of ourselves and others; fears, doubts, regrets, *ad infinitum*.

All of this self-conversation can be very interesting, even fascinating, but when we spend more time living in our minds than in reality, we very often miss the moment. We tend to be inattentive and forgetful, and lose out on a good part of what life has to offer.

While we certainly wouldn't want to fully silence our minds, it's important to take refreshing and sorely needed breaks from these ongoing internal dialogues. This can be accomplished by various forms of meditation, which allow us, at least temporarily, to become anchored in the here and now.

THOUGHT FOR TODAY: Meditation can help when I'm at the mercy of my own brain-chatter.

We forfeit three-fourths of ourselves in order to be like other people.

—Arthur Schopenhauer

At long last, I feel deep down that it is perfectly all right to be myself, even if that means being different than other people. At long last I have begun to value the uniqueness that is me—the uniqueness that is each of us.

Gone are the days, thank heaven, when I would turn myself upside down and inside out to fit in, to be accepted, to win the approval of others. Gone, too, are the painful feelings that went along with such personal compromises.

For quite some time, it was difficult to accept some of my differences. But I ultimately learned that it is far easier to achieve self-acceptance than it is to constantly pretend to be something I'm not. I've come to believe, moreover, that God made me a certain way for a particular set of reasons. I have a special destiny.

Today, it's all right to stand out, to be noticed, even to be talked about as one who is different. When I give others the opportunity to get to know me, they almost always accept and respect me for the person I am.

THOUGHT FOR TODAY: My uniqueness need not isolate me.

September 3

Adversity is the first path to truth.
—George Gordon Byron

There are times when we feel a frightening, even paralyzing loss of control. We become convinced that nothing we do can change the outcome of what we are facing.

Whether it's a serious illness, a layoff, or the self-destructive behavior of a family member, we expect to be swept over a physical or emotional precipice. The sense that we have completely lost control brings with it an enormous amount of negative stress.

Yet in many cases there are actions we can take to regain a sense of control, and thereby reduce stress—actions that at first were not apparent, or seemed out of reach. We can learn all there is to know about our illness, for example. We can aggressively look for a new job. We can arrange an intervention with the troubled family member.

In other cases the best course of action is to concede our powerlessness—to recognize that it is *all right* to give up control over that part of our life. This in itself is bound to reduce stress.

The important thing to remember is that while we may have to give up control over outside issues, it is always possible to regain control of our inner self.

THOUGHT FOR TODAY: God is always in control.

Ignorance is a feeble remedy for our ills.

—Seneca

Growing up, I often heard people say, "What you don't know can't hurt you." I accepted the admonition willingly. As far as I was concerned, life was overwhelming enough without digging up still more problems.

For a long time, the notion that "ignorance is bliss" became one of my primary coping techniques, an all-purpose defense mechanism. But like so many people, I've since learned that our most troubling fear is fear of the unknown, and that in the long run ignorance is far more stressful than blissful.

When I had symptoms of illness in the past, for example, I would pretend that nothing was wrong. All the while my mind would be flooded with fearful speculations. Today if I'm not feeling well, I find out why and quickly put an end to the stress of not knowing.

Similarly, when I used to experience uneasiness, depression, or anger, I almost always refused to face such feelings. Naturally, my negative emotions continued to eat away at me. These days when I'm experiencing emotional turmoil, I seek out the cause—by talking it out, by meditative soul-searching, by inventory. When I determine what's wrong, I look for a solution.

THOUGHT FOR TODAY: Knowledge is freedom from fear.

September 5

To live is not merely to breathe, it is to act; it is to make use of our organs, senses, faculties, of all those parts of ourselves which give us the feeling of existence.

—Jean Jacques Rousseau

There was a time when, day after day, we depleted our bodies and stifled our spirits. We ruined our health by eating on the run, by smoking and drinking too much, by trying to get by without enough sleep. Each day was another silent struggle; we gritted our teeth to get through to the weekend. Only then could we hope to relax and catch up with ourselves.

Then something turned us around; we decided we could no longer go on that way. Slowly but surely we took steps to change our eating habits, to become physically fit, to give up the habits and dependencies that had been dragging us down for so long.

All we wanted initially was to feel better and look better. But because of our constructive new actions, we rediscovered and rekindled our inner spirit. Life began to take on exciting new dimensions.

As our inner spirit flourished and flowed through our being, it allowed us to tap into an abundance of physical and creative energy. We were motivated to further improve the quality of our lives, to learn more about ourselves, to expand our boundaries and widen our horizons.

THOUGHT FOR TODAY: My zest for living is spurred from within.

Just stand aside and watch yourself go by,
Think of yourself as "he" instead of "I."
—Strickland Gillilan

During the first year of recovery, it was exceedingly difficult for me to make decisions. My erratic feelings muddled the facts and confused me. Because the decision-making process was so stressful, I relied on a trusted friend for help.

Time after time he settled me down, helped me separate feelings from facts, and presented issues as they actually were rather than as my imagination distorted them. I relied on his objectivity for months, until we decided I was ready to learn how to be objective on my own.

My friend demonstrated that it *was* possible for me to make decisions with detachment and clarity. He patiently walked me through the process several times.

I learned first that it was essential to become relaxed in mind and body before even examining the issues. He also taught me how to observe a situation impartially, by figuratively stepping outside of myself. Next, he emphasized the importance of writing out a list of pros and cons. Finally, he explained that my biggest challenge was to squelch my negative imaginings, which catapulted me into the future and took me out of the here and now.

THOUGHT FOR TODAY: My emotions and projections—whether negative or positive—can destroy my objectivity.

September 7

Every extension of knowledge arises from making the conscious the unconscious.

—Friedrich Nietzsche

Whether our desire to live a spiritual life came as the result of a sudden awakening or was the outgrowth of gradual educational experience, we were motivated to change our attitudes and behavior in all areas. Spiritual growth, we were taught, would come from seeking humility by putting aside our self-serving ways and striving instead to serve others and God.

To the best of our ability, we consciously tried to be patient with loved ones, to be sensitive, caring, and kind. Each day we established a spiritual agenda, determined to admit our wrongs, to be forgiving, to respect life and the rights of others.

At times it was more difficult than we anticipated. Our inclination was to continue acting as we had in the past—with impatience, resentment, and dishonesty. Before doing the right thing, we sometimes had to restrain ourselves and think it through.

As months and years pass, our reactions and actions along these lines are becoming automatic. More and more these days, it is second nature to recognize and seize opportunities to be of service. Spirituality has become an instinctive way of life.

THOUGHT FOR TODAY: I don't have to wonder, ask, or agonize. I know what to do.

The mind is its own place, and in itself can make a heaven of hell, and a hell of heaven.

—John Milton

We all know what it's like to have an anxiety attack. It doesn't necessarily take a hair-raising experience to bring one on. Sometimes a relatively inconsequential event, blown out of proportion by our imagination, can cause us to panic.

We've found that our breathing, of all things, can quickly bring us around when this happens. The object is to keep our mind occupied—and thereby unable to overpower us—by focusing it on our incoming and outgoing breaths. In fact, learning to control our breathing—its rhythm, depth, and speed—is one of the most useful tools we have for reducing stress.

When we are anxious, our breathing becomes rapid and shallow; it may even stop for a time. When we are relaxed, on the other hand, our breathing is slow, even, and deep.

So the first thing we do when we are beset by anxiety is to direct our mind to our breathing, becoming aware of its rhythm and origin. Next, we make a conscious effort to shift from rapid chest breathing to slow abdominal breathing.

A major advantage of this anxiety-defeating exercise is that we can do it anytime and anywhere—standing, driving, in an airplane, or in our own bed.

THOUGHT FOR TODAY: I can harness the power of my mind.

September 9

We must discover security within ourselves.
—Boris Pasternak

If I were somehow able to journey back through my life and recapture the major fears that plagued me at one time or another, their number would be staggering. If I had the time and inclination to examine each fear—its effect on me and its relation to reality—I would likely find that I had spent years paralyzed and imprisoned by phantoms of my own creation.

My life has changed dramatically in that regard. I'm relatively fearless and feel free to do almost anything. Few days go by when I'm not gratefully aware of the difference between the way it is now and the way it used to be.

How did I get from there to here? How do any of us break way from constant, overpowering fear and become liberated?

First, we courageously identify and admit our fears. This step in itself can bring great relief. We then ask for God's help in becoming rid of our fears. At the same time, we do our best to walk through and beyond them day by day.

Finally, we seek serenity and security within, rather than in outside things. We learn to trust ourselves and our fellows.

THOUGHT FOR TODAY: I can overcome fear by relying on the power of God within me.

The essence of humor is sensibility; warm tender fellow-feeling with all forms of existence.
—Thomas Carlyle

There is something magical about laughter. It is available to everyone, it costs nothing, and it can accomplish in an instant what hours of conscientious effort might never produce. A life filled with laughter is a life rich with rewards.

Few traits bring about a feeling of well-being as quickly as an active sense of humor. A sense of humor helps us see events and interactions in perspective; as the result, we're less likely to take ourselves or anything else too seriously.

We can use laughter as a tool to defuse anger and other unsettling emotions, and to relieve tension. A well-chosen pun, for example, can force a smile on the most dour countenance. Moreover, humor can enliven the most tedious chore, and can be an antidote for boredom or even depression.

Of course, we can't force humor. It is best when it flows out of our own personal sense of fun and our awareness of life's absurdities, ironies, and incongruities. We let it happen naturally, and therein lies its greatest magic.

THOUGHT FOR TODAY: I will find humor in everyday experiences, and look for people I can laugh with.

September 11

*The best way to make your dreams come true is to
wake up.*

—Paul Valéry

It's hard to lose weight; anyone who has ever tried to
change their eating habits can attest to that. To begin
with, we have to get ourselves motivated, and that in
itself can be a formidable challenge.

An excellent method of becoming motivated is to
take an honest and unflinching look at how our weight
adversely affects our life. We can accomplish this by
writing out a detailed inventory of problems in various areas—social, professional, health—that relate
directly to being overweight.

Those of us who have taken such inventories
were surprised to discover, for example, that we
favored job assignments that kept us hidden in the
background. As a consequence, we suffered not only
socially, but also professionally and economically.

The inventory helped us see that being overweight profoundly affected not only our health, but
also our self-esteem; we felt less worthy than thinner
people. We realized, similarly, that our weight severely limited our physical activities.

The more aware we became of the detrimental
effects of being overweight, the easier it was to
develop motivation and begin to move forward.

THOUGHT FOR TODAY: A weight inventory can
help move me from willingness into action.

How good is man's life, the mere living! how
  fit to employ
All the heart and the soul and the senses forever
  in joy!

—Robert Browning

I liked to think of myself as one who lived life to the fullest. Because I had learned to value myself and God's blessings, I tried to put the most into and get the most out of each day.

Then, unexpectedly, I underwent emergency open-heart surgery. That lifesaving procedure was as much a trauma to my mind as to my body; it brought about dramatic emotional changes. And none was greater than the realization that my appreciation of life did not come even close to its potential.

As I say, I had thought of myself as a grateful person. Following the heart surgery, however, I could see that I had been taking a great deal for granted. All too often I had let the little things get to me, had allowed my priorities to go awry, and had let inconsequential fears eat away at my faith.

During the difficult months of healing and rehabilitation, as my body became strong again, I developed a deep conviction that life is truly our ultimate gift. If only I could *always* keep that conviction in the forefront of my mind . . .

THOUGHT FOR TODAY: I will savor the preciousness of my life.

September 13

A good conscience is a continual feast.
—Robert Burton

It wasn't necessarily any major wrongs we committed that caused us so much inner disquiet in the past. It wasn't that we were thieves, or adulterers, or that we caused physical harm to others. Ninety-nine percent of the time, the relatively *minor* acts of commission or omission were the ones that gnawed away at us and frequently kept us awake at night.

It was breaking appointments without calling to cancel. It was forgetting birthdays and anniversaries. It was not showing up for work and not coming home on time without letting anyone know. It was failing to respond to a friend in need of help. *Those* were the things that weighed heavily on our minds.

What a joy to live today with a clear conscience, to have peace of mind and a pervasive sense of emotional well-being. It's so satisfying to go to sleep knowing that we haven't left anything undone, that we don't have to make up for something, that it's not necessary to offer a major nose-in-the-dirt apology.

It's such a relief not to have fresh memories of misbehavior and irresponsibility bubbling through our brains. It's wonderful to have mental freedom!

THOUGHT FOR TODAY: My conscience is clear, and I intend to keep it that way.

We may with advantage at times forget what we know.

—Publilius Syrus

Second only to faith in God, the pursuit of self-awareness has brought about remarkable changes in my life. Day in and day out, self-awareness puts me in touch with my likes and dislikes, my aspirations and priorities, as well as my patterns of behavior and character defects.

But I have discovered that at times there can be too much of a good thing, so to speak. When I get carried away and become hyperaware of "me, me, me"—to the point of preoccupation—I am in danger of returning to the extreme self-centeredness of my past.

When I begin to dissect and analyze my every thought, feeling, action, and reaction, I again become the center of my own limited universe. When self-awareness turns into self-obsession, I am not unlike a snake trying to eat its own tail.

Thankfully, I don't fall into this mind-set very often. But when I do, I always emerge defeated, exhausted, and sick of myself. When I recover from my emotional slump, I realize once again that some-times it's necessary to just let myself be—to live, to let live, and to enjoy life as it unfolds.

THOUGHT FOR TODAY: When self-awareness be-comes all-encompassing, it's time to let up.

September 15

O heavy burden of a doubtful mind!
—Francis Quarles

We know from personal experience that our health can be strongly influenced by the kinds of personal messages we transmit to ourselves. So we try to stay tuned in to our inner dialogue. That way, when we become aware of a trend of negativity, we can take steps to change our attitude, thinking, and course of action.

At one time or another, we've all pressured ourselves by saying, for example, "I'll get promoted out of this job if it kills me!" or, "I'll make this relationship work if it's the last thing I do!" When we send ourselves rigid ultimatums along these lines— using such threatening phrases as "come hell or high water," or "no matter what"—we're bound to jeopardize our emotional and physical health in some way, even though it may not be readily apparent.

It's a part of human nature to have ambitious goals and aspirations. However, before we pursue them we should be certain that we can approach them positively and flexibly, and that we're emotionally, physically, and spiritually prepared to undertake the challenge.

THOUGHT FOR TODAY: Am I damaging myself with negative internal messages?

Rejoice that man is hurled
From change to change unceasingly,
His soul's wings never furled.

—Robert Browning

In the years prior to recovery, my mind was constantly ablaze with self-directed disappointment and disgust. Beyond my hateful feelings for myself, I couldn't escape the reality that my life was careening rapidly downhill. That was frightening enough, but even more terrifying was the sense that I was powerless to keep things from becoming worse and worse in every way.

In truth, I *was* utterly powerless, not only over my addictions and behavior patterns, but over my self-destructive thinking as well. It was only when I surrendered to that reality—and decided to turn my will and life over to the care of a Power greater than myself—that my rebirth and metamorphosis could begin.

Today my life is constantly changing, and almost always for the better. Where once I was loveless and friendless, my days are now rich with caring, giving, and fellowship. Where once I could only helplessly witness my physical and mental deterioration, today I take great pride in the health and fitness I've achieved. Where once I was embittered and despairing, I have become enthusiastic, joyful, and grateful.

THOUGHT FOR TODAY: Lack of power was once my dilemma; it has since become my salvation.

September 17

Life is the coordination of actions.
—Herbert Spencer

Most of us learned about the "fight or flight response" in junior high school. Our teachers usually used primitive man to illustrate the lesson: Caveman sees tiger; caveman's mind and body prepare him to either fight or run away by releasing adrenaline and increasing his heart rate and blood flow.

We all occasionally experience the fight or flight response in our own lives. We feel the rush of adrenaline when we almost fall or when a car swerves into our path. And as we well know, the same high-stress response is also triggered by emotions other than the fear of physical harm—the kind of negative emotions caused by living with a violent alcoholic, for example, or prolonged financial troubles, or trying to live up to another person's impossible expectations.

When these emotions and the conditions causing them go on for months or years, we remain in the fight or flight mode continually—not just briefly to deal with an occasional "tiger." And the problem with long-term unremitting stress of this kind is that it can lead to severe suppression of the body's immune system—and illness.

THOUGHT FOR TODAY: Long-term stress can cause long-term health problems.

No one can harm the man who does himself no wrong.
—St. Chrysostom

It seems so long ago—thank God for that—yet we don't ever want to forget the way we treated ourselves and allowed others to treat us. We had such low self-esteem that over and over again we unwittingly set ourselves up to be harmed.

We also willingly soaked up abuse from others because of our deep-down conviction that we were somehow guilty and therefore deserved it. We might as well have plastered ourselves with "KICK ME" signs and then, day after day, stepped out onto the same crowded street.

In recovery, because we've been taking steps and actions that are right and good for us, we've become increasingly self-aware and self-honest. Our self-esteem has steadily risen, and we hardly ever put ourselves in positions that invite derogation and deprecation.

These days, we are far less fragile than we once were. It takes a lot more than a snide remark or a disdainful glance to bring us to our knees. Indeed, the occasions are few and far between when we allow ourselves to be manipulated or taken advantage of in *any* way. We feel proud to stand up for ourselves.

THOUGHT FOR TODAY: I am no longer a doormat—for myself or anyone else.

September 19

Faith is the root of all blessings. Believe, and you shall be saved; believe, and you will be satisfied; believe, and you cannot but be comforted and happy.
—Jeremy Taylor

Today I will visualize my body as a vessel in which God's spirit dwells. I will see myself brimming over with health, strength, and vitality. *I feel completely alive and whole.*

I will visualize the power of God working in and through me. I will fully avail myself of His help by relaxing and releasing all anxiety about my health and well-being. I will let go of my concerns and let God care for me only as He can. *I feel completely serene.*

I am confident that God's healing power stands ready within me, always potent and available. It need only be activated by my faith. I visualize every organ, every fiber, every cell in my body responding to God's healing grace. If I experience a health challenge, I know that His love will renew and revitalize me. *I feel completely secure.*

I believe unreservedly that God's healing power is my ultimate resource. He offers it as an unconditional gift, and I accept it with gratitude. *I feel completely blessed.*

THOUGHT FOR TODAY: By caring for my body, I affirm my Divine birthright of good health.

We should be taught not to wait for inspiration to start a thing. Action always generates inspiration. Inspiration seldom generates action.

—Frank Tibolt

There were things we wanted to do that we knew would enrich our lives. We had always been fascinated by literature, and felt we had the talent to write poetry or short stories. For years we'd dreamed of learning to sail and scuba dive, and running a marathon.

So what did we do? We waited and waited. We kept on dreaming, in anticipation of the perfect set of circumstances, that magic moment when we would be inspired to move ahead. Most of the time, of course, nothing happened. We continued to wait, neither fulfilling our desire nor living our dream.

Ultimately, we discovered that action and action alone was the catalytic ingredient. When we picked up the phone to enroll in a writing class, we were on our way to becoming writers. When we joined a running club or took scuba lessons, our dreams had a chance of materializing. When we finally forced ourselves to our feet and jumped in—fears, misgivings, doubts, and all—that's when we were finally able to make a start.

THOUGHT FOR TODAY: Action gets us started; inspiration keeps us going.

September 21

No one is wise enough by himself.
>   —Titus Maccius Plautus

A friend and I were standing in the buffet line at a wedding reception. We became aware that many people were expressing concern that all the appetizing foods would "ruin their diets."

Later, my friend told me about her own experiences with overeating and abstaining. "I went on my first diet when I was eight," she said. "I remember losing quite a bit of weight during that school year, gaining it back in the summer, then having to start all over again in the fall.

"It went on like that for the next twenty years. Big gains and big losses. I was always frustrated, yet driven by the illusion that if only I could keep the weight off permanently, all my problems would be solved."

Just before she turned thirty, my friend joined a Twelve-Step support group for overeaters. "The most important thing I learned," she emphasized, "was that overeating had never been my *real* problem. The real problems, in a nutshell, were the way I felt about myself and my inability to cope with life from day to day. In order to recover, I had to first become self-honest. And from that point on, my whole outlook began to change."

THOUGHT FOR TODAY: Am I treating the problem—or merely the symptom?

We should stop kidding ourselves. We should let go of things that aren't true. It's always better with the truth.

—Buckminster Fuller

We are all familiar with how powerful and punishing old ideas can be. That's why, in our new life, we work steadily to become free of them. Sometimes, however, we've clung to an old idea for so long that it seems to be part of our identity.

Rooted deeply in our mind may be the conviction, for example, that we are and always will be unattractive. Or we may believe that whatever we do, it won't be enough. Each time the idea surfaces, it causes an emotional setback.

We may have periodically tried to replace the tenacious old idea with a new and accurate one. If we've been unsuccessful to this point, we might ask: Have my efforts in the past been sincere and thorough? If not, then it's time to make a *total* commitment.

It can be extremely helpful to reveal the self-destructive idea to a close friend or to members of our support group. This act of forthrightness will not only dilute the potency of the old idea, but further inspire and motivate us to work toward a solution. Concurrently, we can ask our Higher Power to help us become free of the limiting belief.

THOUGHT FOR TODAY: I will put the truth about myself into practice.

September 23

We know God easily, if we do not constrain ourselves to define Him.

—Joseph Joubert

In addition to my dyed-in-the-wool atheism, still another philosophical issue closed my mind and prevented me from seeking a Higher Power. To be sure, my ideas didn't come from theological knowledge or experience of any kind. Yet I had the impression that traditional conceptions of a Supreme Being, along with the strict "rules" of various doctrines, made it exceedingly difficult for people to feel comfortable with God in their lives.

I had heard people talk about being raised to believe in a harsh, punishing God—or a God who is selective as to whom He blesses—or a God who "keeps score" and turns His back on sinners. I wanted no part of it.

One day, I was presented with the revelationary idea that I could choose a God of my own understanding. That reality, more than anything else, made it possible for me to eventually develop a spiritual consciousness. My conception of God became a highly personal matter, not at all reflective of my own upbringing or the beliefs of anyone else.

In order to secure the limitless benefits that faith could provide, I discovered, all I had to do was open my mind, follow my heart, and trust my inner voice.

THOUGHT FOR TODAY: I'm free to seek a Higher Power of my own understanding.

Friendship's a noble name, 'tis love refined.
—Susannah Centlivre

Few situations in daily life are more gut-wrenching than a discordant or deteriorating relationship with a loved one. The emotional toll can be devastating; every one of us is familiar with the quick-acting, high-impact stress that turns our world upside down.

That's why we work so hard to keep our relationships healthy. With time and practice, we've learned about the necessary ingredients. Here are several:

The importance of honest and free-flowing communications can't be overemphasized. If we express our feelings and talk out minor conflicts, we can prevent them from turning into major crises. Communication of this type encourages us to quickly apologize when we have behaved badly or, conversely, to state our case when we feel we have been hurt in some way.

No less essential is the active desire to be empathetic toward a partner. When we walk in another person's shoes, we're certainly better able to be accepting and supportive.

A high degree of selflessness is also vital to successful relationships. That means being consistently thoughtful and considerate of a partner's wants and needs without losing sight of our own priorities.

THOUGHT FOR TODAY: The quality of my relationships has a profound impact on my well-being and productivity.

Nothing is worth more than this day.
— Johann Wolfgang von Goethe

At long last we've become committed to losing weight, to giving up smoking, to improving our overall health and fitness. We've made good progress, to be sure. Yet there are times when we feel overwhelmed at the prospect of having to keep on doing what we've been doing—for the rest of our lives. *Forever.*

Certainly this perspective can be very frightening—frightening enough, perhaps, to send us scurrying back to our old ways. And that's exactly why we have to do our utmost to change this self-defeating point of view whenever it surfaces.

The way to accomplish this is by keeping our commitments and working toward our goals one day at a time. As obvious or even pedestrian as this approach may sound, it nevertheless can be a sure path to success in any number of endeavors—from overcoming addiction to improving physical fitness and self-esteem through disciplined and consistent workouts.

Yesterday is gone and tomorrow hasn't yet arrived, but today is *always* here, and it's all we need to be concerned with. For just one day, we can do whatever is necessary to fulfill our commitments to ourself and move forward on the road to good health.

THOUGHT FOR TODAY: I can meet my lifetime goals a day at a time.

It is good for us to be here.
            —New Testament: Matthew, xvii, 4.

A friend once told me about his grandmother's favorite parable: "We all have our crosses to bear. But if we were to put them down in the middle of a room and mix them up, each of us would gladly go back to our own and pick it up."

Every so often, when things aren't going my way, the image of those crosses comes to mind. The first thing I realize is that I am all too willing to pick up my own cross when I compare it with the far heavier load of so many other people. In other words, I am able to see my problems, difficulties, and dilemmas in true perspective.

Going further, it also becomes clear that the overwhelming majority of my troubles are of my own making. They are the direct outgrowth of old ideas, reemerging character defects, or negative attitudes and reactions.

From that standpoint, I frequently custom-create my own cross, and that's why it's so easy to spot in the pile. Thankfully, however, these days I have a choice; I can either pick up the same old cross, or apply spiritual solutions and lighten my burden.

THOUGHT FOR TODAY: I can start right now to put seeming adversities into perspective.

September 27

*No one can with safety expose himself often to danger
The man who has often escaped is caught at last.*
—Seneca

We used to think we were invincible. We took risks just for the thrill of it; we drove recklessly, experimented with drugs, thrived on danger. We lived on the edge and thought that we would go on like that forever.

Those of us who survived that period, or came through it relatively unscathed, have since developed reverence for life and respect for our bodies. As the result our behavior has changed dramatically. It's not that all the fun and excitement has gone out of our lives; to the contrary. It's just that we no longer take foolish risks and put ourselves in jeopardy unnecessarily.

One fairly obvious reason for this change in attitudes and behavior is that we've become more mature. We've become increasingly aware of our responsibility—not just to ourselves, but to those around us. We've outgrown the need to prove ourselves with self-indulgent thrill-seeking.

Another reason for our changed lifestyle is our deepening faith in God. It is now our sincere conviction that life is His ultimate gift to us, and we treasure it accordingly.

THOUGHT FOR TODAY: Sometimes it's thrilling enough just to be alive.

The first and worst of all frauds is to cheat one's self.
—Gamaliel Bailey

You've made phenomenal progress in the areas of self-discovery and self-renewal. Many positive physical and emotional changes have taken place. But because your self-image is out of date, you may be getting only limited satisfaction from these achievements.

You're toned up and at an ideal weight, but still see yourself as fat and flabby. You're more at ease with people than ever, but still see yourself as shy and withdrawn. Your life is filled with love, but you still see yourself as unloved and unloving.

Perhaps it's time to write an inventory, objectively contrasting the person you were with the person you've become. Make careful note of how you've changed physically—weight, muscle tone, appearance. Ask yourself probing questions: Do I have a greater sense of well-being? Do I react with less volatility in situations that previously caused me to explode? Do I know what to do in times of trouble? Do I turn to spiritual solutions instead of behavioral and chemical crutches?

Those of us who have brought our self-images up to date in this way have found that the quality of our lives has improved dramatically. Certainly it's worth trying.

THOUGHT FOR TODAY: Is my self-image up to date?

September 29

Patience is power; with time and patience the mulberry leaf becomes silk.

—Chinese proverb

One summer while I was watching a game of beach volleyball, a friend of mind injured his shoulder while diving for a ball. I didn't see him again until fall. As we both watched a volleyball tournament, I asked him when he would be able to play again.

He told me ruefully that if he hadn't rushed himself he'd be playing already. He was supposed to stay off the court for at least a month, and do a series of stretching and strengthening exercises at home.

"But after a couple of weeks, when my shoulder didn't hurt as much, I got impatient," my friend continued. "So I tried playing again. The very first game, I reinjured it. Now I'll be out for another three weeks.

"No, wait, erase that," he added quickly. "The biggest lesson I've learned from this whole experience is not to put a timetable on my recovery. The thing is, this is my first real injury, and it's hard to be patient. But now I know how important it is to put in the time and effort on the rehab process. And when I finally am healed this time, believe me, I'm going to start back slowly."

THOUGHT FOR TODAY: I won't let impatience sideline me.

Every blade of grass in the field is measured; the green cups and colored crowns of every flower are curiously counted; the stars of the firmament wheel in cunningly calculated orbit; even the storms have their laws.

—William Garden Blaikie

Not long ago, I read an article describing the genetic blueprints of various life forms. An imaginative diagram revealed how each individual cell is encoded with specific instructions, so that it knows in effect what it is, where it belongs, and what it is supposed to do. The article started me thinking about my own blueprint—my own "inner director"—which makes my life so secure and purposeful today.

For a long period, that wasn't the case at all. Most of the time I drifted aimlessly and was lost and confused. I had no real idea of my place, my worth, or my function.

Gradually, I came to believe in a Power greater than myself. I became convinced that the miraculous reality of God can be found deep within each of us. Today I envision that Power as my spiritual blueprint, from which I receive guidance, direction, and motivation.

The more I pay attention to and trust that part of me, the more clearly I know who I am, where I belong, and what my destiny is.

THOUGHT FOR TODAY: No matter where, no matter what, no matter when—I will trust my inner voice.

October 1

Knowledge is the action of the soul.

—Ben Jonson

In many Twelve-Step support groups, there is a familiar expression along these lines: "This program will sure mess up your drinking (drug use, overeating, gambling, codependency)." What it means, in essence, is that once a person discovers there is a solution and a new way to live, he or she will never be able to comfortably return to the old life.

In the same way, once we develop self-awareness and acquire new knowledge, our old ways of thinking and acting become untenable. For example, as our self-image improves and we recognize and appreciate our value, it becomes less likely that negative thinking will persuade us again that we don't measure up.

Similarly, once we've learned how physically harmful stress is—how it diminishes the capability of our immune system, saps our energy, and impairs our powers of concentration—we no longer can ignore or accept ongoing stress in our lives.

And once we come to believe that God has always cared for us, and always will—despite our prior lack of faith—it's hard to return to a life fueled by self-centeredness.

THOUGHT FOR TODAY: Now that I've awakened, I don't want to go back to sleep.

*It is one of the illusions, that the present hour is not
the critical, decisive hour.*

—Thomas Carlyle

"If only"—this can be the most poignant yet also most
poisonous phrase in our vocabulary. We use it in the
mistaken belief that we will be happy—once and for
all—when certain things occur in our life. If only we
could find a better place to live, a higher-paying job,
a more understanding mate. *Then* we'd be happy.

The biggest problem with this kind of thinking is
that it causes us to put our happiness on hold until
certain conditions are met. And then, after we get
what we want, a whole new array of desires and
contingencies take over.

We end up in a limbo of constantly unfulfilled
desires, and are unable to appreciate what we have
right now. The present becomes little more than a
misty tunnel of time—something we must bear with
and pass through in order to get somewhere else.
What a sad and frustrating way to live!

But we don't have to live that way. When we put
aside thoughts of what we want or don't want to
happen, and become attentive to the joys and blessings of the present, it is then we find true happiness.

THOUGHT FOR TODAY: I will live in the now and
enjoy the miracles of this moment.

October 3

*A man's body and his mind, with the utmost reverence
to both I speak it, are exactly like a jerkin and a
jerkin's lining; rumple the one, you rumple the other.*
—Laurence Sterne

For years my distressful feelings ate me alive with
physical symptoms. On any given day my jaws would
ache from clenching, and I would have a burning pain
in my stomach. But I rarely connected those reactions
to my underlying emotions of anger, self-consciousness,
or anxiety.

I've since learned that certain kinds of physical
discomfort are often a dead giveaway to emotional
discomfort, and can help me become more quickly
aware of my true feelings.

In various social situations, for example, an ac-
celerated heart rate and sweaty palms can make it
clear that I am self-conscious and fearful. Similarly,
my repressed anger usually manifests itself physically
through tight muscles and a headache.

When a physical reaction allows me to identify a
negative feeling, it becomes possible to reverse the
process, so to speak. As a typical example, if my
emotional response to a particular event has caused
my shoulder and neck muscles to knot up, I try to
stretch and relax those muscles. Even if I'm only
partially successful, the effort can help me relax
emotionally as well.

THOUGHT FOR TODAY: An awareness of my body
can lead to an awareness of my feelings.

Comparisons do oft-time great grievance.
—John Lydgate

No matter how much progress we make on the road to physical, emotional, and spiritual well-being, some of us still have a tendency to unfairly compare ourselves to others. We've reached and maintained our weight-loss goal, for example, but feel that our aerobics partner has a much nicer body. We have a lot more composure than before, but doubt that we'll ever have the unflappability of some of our friends.

It's always damaging to us when we compare ourselves in these ways. Our self-confidence becomes eroded, and is sometimes completely shattered. We feel discouraged and disillusioned.

That's why, when these competitive feelings surface, it's important for us to step back and reaffirm that we are not in a contest with anyone. Rather, we are on a personal journey to self-discovery and self-expansion.

We can remind ourselves, moreover, that each of us is an exceptional individual, possessing a unique set of God-given talents and capabilities. Our purpose is to fully discover and develop the special potential that is ours alone. At the same time, we can learn to respect rather than envy the uniqueness and special potential of each of our fellows.

THOUGHT FOR TODAY: We each grow in our own way, and in our own time.

October 5

They never fail who light
Their lamp of faith at the unwavering flame
Burnt for the altar service of the Race
Since the beginning.

—Elsa Barker

At some point today I will sit quietly, breathe deeply, close my eyes, and visualize the essence of my spiritual being. I will see myself as God sees me, deserving of all the good that comes my way, and worthy of His boundless love.

I will visualize myself as a person with great potential. With God as my guiding force, I can actualize that potential and become greatly fulfilled. A future of unlimited possibilities lies before me.

I will see myself as a whole and complete individual, with an array of God-given talents and capabilities. I have been endowed by my Higher Power with everything I need for a full and productive life.

If I am set back by any flaw, failure, or circumstance, I will view my slowed pace as only temporary. I can always turn and return to God within me for new inspiration and impetus.

Through today's visualization I will cancel any thoughts and feelings of unworthiness or inadequacy. I will affirm that I am a valued child of God, blessed by Him with uniqueness and importance.

THOUGHT FOR TODAY: I am a grateful beneficiary of my Father's precious and abundant gifts.

Knowledge is a treasure, but practice is the key to it.
—Thomas Fuller

We have accumulated a wide range of new knowledge and ideas during our recovery. By reading, by attending lectures—mostly by talking to other people and learning from their experiences—we've been introduced to new ways of thinking and acting.

For some of us, however, that's as far as we've gone. Our new knowledge hasn't developed or evolved because we haven't yet put it to use. Consequently, nothing in our lives has really changed.

If that's the case, today is a good day to put one or two of our new ideas into practice. Perhaps weight loss is a long-standing goal. If so, today is a good day to prepare a meal plan, and to start exercising, based on the knowledge we've acquired.

If stress reduction is high on our list of priorities, today is a good day to write a stress inventory, to experiment with breathing exercises, or to commit to a new mind-set concerning the way we react to certain situations.

If we've been planning to begin meditating, today is a good day to choose a method that seems right for us, to set aside some time, to finally put some of our new knowledge into practice.

THOUGHT FOR TODAY: I've become educated, but have I become motivated?

October 7

Health is the first muse.

—Ralph Waldo Emerson

As a practicing alcoholic, the most exercise I ever got was wandering through unfamiliar streets trying to find my lost car. Not surprisingly, when I finally quit drinking I was considerably overweight, out of shape, and unhealthy.

For the first time in years, I began to care about the way I looked and felt. That's why I started exercising. Since I lived in a coastal town, I began by taking long early-morning walks on the beach. Gradually, very gradually, I worked up to slow jogs along the hard-packed sand at the water's edge.

I wasn't out to prove anything or to break any records. When I got tired or my muscles started to ache, I rested. Looking back, I'm grateful that I didn't push myself too hard; had I done so, I surely would have become discouraged and quickly given up.

I have fond memories of those mornings on the beach. I was doing perhaps one-tenth as much exercise as I do today, but at the time it seemed like such an enormous accomplishment. And it truly was, because it formed the foundation for what has become an extremely important part of my life.

THOUGHT FOR TODAY: The way to build my house of health is from the bottom up, slowly but steadily.

The greater the obstacle, the greater the glory we have in overcoming it.

—Molière

Some of us still smoke. We've been smoking for a long time, and for one reason or another are just not ready to give it up. But maybe we can bring ourselves closer to the day of surrender by thinking about some proven benefits we can look forward to when we become nonsmokers.

For each cigarette you *do not* smoke you will live five minutes longer.

When you give up smoking your body will start healing itself immediately. The irritated cells in your lungs, throat, sinuses, and elsewhere will start growing normally again.

You'll probably get fewer colds. When you do get one, it probably won't last as long and will be less likely to develop into something more serious.

You won't become short of breath because of such minor exertions as stair-climbing. In fact, your breathing will become much easier overall. As a result, physical activities including walking, biking, tennis, and swimming will be far more enjoyable.

Your skin, hair, and clothes will stop smelling of stale smoke. Your house, office, and car will also be cleaner and smell better. Your fingers and teeth will no longer be nicotine stained.

Your self-esteem will soar.

THOUGHT FOR TODAY: The best way to give up smoking is the way that's best for you.

October 9

Love in its essence is spiritual fire.
—Emanuel Swedenborg

We all know how wonderful it is to love someone or something. We have warm, good feelings inside of us. Love is exciting, joyful, uplifting. To be sure, we cherish these feelings and want them to be with us forever. Yet if we only feel love in a passive way within ourselves, and don't openly and actively express it, we don't experience it to the fullest.

Real, expansive love—the special love we learn about in our spiritual quest—flows out of us, touches and affects others, and hopefully enhances the quality of their lives in some way. If what we call love is not actively expressed in this fashion—in service to others—then we are simply experiencing good feelings within ourselves.

Going further, all too often we think of expressive love solely in romantic terms—a kiss, a hug, a caress. But love can also be expressed to friends, acquaintances, and even strangers through acts of service and compassion. We can volunteer, donate blood, help neighbors, offer encouragement, and work to improve the environment. Love can be expressed in limitless ways.

THOUGHT FOR TODAY: True love is putting good feelings into action.

The very commonplaces of life are components of its eternal mystery.

—Gertrude Atherton

When we think of meditation, we usually picture a darkened room, a quiet environment, or a shrine-like setting. We imagine ourselves with our eyes closed in a special place at a special time.

Certainly this approach can help any of us find inner peace. But meditation need not be limited to a fixed ritual during which we sit motionless in a confined space. The truth is that any activity which calms the body and focuses the mind can be helpful in achieving a meditative state. Any endeavor which keeps our attention tranquilly fixed in the present moment can provide the basis for meditation.

When we practice "meditation in motion," we become fully connected to a particular activity—such as running—without allowing our thoughts to become diverted. We become sharply focused and completely open to each moment as it occurs. Ultimately, we achieve a reflective state of attentiveness—not only to our inner voice, but also to the action itself and its related perceptions and sensations.

To bring about this state, some of us favor hiking, swimming, or fishing; others find success while painting, sewing, or gardening. Needless to say, it's up to each of us to discover the activities that work best.

THOUGHT FOR TODAY: There are no limits to the forms or benefits of meditation.

October 11

I have learned to use the word impossible *with the greatest caution.*

—Wernher von Braun

On a foggy morning not long ago, I spent a couple of hours learning to ride a mountain bike in a canyon near my home. Later that day a neighbor said she had seen me. "That's wonderful," she enthused. "That's what I've got to do." The exchange made me feel really good about myself.

Experiences like that mean a great deal, because I spent half my life convinced that I would never have positive feelings toward myself. I thought low self-worth was my permanent lot.

But what had always seemed impossible has become reality. Granted, it has taken years, but today I value myself as a worthy person. For the most part, I've been able to put to rest my once-chronic feelings of self-hatred.

This metamorphosis has come about through action, not by thought. Each day, a major priority is to actively improve my physical, emotional, and spiritual well-being. Learning to ride a mountain bike off-road is the most recent example.

That's how we gain self-esteem, I've learned—by taking risks, pushing back limits, expanding boundaries. By doing the things that nourish our souls and lift our spirits.

THOUGHT FOR TODAY: The greatest miracle is the one within.

Look twice before you leap.

—Charlotte Brontë

One of the most significant truths that newly recovering alcoholics and addicts learn is: "If you don't take the first drink (pill, fix, snort, puff) you won't get loaded."

Thinking back, it's hard to believe that so many of us couldn't figure that out for ourselves before we threw in the towel and sought help. The thing is, we never understood that the first drink triggered an irresistible compulsion; any efforts to limit ourselves after that were bound to fail.

Now that we're clean and sober, we've learned, in effect, how to lock the barn door securely *before* the horse gets out and runs away. This applies not only to alcohol and other drugs, but also to damaging substances and behavioral patterns in many other areas of our lives.

As one example, we don't take the first step into a place that will be emotionally "slippery" for us. We don't take the first bite of a certain food that may trigger an eating binge. We don't nurture the seeds of negative thoughts, resentments, or harsh judgments and allow them to take root. And since one lie inevitably leads to another, we don't tell the first one.

THOUGHT FOR TODAY: "One too many" means exactly that.

October 13

In contemplation of created things, by steps we may ascend to God.

—John Milton

Whenever I travel, whether for business or pleasure, I always make it a point to seek out the most scenic local areas and explore them. I usually do so by hiking, but if time is short I drive to my destination, get out of the car, and simply soak up my surroundings.

It's hard not to be inspired when I'm surrounded by wild orchids in a mile-high cloud forest. It's hard not to see myself right-size, in proper perspective, when I'm overlooking a towering waterfall or when I'm shadowed by a giant redwood tree.

Almost always during these excursions, I feel close to my Creator. I become keenly aware of His presence and power. And it's easy to imagine that He has drawn me to a particular place so that my spirit can be nourished and refreshed.

When I retreat to a wooded hilltop, hidden lake, or remote canyon, a harmonious chord is struck within me. I feel a unity of mind, body, and spirit. At the deepest level of my being, I have an unshakable sense of belonging.

THOUGHT FOR TODAY: By experiencing God's wonders, I can become spiritually renewed.

Remember you have not a sinew whose law of strength is not action; not a faculty of body, mind, or soul whose law of improvement is not energy.

—E. B. Hall

We really thought we were committed when we first set out to revitalize ourselves. We spent a lot of time and energy choosing the diet and fitness programs that seemed right for us. We researched stress-reduction techniques and avenues for spiritual growth. We told anyone who was willing to listen exactly what we were going to do for ourselves.

The problem for some of us was that our commitment was only a conditional one. We may not have been aware of it, but most of our planned activities were contingent on other things taking place in our lives and the lives of others. We played the "if" game.

We'd eat right *if* we could fix meals at home; eating out was different. We'd exercise *if* we could conveniently arrange the time, or *if* we could get our spouse or pal to keep us company. We'd pray and meditate *if* our backs were against the wall.

Needless to say we didn't get very far taking that approach. We are not automatically graced with physical, emotional, and spiritual well-being just because of our good intentions. It is only achievable through discipline and total commitment.

THOUGHT FOR TODAY: Action alone can bring my good intentions to fruition.

October 15

If anything is sacred the human body is sacred.
                                    —Walt Whitman

Some years ago my doctor recommended that I undergo an elective surgical procedure. It would likely prevent a developing condition from becoming serious, he said, and might even alleviate it entirely. I agonized over the decision, but eventually agreed to check in to the hospital.

On the morning of the surgery, as I was being prepped, I became extremely anxious. Negative thoughts flooded my mind; I began to have serious regrets about my decision.

As I waited to be wheeled to the operating room, a nun walked in and wished me well. At one point she took my hand and said, "You're doing a wonderful thing for yourself. It shows that you have reverence for life, and that you have great respect for the body God has given you."

I don't know whether the nun says the same thing to all surgical patients. It doesn't matter, for her words had a magical effect on me. Not only did they ease my fears that day, but they have remained with me over the years. When I remember the sister's visit, I think about God's gift of life. And I am motivated to treat my physical being with the respect it deserves.

THOUGHT FOR TODAY: In a very real sense, my pursuit of physical well-being is an expression of gratitude.

Grace comes into the soul, as the morning sun into the world; first a dawning; then a light; and at last the sun in his full and excellent brightness.

—Thomas Adams

For relatively few people, spiritual awakenings take place suddenly and spectacularly. These individuals seem to acquire belief and trust in a Higher Power all at once, and with equal speed undergo dramatic changes in attitude, outlook, and behavior.

For most of us, however, such transformations develop over a long period of time—months or years. Very often, the process begins with a profound awareness that we must change because the ways in which we've been thinking, acting, and living are leading to a figurative or even literal downfall.

When we reach out for help, it's a relief to learn that we don't have to change on our own; our resources are not limited to willpower and self-discipline. If we're willing to put our faith in a Power greater than ourselves, close friends assure us, the changes we previously couldn't bring about will come to pass.

That is is exactly what happens over time. When we turn to God for guidance, strength, and support, He comes through for us. He does for us what we are unable to do for ourselves.

THOUGHT FOR TODAY: Thank God I don't have to change on my own.

October 17

Do you count your birthdays thankfully?

—Horace

It's one of those milestone birthdays—thirty, forty, fifty, sixty. At work and at home, people have begun to tease us. We've received one too many cynical birthday cards.

Now we're beginning to feel depressed. We're newly aware of every gray hair, each line and wrinkle. We see our cup as half empty rather than half full and reflect negatively on our life, thinking, "I'm already thirty and still not married."—"I've hit forty and I'm not yet successful."

Why do we react in these maudlin and expected ways, even though we know that such thoughts and feelings are truly nonsensical? After all, the substance and quality of life has nothing to do with numbers, round or otherwise. It has to do with what we put into and take out of each day, with our attitude toward life and how we choose to experience it.

Depending on our approach, we can be "old" in spirit at forty or "young" at heart at seventy. The better we feel about ourselves, the less likely we are to buckle under to such societal pressures as "twenty-nine and holding."

THOUGHT FOR TODAY: I value and appreciate each new day, no matter where in my life span it falls.

Great is the human who has not lost his childlike heart.

—Mencius

Not so very long ago, I would automatically flinch at the admonition, "You're acting like a child!" But I've come to see that there are two kinds of childishness— the kind I want to grow out of, and the kind I want to carry with me as an adult.

The child I want to leave behind is self-centered and self-indulgent, thoughtless and inconsiderate. His number one concern is personal gratification; when he doesn't get his way he loses control and throws a tantrum. The child I want to outgrow has a need to be the center of attention. He is frequently reckless, greedy, and irresponsible.

The child I hope will be with me throughout my life is free spirited and lighthearted, enthusiastic and playful. He has the ability to live completely in the present—to bring his entire self into the activity of the moment.

That child has an active sense of wonder and curiosity, plus a knack for deriving genuine pleasure from the simplest things. He lacks self-consciousness and is uninhibited. He is open, trusting, and teachable.

THOUGHT FOR TODAY: My maturity is enhanced, not diminished, by my free-spirited inner child.

October 19

I vow and protest there's more plague than pleasure with a secret.

—George Coleman

In order to experience personal and spiritual freedom to the greatest extent possible, we had to carefully examine our inner lives. There were many things weighing us down that had to be uncovered, explored, and changed. Some were obvious, some were not.

We knew we had secrets, far too many of them, but it never occurred to us that they were a major source of stress for us. Yet for years we had been using up a tremendous amount of energy to hide our feelings, fears, and wrongful behavior.

Once we committed ourselves, it wasn't too difficult to make a list of our secrets. But following that, many of us were reluctant to reveal them and let them go. They were secrets for a reason; we feared that if people knew about them, they would lose respect for us.

As it turned out, in order to unburden ourselves all we really needed to do was confide in one person we trusted. Once we were able to do that, we experienced great relief. These days, we make it a point not to accumulate new secrets. We continue to talk about our feelings, fears, and actions.

THOUGHT FOR TODAY: Secrets can cause stress.

We should often have reason to be ashamed of our most brilliant actions if the world could see the motives from which they spring.
— Duc de La Rochefoucauld

I ran into a friend who had lost sixty pounds since I last saw him. Naturally, I wondered how he had done it. He explained that his initial motivation to lose weight was completely negative, based on shame and embarrassment. But after a while, as he began to change his eating habits and slim down, the motivation turned positive.

"It all began when I overheard a whispered remark about me," he said. "The operative word was *blimp*. I was devastated."

Many of us have similar experiences. We are first motivated to make major changes in our lives because of unbearable self-loathing, because of a physician's ominous warning, or because of societal pressures. Along the way, we find that while this sort of negative impetus can get us started, it doesn't sustain us long enough to reach our goal.

Fortunately, our negative motives for changing often evolve into positive ones. We may start out because of shame and embarrassment, but before long we are motivated by life-affirming reasons. We begin to look better and feel better. We regain self-worth because we're doing something to improve the quality of our lives. We sense that we are once again in control of ourselves.

THOUGHT FOR TODAY: I'm doing it for the best reason; I'm doing it for me.

October 21

The whole life of man is but a point of time; let us enjoy it, therefore, while it lasts, and not spend it to no purpose.

—Plutarch

As we grow spiritually and move from the narrow world of self into God's wider world, our perspective changes. We realize that life is God's ultimate gift to us. It is His intention, we believe, that we spend it freely, joyously, and purposefully.

We therefore try to live each day and each hour to the fullest. We seek out relationships and activities that will energize and enrich our life, rather than deplete and diminish it. We try to be of service to our fellows, to be kind, giving, and loving. We do our utmost to avoid getting caught up in pettiness, with all its self-destructive ramifications. In short, we do our best to live as God would have us live.

Our destiny, as we understand it, is to exist in this life for a finite period. This does not mean that we view the future with fear or apprehension but, rather, that we no longer take any waking moment for granted. We concern ourself more with life's quality than its length.

THOUGHT FOR TODAY: I will show my gratitude to God by living this precious day to the fullest.

Nor on one string are all life's jewels strung.
—William Morris

We've been in recovery for several months, or perhaps several years. We have learned to deal with the addictions and compulsions that were destroying our lives. And we are deeply grateful.

But some of us have switched to other, seemingly innocuous forms of behavior that enable us to escape the world and our feelings. Without fully realizing it, we use work to shield ourselves from unresolved problems and uncomfortable emotions; we are so immersed in the job that it becomes our whole life.

In the same way, some of us find escape in sports, relationships, and even the support groups which have kept us on the broad road of recovery.

If we are relaxed and fulfilled only when we are involved in a sport we've come to love, we may be overlooking other areas of our inner selves that need attention and nurturing. If we feel secure and at ease only when we are with support group friends, perhaps it's an indication that we need to develop more "outside" relationships. Or if we are truly happy only when we're on the job, clearly it's time to seek greater balance in our lives.

THOUGHT FOR TODAY: Balance is a key ingredient, if not a prerequisite, for continuing growth in recovery.

October 23

As a child misses the unsaid Goodnight
And falls asleep with heartache.

—Robert Frost

Like many youngsters, I was hardly ever touched affectionately by my mother and father when I was little, and even less so as a teenager. I didn't think much about it, at least not consciously, but I'm certain that the absence of warm physical contact had a profoundly adverse effect on my emotional foundation.

Early in recovery I realized that my parents were simply incapable of being physically demonstrative. They couldn't pass along something they themselves had never received. They did the best they could with what they had.

Clearly, there is far more to touching than physical expressiveness. Research going back a century or more proves, and I truly believe, that the language of touch can be amazingly therapeutic. We all know from personal experience that there is nothing more calming and reassuring than a warm, gentle hug when we are distraught, depressed, or otherwise emotionally upset.

Touching can also provide physical benefits. During the past decade, any number of studies have demonstrated that human touch can reduce anxiety and speed healing by activating the body's immune system.

THOUGHT FOR TODAY: Touch can warm the heart, calm the mind, and heal the body.

The mystery of life is not a problem to be solved, it is a reality to be experienced.
—Jacobus Johannes Van der Leeuw

We used to sit around in bars, dormitories, and coffee shops pondering and debating the "big picture." "Why are we here?" we asked. "What does it all mean?" "Am I doing what I'm supposed to be doing? How will I ever know?"

We tended to look on the dark side, viewing the world and our place in it with unremitting seriousness. We approached almost everything as a challenge to be met, a problem to be solved, a puzzle to be analyzed.

What a waste of time and energy! Instead of recognizing and appreciating our joys as we found and lived them, we frequently let them slip through our fingers because of our overly analytical approach.

Now that we have become more mature, we value life in an entirely different way. We leave the big picture to God and focus instead on the numerous and varied opportunities He puts in front of us each day. We experience and relish each activity as it occurs, rather than extracting our joy solely from pleasant memories. We live and love in the reality of here and now.

THOUGHT FOR TODAY: One way to express my gratitude for life is to live it fully.

October 25

I am myself, my own nearest of kin; I am dearest to myself.

—Terence

Day by day our self-image is changing for the better. We're beginning to really like ourselves and to have a sense of importance as individuals. The more progress we make along these lines, the easier it becomes to recognize our physical, emotional, and spiritual needs and to assert ourselves accordingly.

In the past, the hour we set aside for exercise or meditation was the first thing to be canceled if someone needed something done. Today we take the time that's necessary for our well-being, and don't automatically give top priority to the demands of others.

We used to stay out when we didn't really want to, and stay up when we were dead on our feet. These days we don't let others decide our playtime or bedtime. We quit working when we're worn out and go home when we want to be alone.

In the same way, we've learned to say no to the foods, beverages, and activities that are not good for us. It doesn't matter who offers them up—an acquaintance or our grandmother.

Whenever possible we create our own challenges and opportunities. We do the things that make us feel good about ourselves.

THOUGHT FOR TODAY: There's a difference between selfishness and honoring one's self.

A mind forever
Voyaging through strange seas of thoughts alone.
—William Wordsworth

No matter how often I speculate or write about it, I'll never cease to be surprised by my mind's tendency to rambunctiously run off and take me along on a wild emotional ride.

In a typical scenario, I begin to feel anxious, rushed, and "hyper"—for no real reason. Life has been proceeding normally, with no unusual pressures. My mind alone is responsible for the negative emotional energy surging through me. To compound the problem, I bring that manic energy, and the erratic behavior it triggers, into everything I do. Even pleasurable activities become frantic and stressful.

In order to turn things around, it's necessary to bring about a major energy shift within myself. I breathe deeply and say sharply, "This is absurd—there's absolutely no reason for me to feel this way!"

I force myself to concentrate on my surroundings, on what I'm actually doing, in order to return to the here and now. Sometimes, I go so far as to slow down my physical movements, temporarily functioning at half speed. By that time, I'm usually able to rein in my mind, regain control, and come back to reality and serenity.

THOUGHT FOR TODAY: My mind has incredible power, but that doesn't mean I'm powerless over it.

October 27

The world belongs to the enthusiast who keeps cool.
—William McFee

I once swam with a friend at a local pool and she completed twice as many laps as I did. "I'm glad I don't feel the need to compete with you," I said jokingly. "I'd do myself in."

She laughed, then admitted that her competitiveness had often worked to her disadvantage. By way of example, she told me what happened when she took up surfing.

"It's such a difficult sport to learn," she recalled. "So when I first started I was thrilled just to be able to catch a wave and stand up. But within a few months I began comparing myself to some of the other surfers. They were doing incredible maneuvers on practically every wave.

"I began pressuring myself to improve quickly. And for the next three months, surfing became sheer frustration and torment.

"It finally dawned on me why I was out there in the first place—for enjoyment and exercise. It was ridiculous to try to compete with those guys. They're half my age, they've been surfing for years, and they practically live in the water.

"Once I had that realization, the pressure was off. I began surfing to achieve my own personal best and started having fun again."

THOUGHT FOR TODAY: I will keep my goals within reason, based on my personal capabilities.

Joy is an elation of spirit—of a spirit which trusts in the goodness and truth of its own possessions.
—Seneca

We've all had the pleasure of watching children on a carnival ride, playing in the water, or trying out a new bicycle. We smile automatically at their exclamations of delight and at the joy expressed in their faces.

It's easy to relate to the joy of a child doing something exciting. But as we've grown and matured, joy for us has taken on deeper meaning and new dimensions.

Our joyful feelings flow most freely when we have a positive attitude and approach to life. They derive from the "process" of our spirit-enhancing activities and are not contingent on expectations of a particular result. In other words, the joy is in playing the game, not in winning. From that standpoint, joy is unrestricted to us—it is always freely available.

As adults, we've developed the ability to find joy and spontaneous pleasure in the little things. It doesn't take something extraordinary or expensive to bring about a peak experience.

There is the greatest potential for joy when our minds are free of distraction and our senses are finely tuned. It is then that we are most receptive to the wondrous subtleties of the natural world.

THOUGHT FOR TODAY: My inner spirit is the wellspring of joy in my life.

October 29

Life shrinks or expands in proportion to one's courage.

—Anaïs Nin

There are major turning points when we need to make critical decisions—decisions with the potential to affect the quality of our lives for years to come. The dilemma may involve financial security, a significant career move, or a controversial surgical procedure.

Almost automatically, we turn to prayer and meditation, because we know from experience that is how we will receive God's guidance. Then, at a certain point, we feel we have been given the answer, and it is time for action.

We know exactly what to do, but suddenly we are paralyzed by fear. We reach inside ourselves for courage and strength, but there doesn't seem to be anything there.

This is when we need to turn again to God, for He can provide the courage that we lack. It's not that God will take the required actions on our behalf. Rather, He will provide us with the ability to *see* ourselves as courageous, and to *be* courageous.

God will give us the inner confidence to take control of our lives. No matter what the challenge, His grace will enable us to experience it as a bridge to ever greater personal growth.

THOUGHT FOR TODAY: God can lead me back to my own inner courage.

Zeal is like fire; it wants both feeding and watching.
—W. Gurney Benham

I skipped a day of exercise last week and paid an enormous price for doing so. No, I didn't suddenly lose all my muscle tone and become short of breath. I didn't gain weight or lose sleep. Rather, the price I paid was an emotional one; I beat myself unmercifully for taking that day off.

Never mind that I had been busy all day long, or that I had exercised twelve days in a row. Never mind that my muscles and tendons were screaming for a rest.

It wasn't the first time I had heaped guilt on myself for "missing" a workout. The thing is, I should know better. I've learned that when I become obsessed with my physical fitness program, I end up turning a very positive and life-affirming endeavor into a negative experience. Indeed, my occasional fanaticism can easily override not only the pleasure of my workouts, but also the satisfaction I get from being disciplined and consistent.

I have to remind myself periodically that I exercise to achieve health and well-being—not because of obligation, not to make up for lost time, and certainly not to avoid guilt.

THOUGHT FOR TODAY: My goal is a physical workout, not an emotional wipeout.

October 31

Beware, as long as you live, of judging people by appearances.

—Jean de La Fontaine

No one will disagree, at least in theory, that it's wrong to judge or value people based on their physical appearance. Yet for various reasons—cultural conditioning in particular—many of us find it difficult to put into practice what we believe in principle. And as the result, we short-change ourselves in ways that might not be immediately obvious.

The more we judge others solely by the way they look, the more we tend to feel that we're being judged in the same way. We may become uncomfortable and self-conscious, for example, without realizing why. Similarly, when we put someone up on a pedestal, we can't help but feel that they are looking down on us.

We are also likely to make unsound relationship choices when we pursue people and develop friendships based on outward appearances. True compatibility is based on such *inner* qualities as personality, ideals, tastes, and even sense of humor.

Moreover, when we are preoccupied with material considerations, we overlook people's spiritual qualities, including understanding, empathy, and kindness. In so doing, we deprive ourselves of an abundant source of personal enrichment.

THOUGHT FOR TODAY: I will try to value you as I would have you value me—by what is within.

Self-respect—that cornerstone of all virtue.
                              —Sir John Herschel

When a woman suggested during the first month of my recovery that I would eventually come to love myself, I told her I could never see that happening. She smiled tolerantly and said, "For now, how about working on liking yourself just a little more?"

Learning to love myself in the sense she described has been a gradual, evolutionary process. From rock-bottom self-loathing, I slowly reached a point where I could actually tolerate myself, and even think of myself as an "okay" person. It took years, but in time I developed real self-acceptance and self-respect.

The dramatic change in my feelings toward myself came about not by thinking in a new way, but by living in a new way. I developed a sense of worthiness by doing worthy things—by staying clean and sober, by being honest, by helping others.

Self-love, which I once saw as an impossibility, has become a reality. In fact, these days I am not only able to have kind and loving personal feelings, but to express those feelings by taking kind and loving actions toward myself.

THOUGHT FOR TODAY: The first step is to say nice things about myself. The second is to do nice things for myself.

November 2

Look upon every day as the whole of life, not merely a section; and enjoy and improve the present without wishing, through haste, to rush on to another.
—Jean Paul Richter

Living in the now—everyone agrees that it's the thing to do and the place to be. Life would be so much simpler, so much more productive and fulfilling if we could just keep ourselves anchored in the present moment.

Unfortunately, what we believe and what we end up doing are sometimes worlds apart. Most of us usually devote only a portion of ourselves to what we are doing and what's happening right now. The remainder of our thoughts and attention shifts back and forth between the past and future. To make matters worse, our ruminations about yesterday and speculations about tomorrow tend to be negative in nature.

The result is that we create unnecessary stress for ourselves. Isn't it challenging enough to concentrate on and deal with what is going on at this moment? Aren't we doubling our mental and emotional workload, and quadrupling stress, when we concern ourselves with what *has* happened or what *may* happen?

We find freedom and peace of mind by doing all we can to stay centered in the here and now. We may not always be successful, but the effort alone can go a long way toward reducing stress in our lives.

THOUGHT FOR TODAY: Am I creating unnecessary stress for myself by wandering out of the present?

But happy they, the happiest of their kind, whom gentle stars unite; and in one fate their hearts, their fortunes and their beings blend!

—James Thomson

We've all been at gatherings and support group meetings where an individual shares about progress he or she has made in certain areas. Then, in closing, voice trailing off, the person says, "But relationships, that's a whole different matter. . . ."

Relationships can be extremely difficult, there's certainly no question about that. We come together from different backgrounds and with divergent wants and needs. We frequently have trouble communicating, adapting, agreeing, or compromising. Additionally, each of us brings our own character traits and unresolved problems into the relationship. It's no wonder that relationships are as challenging as they are.

Looking at it in an entirely different light, participation in a relationship can be one of the fastest ways to grow emotionally and spiritually. In a very real sense, marriage or other close partnerships offer us endless opportunities to learn and to change. They allow us to see our progress (or the lack of it) in the perfect mirror of our partner.

We have learned that successful relationships require a willingness to look fearlessly into that mirror. And they also require an unwavering commitment to personal growth.

THOUGHT FOR TODAY: To have a successful relationship, I must actively concern myself more with giving than receiving.

November 4

Look how we can, or sad or merrily, Interpretation will misquote our looks.

—William Shakespeare

A woman friend and I were invited to go sailing on a neighbor's new boat. I took along a camera. When my friend noticed that I was about to photograph her, she reflexively turned away and said, *"Don't."*

I urged her to let me take just one photo, and she finally relented. But when I raised the camera, a frown crossed her face and her body went rigid.

Later, I apologized for making an issue about it, and she began to open up. "I should have just let you take the picture in the first place." She laughed. "It would have been much easier. But I'm terribly camera-shy, because I've always hated my looks."

When I expressed amazement that she considered herself unattractive, she paused for a moment, then conceded that the way she perceives herself is not the way others perceive her.

She went on, "Whenever I feel self-conscious, like today, I need to remember that what I see as major flaws in my looks are of very little concern to anyone else. Provided," she added with a smile, "that I don't behave in a way that calls attention to them."

THOUGHT FOR TODAY: If I haven't yet begun to refocus my self-image, now is the time.

Reflect upon your present blessings, of which every man has many; not on your past misfortunes, of which all men have some.

—Charles Dickens

Today I will make an effort to set aside any lingering doubts about my capabilities. I will visualize myself as the intellectually sound person I truly am.

Thanks to God, there are no limits on my ability to learn and reason—to acquire new knowledge and apply it in life-affirming pursuits. I have also been blessed with a growing willingness to develop new skills, to seek out new solutions, to find new ways of expressing myself.

I will visualize myself as a confident, self-assured individual. I can make choices and decisions without fear. However, if the road ahead is not clearly marked, and if for a time I am uncertain, I will not hesitate to ask God for guidance. I will turn to the Divine intelligence within; I will listen to my inner voice.

I see myself as a free spirit. My newfound ability to accept reality—to be discerning and objective—in no way detracts from my powers of imagination and creativity. I draw inspiration from God's wonders in and around me, from nature's seasonal cycles to the intricate miracles of my own life process.

THOUGHT FOR TODAY: I am capable, confident, and free.

November 6

Let a man be but as earnest in praying against a temptation as the tempter is in pressing it, and he needs not proceed by a surer measure.

—Robert South

Those of us who are trying to lose weight face many challenges and temptations. Some of the most formidable ones are created by family members or close friends who unwittingly sabotage our efforts.

Most of us have had encounters with friends or relatives who bring gifts of food—seemingly as a way of showing affection. When we decline their offerings, they act terribly hurt.

Then there's the overweight friend who becomes envious when we successfully slim down while he or she is unable to shed a pound. Before long our friend turns aloof and resentful, implying that by changing, we've ruined a relationship based on "common suffering."

Sometimes we're challenged by a well-intentioned parent or sibling who encourages us to put off dieting until we have resolved other "more pressing" problems.

Or perhaps the saboteur is our spouse or partner, who snidely reminds us over and over that we're not fun anymore. They've lost their eating partner and try to make us feel guilty for "spoiling the party."

Most often, these people are unaware that they are making things difficult for us. But it's important that *we* remain aware, standing our ground and taking action to ward off potential sabotage.

THOUGHT FOR TODAY: Support and encouragement is always welcome, but in the end it's up to me.

I will neither yield to the song of the siren nor the voice of the hyena, the tears of the crocodile nor the howling of the wolf.

—George Chapman

It would be wonderful if every one of our friends and relatives were unfailingly supportive of our physical and emotional needs as we work toward losing weight. But the reality is that there will always be those who try to tempt us.

Since it's unlikely that many of these potential saboteurs will change their behavior, it's up to us to find ways to deal with them. Here are some basics that can be applied to just about any situation. . . .

When a person insists on bringing gifts of food even after we've asked them not to do so, we have to remind ourselves of our priorities. In this case, our health and well-being must come first, rather than someone else's "hurt" feelings.

With those who envy us, or who insist that we're killjoys because we won't eat with them, a confrontation may help. After noting their behavior, we can say something like, "I really need your encouragement. You can't do it for me, but you can help me stay committed."

Above all, we must recognize that it is always our hand that puts the food in our mouth. No matter how manipulative another person is, we alone are responsible for what we eat.

THOUGHT FOR TODAY: I will state my case and stand my ground.

November 8

Everyone stamps his own value on himself.
—Johann Christoph Friedrich von Schiller

Not until I lost weight, toned up, and in general became physically fit did I realize how much stress and unhappiness my body image had caused me over the years.

Every day, in one way or another, I bitterly chastised myself for the way I looked. I would angrily pinch the "spare tire" that encircled my waist. I would shake my head in disgust if I glimpsed myself in the mirror on the way to the shower. To make matters worse, I further belittled myself for failing to do anything about my physical condition and appearance.

It finally began to change when exercise became an important and regular part of my life. As my body became leaner and more muscular, my spirits soared. As I progressed—losing more weight and becoming healthier—my self-image also improved.

I bought new clothes and wore them proudly. From time to time, I actually found myself nodding approvingly at my reflection. As with all other rewards of regular exercise, my improved body-image and the peace of mind that comes with it is a benefit I enjoy each and every day.

THOUGHT FOR TODAY: I can change the way I feel about the way I look.

Take rest; a field that has rested gives a bountiful crop.

—Ovid

Some of us took secret pride in our ability to go and go and go without rest. We felt we could get away with burning the candle at both ends, that it couldn't really hurt us. But we've since become much more sensitive to our bodies and minds, and we know better.

What happens when we don't get enough rest? We become edgy. We overreact and frequently say or do things we may regret. We become easily confused, and our problems seem larger and more complicated than they actually are.

When we're overtired, we can't perform up to our potential. We tend to have poor judgment and to make mistakes—at work, on the road, on the playing field.

We're vulnerable to old ideas when we're in need of rest. Those of us recovering from dependencies may find ourselves tempted to take a drink, to smoke a cigarette, to eat sugar. Moreover, we simply don't feel well when we are tired. And these days, feeling well is a priority.

For all of these reasons, it's vitally important to get our lives on a health-enhancing schedule that includes a sufficient and regular amount of rest every single day.

THOUGHT FOR TODAY: Rest is an expression of self-respect.

What ardently we wish, we soon believe.
—Edward Young

Our attitudes, convictions, and belief systems have no material substance, yet they can have the impact of a wrecking ball on our lives. Attitudes and beliefs become thoughts, which not only influence our experiences, but actually create them.

For example, some of us have difficulty shopping for clothes. The entire process—selecting, trying on, spending money—is almost always an ordeal. The beliefs that we are unattractive and/or unworthy come to life in negative thoughts, which all but guarantee a tormenting shopping experience.

Affirmations can be an effective tool in our continuing struggle to overcome such deep-rooted negative convictions about ourselves. An affirmation is, of course, a positive statement used repeatedly to counteract a false, outdated, or damaging belief.

Typically, an affirmation might go something like this: "I am an attractive, worthy person, deserving of nice new clothes." We can repeatedly think the affirmation, say it aloud, or write it.

If we are serious and consistent, our affirmations will eventually become our new beliefs. They will become ingrained in our thought processes and create joyful rather than tormenting experiences.

THOUGHT FOR TODAY: I have the power to change my beliefs, my thoughts, and my experiences.

*Be glad of life because it gives you the chance to love
and to work and to play and to look up at the stars.*
—Henry Van Dyke

A week after my heart attack, the cardiologist presented me with a list of *musts*. I needed to quit smoking, lose twenty-five pounds, reduce fat in my diet, and start exercising regularly.

My first reaction was total willingness; I would do whatever it took to stay alive. Several weeks later, a second, more powerful reaction kicked in. I was awash with self-pity. I felt especially sorry for myself because of the dietary restrictions.

Most of us have similar reactions when faced with the need to make major changes in our habits in order to improve our health. A certain amount of self-pity is understandable. But if we give power to this dangerous emotion, it can lead us back to our self-destructive ways.

When we find ourselves sinking into the seductive swamp of poor-me-ism, we can pull ourselves out by taking a hard look at what's really going on. Once we acknowledge feeling sorry for ourselves, we can do something about it.

In my own case, I try to use gratitude as an antidote to self-pity. How fortunate I am that there are specific actions I can take to improve my health and prolong my life!

THOUGHT FOR TODAY: If I give self-pity a toehold, it could lead to a stranglehold.

November 12

Still I am learning.

—Michelangelo

The weekend visit is over, and now that we are back home we can begin to calm down. Mother knows just how to push our buttons, and this time she went all out. As usual, we immediately went on the defensive. We became guilt-ridden and anxious, furious at our mother's words and actions and the harm they caused us.

Hopefully, someday we'll be able to grow in such a way that we can feel and behave differently during our visits. Hopefully, someday we will be able to turn each "button-pushing" incident into a learning experience.

Is it actually possible to do this? Yes, but only if we become convinced that the problem is not with the button-pusher, but with ourselves. Each time our negative emotions are triggered by a jibe or innuendo, aren't we being shown an area that needs work? Indeed, we might ask ourselves specifically, "What character defect or unresolved issue bubbles to the surface each time my mother brings up a certain subject?"

If we are truly committed to emotional and spiritual growth, there is no reason why painful experiences of this type can't be turned into opportunities for personal awareness and change.

THOUGHT FOR TODAY: If I remove the fuel, the fire will die.

The thoughts that come often unsought, and, as it were, drop into the mind, are commonly the most valuable of any we have.

—John Locke

Several times a week, I leave my home early in the morning and set out on a five- or six-mile walk. I find that some of my most effective problem-solving takes place on these occasions.

Perhaps solutions come more easily because I am not forcing the issue. I'm out to get exercise and fresh air; my intention is walking, not thinking. So the results are a lot different than when I consciously sit down to *think*—which is my least effective problem-solving technique.

When I am outdoors and surrounded by God's wonders—clouds, trees, the ocean, humanity itself—I'm better able to put my problems and myself into proper perspective. I'm soon reminded, once again, that I'm but one small part of a very large world.

As my walk progresses, a natural muscular action takes over. That rhythm—step after step and breath after breath—seems to sweep away confusion and unlock my subconscious. Thoughts float in and out, unstructured and unfettered. At that point, it becomes relatively easy to slip into a meditational state and listen for my inner voice.

THOUGHT FOR TODAY: A relaxed body leads to a relaxed mind and spirit.

November 14

There smiles no Paradise on earth so fair
But guilt will raise avenging phantoms there.
　　　　　　　　　—Felicia Dorothea Hemans

Because we are human, at some point in our life each of us has made serious mistakes, treated others badly, failed to achieve important goals we had set for ourselves, or wasted a great deal of time and money. It doesn't take much to dredge up those painful memories and ruin the present moment or entire day by layering ourselves with guilt.

There's no question that guilt can have an extremely detrimental effect on our health and well-being. The worst thing about this destructive emotion is that it tends to make us feel unworthy and undeserving of the good things in life. We may feel, for example, that we don't deserve companionship or love. Our burden of self-blame may prevent us from taking good care of ourselves physically, emotionally, and spiritually.

What can we do to free ourselves of the past in order to live more comfortably and joyously in the present? We can divulge our secrets and make amends for any past wrongs. We can surrender our guilt and ask for God's help in letting go. Finally, and most important, we can work on forgiving ourselves once and for all.

THOUGHT FOR TODAY: God has forgiven me. Can I forgive myself?

Haste trips its own heels, and fetters and stops itself.
—Seneca

When I first started exercising seriously after many years of inactivity, it seemed that every muscle in my body was conspiring against me. That's how sore I was. Within several weeks I was completely discouraged and ready to go back to my sedentary ways.

When I complained to a friend who was a runner, he showed me a series of stretching exercises and suggested I work them into my daily routine. He emphasized the importance of learning the proper stretching techniques, and following through, so that I wouldn't hurt myself.

Even after agreeing with the logic of his advice, my inclination was to skip the stretching and just get on with the workout. It took me a while to become disciplined. Once I got into the habit of stretching, however, it made a considerable difference in how I felt—not only during exercise, but overall.

Stretching has gone a long way toward reducing the soreness and increasing the flexibility of my muscles, tendons, and ligaments. It has also helped me to stay relatively injury-free. Beyond that, stretching is something I can do whenever I want to simply relax my body and mind.

THOUGHT FOR TODAY: The more I respect my body, the better it will serve me.

November 16

There is no such thing as chance; and what seems to us the merest accident springs from the deepest source of destiny.

—Johann Christoph Friedrich von Schiller

From early childhood, most of us hear over and over that "God works in mysterious ways." Although the idea is comforting, it's hard to know and understand exactly how God does work in our lives.

How, for example, are we brought to the threshold of recovery? How did we find that job that so perfectly matches our capabilities? How did we become linked with that very special person?

When we wonder about such momentous turning points, we may initially believe they were the result of extraordinary luck or mere coincidence. But if we take the time to carefully look back at the series of events preceding each turning point, chances are we will see a Divine plan at work.

More often than not, we'll find that we were being prepared and guided—step by step, and experience by experience—toward a very special personal destiny. We were somehow led to a certain place at a certain time. Something made us listen carefully to what was being said. We knew instinctively that this time we shouldn't say no.

God may indeed work in mysterious ways, but there is no mystery to the goodness and abundance He brings into our lives.

THOUGHT FOR TODAY: God is guiding me.

God made the human body, and it is the most exquisite and wonderful organization which has come to us from the Divine hand.

—Henry Ward Beecher

It began in junior high school. We became painfully self-conscious. The combination of peer pressure and our own adolescent insecurity made us extremely uncomfortable with our bodies and looks.

More than a few of us carried our poor body-image into adulthood. We continued to dwell on perceived defects in our physical appearance—bone structure, height, weight, skin tone, whatever. The bottom line was that we couldn't accept our bodies, and as a result we experienced a great deal of emotional distress.

Naturally, all of this affected the way we related to other people and the world around us. Our feelings about our looks continued to erode our self-confidence and inhibited our growth in many areas.

Today we're working hard to become more accepting of our physical being. This is the body that God has given us, we often tell ourselves; our goal is to respect it and care for it in the best ways possible.

As we continue to take actions to improve our physical well-being—by exercising and becoming fit, by eating right and becoming healthy—we are more and more able to accept our bodies and ourselves.

THOUGHT FOR TODAY: I will focus on my true assets rather than on my imagined defects.

November 18

In my belief, you cannot deal with the most serious things in the world unless you also understand the most amusing.

—Winston Churchill

For years my expression was frozen in a perpetual scowl. I was preoccupied with problems and almost always felt miserable. It wasn't until I joined a recovery group to get help for my alcoholism that I was able to let myself go. I finally learned to laugh.

For a long time after that breakthrough, I enjoyed laughter for its own sake. Recently, though, I've discovered there is far more to it than I realized.

To begin with, laughter seems to have a beneficial effect on my health. When I'm able to laugh at the irony of a situation—a patient being awakened to be given sleeping pills, for example—I tend to feel better. Moreover, when *I'm* the patient, an active sense of humor brings me out of myself and helps me forget my problems.

Laughter also relieves stress for me. I've read many times that stress weakens the immune system, and from that standpoint I've become convinced that laughter helps my body heal itself.

Beyond all of that, now that life has become so precious to me, it's important to get as much as possible out of each experience. The sound of my own laughter prolongs each joyful moment.

THOUGHT FOR TODAY: Laughter is therapeutic.

Our bodies are our gardens, to which our wills are gardeners.

—William Shakespeare

After years of putting up with a chronic injury such as a bad back, or dealing with a recurring health problem, some of us began to feel that our body had become our enemy. It had turned on us by breaking down, by causing us pain, by disrupting our lives. At times we felt alienated and detached from our body; we lost confidence in its healing powers.

Eventually we realized that these feelings were actually compounding our physical problems. By perceiving and treating our body as an enemy, we were becoming our own enemy. Having had a change of heart, we tried to accept our body, and began working in partnership with it to mitigate our ailments and become as healthy as possible.

We tried to adopt a more relaxed attitude concerning our physical problems and limitations. We did all we could—through meditation and mental imagery, for example—to harness our body's self-healing capabilities. And we became willing once again to listen and respond to our body, as we would to a trusted friend, in order to learn what further actions we could take to help ourselves.

THOUGHT FOR TODAY: My body is not my enemy.

November 20

A grain of sand includes the universe.
—Samuel Taylor Coleridge

The feeling of being connected to others, to God, and to ourselves is among the most meaningful components of our sense of well-being today. For some of us, participation in support groups brings about a very special feeling of connectedness. By attending sharing meetings and becoming actively involved, we form bonds not only with one another, but with the more powerful entity of the group itself.

Initially, we may join solely to gain hope and encouragement. Soon, however, we find that we are tapping into a unified energy source that puts the power of the universe within reach.

We also achieve a sense of connectedness through our involvement with nature—either with specialized sports such as fishing, surfing, and climbing, or more widely available activities such as walking, biking, and picnicking.

When we are in direct contact with the natural world in these ways, it takes but a small surge of the imagination to feel truly connected to the earth, the solar system, the universe—to everything that exists. We are at one with the source of creation and acquire an indescribable aura of wholeness, security, and inner power.

THOUGHT FOR TODAY: I choose connectedness and involvement, not aloneness and alienation.

*We find comfort among those who agree with us—
growth among those who don't.*

—Frank A. Clark

I had no idea how to live, how to love, or how to relate to other people when I began my recovery. Yet at the same time I thought I had all the answers. My self-image, or the one I tried to project, combined knowledgeability, sophistication, and self-sufficiency.

The members of my support group may well have been tempted to "pull my covers" during those first shaky weeks. Thankfully, they chose not to do so, knowing that I would have bolted.

What they did instead, over time, was help me realize on my own how distorted and out of touch with reality my perceptions were. Gently and patiently, they pointed out ironies and inconsistencies in my beliefs about myself, while reminding me of my inability to get along in the world.

I was sensitive, defensive, and at times almost hostile. But my new friends always seemed to know exactly how far to go, when to pull back, and when it was time for me to face another reality. They eased me along the path of spiritual growth and emotional well-being, and over the years they have remained at my side.

THOUGHT FOR TODAY: My most valued friends are those who see the real me—even when I cannot.

God asks no man whether he will accept life. That is not the choice. You must take it. The only choice is how.

—Henry Ward Beecher

Yes, we are powerless over many things, and God is ultimately in charge of our destiny. We are powerless over the actions and beliefs of others, over the chronology of events, and over the forces of nature. But this doesn't mean we lack control over our own lives. Nor does it mean that God's design includes passivity and inaction on our part.

To be sure, there was a time when many of us did sit by, letting others take responsibility and make decisions for us. We saw ourselves as victims, and refused to take interest in the form and flow of our lives. We blamed other people and institutions for the way things were.

We have since come to see that powerlessness does not preclude free will, nor does it absolve us from responsibility. To the contrary, we now enjoy an abundance of life-enriching choices. We have the power, moment by moment, to choose friends, directions, destinations, activities, and attitudes to shape a quality life.

We are not only certain that God has a plan for each of us, but are equally certain that He expects us to participate fully, freely, and joyously.

THOUGHT FOR TODAY: I take my power of choice very seriously.

Best of all is to preserve everything in a pure, still heart, and let there be for every pulse a thanksgiving, and for every breath a song.

—Konrad von Gesner

When Thanksgiving rolls around this week, the last thing we'll probably think about doing is writing down the things for which we're grateful. There's too much to do. The house needs to be cleaned and decorated, the cooking has to be done, and so on. There's hardly time enough to prepare a shopping list, let alone a "gratitude list."

All of these responsibilities notwithstanding, those of us who take a few quiet moments to list and reflect on our blessings find that the practice can add a great deal of personal meaning and spiritual substance to our holiday.

As friends and relatives arrive, we are newly aware of what they have meant to us over the years. We are aware and grateful, too, for the part we've been able to play in their lives. We are thankful that we can be there, healthy and whole, for our family and friends; that we can give of ourselves; that we can bring good feelings and warmth to the gathering.

Because of the time we took earlier to reflect on our many blessings, we feel God's presence throughout the day. His grace has made it all possible.

THOUGHT FOR TODAY: I can enrich any day by counting my blessings.

November 24

How can we expect a harvest of thought who have not had a seedtime of character?
— Henry David Thoreau

A student at the local university once shared with me some problems he had been having in school. He found it difficult to be disciplined and to take his studies seriously. Several mornings a week he overslept and was late for class. Although he had been receiving sufficient spending money from home, he was always broke and ended up borrowing from friends.

"Last year I put a lot of energy into getting in touch with my inner child," he confided. "Learning to loosen up and to laugh—you know, letting myself feel the excitement and wonder I missed as a kid."

He told me he still tries to nourish the childlike qualities that never fully emerged in his alcoholic home. But because of the way he had been feeling and acting recently, he decided it was time to begin taking his education and responsibilities more seriously. He made a commitment to rely less on others and to depend more on himself.

"It's time to stop putting things off, and to grow up," he concluded. "What I'm saying, is that now that I've brought out my inner child, I need to find and give encouragement to my *inner adult*."

THOUGHT FOR TODAY: Maturity is not bestowed; it is developed.

Nature, time, and patience are the three greatest physicians.

—Henry George Bohn

Now that we're enjoying a regular exercise routine, it's hard to believe we resisted and procrastinated as long as we did. We never thought we could feel this good.

Suddenly, we injure ourselves. It's not terribly serious, and it will heal completely if we rest for several weeks. We say, "That's life," and try to make the best of it, but within a few days we're climbing the walls because of all the unforeseen changes that are taking place.

To begin with, we're worried about gaining weight because we're not burning as many calories. We're also concerned about losing muscle tone and getting out of shape. We don't know what to do with our excess energy, and we're feeling depressed.

When we've finally had as much self-pity and short-temperedness as we can stand, we move out of the problem and into the solution by surrendering. We accept the fact that injuries can be part of an active person's life. And we become willing to make whatever adjustments are necessary to keep ourselves physically and emotionally comfortable.

Last but not least, we try to eliminate fear, impatience, and other negative emotions from our minds and, instead, begin to generate positive, healing energy.

THOUGHT FOR TODAY: I will respect rather than resist my body's healing power.

There is a great deal of unmapped country within us.
—George Eliot

Societal rules often bring out a strong reaction of rebelliousness in some of us. The movie usher tells us to form a line, but we find a way to defy him and enter the theater immediately. The sign says, "No dogs on the beach," but we feel that our dog is special and that our case is different.

Yet ironically, most of us create, accept, and rigidly adhere to rules in our private lives that are out of sync with reality, necessity, or even common sense.

We follow self-imposed rules about love, for example, which tell us to never open up completely—and to always hold something back. We adhere to long-standing rules about our feelings which tell us that certain emotions are unacceptable and should not be expressed.

Some of the outdated private rules we cling to were self-created, while others had their origins in our family backgrounds. In either case, perhaps it's time to identify and examine *all* the rules we live by, especially in our relationships. Then we can keep the ones that work to our benefit and become willing to discard those that are detrimental.

THOUGHT FOR TODAY: If my private rules are out of date and growth inhibiting, I need not live by them any longer.

Outside show is a poor substitute for inner worth.
—Aesop

A friend and I were talking about a mutual acquaintance known for endless discourses designed to make him look good to others. "You ask him what time it is, and he tells you how to build a watch," my friend concluded snidely.

I became slightly uncomfortable for a moment because for years I, too, had practiced various forms of one-upmanship to attract attention and gain approval. I worked hard to be smarter, funnier, tougher, and, in general, more "hip, slick, and cool" than the people around me.

It took quite some time in recovery to become aware that my offensive behavior was a reflection of emotional insecurity. Only then did change become possible.

When I first began to gain a little humility along those lines, I found myself reacting with hostility to arrogant people—probably because they reminded me of how I had acted for so long. But now that some time has passed, I'm able to be more understanding and empathetic. I've walked in those same shoes. I know from my own learning process that such behavior—such "outside show"—is more likely than not a way of compensating for low self-worth.

THOUGHT FOR TODAY: I'm so grateful that I no longer have to "put on airs."

November 28

Hurry is only good for catching flies.

—Russian proverb

Many of us unknowingly fall into the habit of racing through life. If we are fortunate, a single incident or series of events will alert us to our self-defeating behavior. One too many speeding tickets or a doctor's admonition that we are "running ourselves into the ground" just might force us to take a look at our frenetic pace.

We may find that in everything we do—eating, talking, working, studying—we push ourselves to the limit. Even on a day off, we rush from one recreational activity to another. No matter what our sport, we feel that we are not really getting a workout unless we're speeding along and suffering.

When we look deeper, we may realize that our race against time creates a tremendous amount of stress. We waste energy, become exhausted, and find little enjoyment in what we do.

It may take a while to slow down and learn to pace ourselves, but the rewards will be worth the effort. We'll have more energy at the end of the day and feel relaxed rather than overwrought. Instead of rushing blindly through our activities, we'll begin to savor and appreciate them.

THOUGHT FOR TODAY: What's the hurry?

There is more to life than increasing its speed.
　　　　　　　　　　　　—Mahatma Gandhi

Relaxation of my mind and body is one of my top priorities today. There are many techniques to help me accomplish this, and I will take the time to practice some of them.

I will find a quiet place away from glare and distraction. Once I am positioned comfortably, I will close my eyes and concentrate on my breathing. I will picture my lungs expanding and contracting, sending oxygen through my bloodstream to all parts of my body.

Starting at the crown of my head, I will experience every part of myself to reveal any tension that may be present. When I find such an area, I will visualize it: clenched, tight, rigid. I will then deliberately relax the tense muscle group.

Starting again with my forehead and eyes, moving systematically down my body, I will tighten and then relax each area as I come to it—my jaw, neck, shoulders, arms, hands, chest, abdomen, pelvis, thighs, calves, feet. With each release, I will feel that part of my body becoming unbound.

When I am completely relaxed, I will rest quietly and focus my mind on soothing images, such as an open field, a billowing cloud, a breaking wave.

THOUGHT FOR TODAY: My mind can help my body become unbound.

November 30

It is not the lie that passeth through the mind, but the lie that sinketh in, and settleth in it, that doth the hurt.

—Francis Bacon

One of the most painful aspects of being overweight is the effect it can have on one's self-esteem. Many of us who have had a weight problem know what it's like to deprecate ourselves by unfairly comparing our bodies and lives not only to those of other people, but also to societal ideals. We're familiar with related feelings of failure, unworthiness, and guilt.

As if those psychic wounds were not painful enough, some of us were compelled to rub salt in them by believing that being overweight, in addition to all else, is a sin. Of course, this is a poisonous untruth. Nobody ever suffered an eating disorder because they were a bad person; nobody ever recovered by being good. It is simply not a moral issue.

Granted, it is difficult to overcome these self-defeating beliefs. However, it is all but impossible to make any meaningful progress in a weight control program unless we first learn to lovingly accept ourselves as we are.

When we put aside the straw man of morality, and focus instead on loving ourselves enough to truly want to change, then it becomes possible to do so.

THOUGHT FOR TODAY: I am changing because I am a worthy person, not to become one.

Things do not change; we change.
—Henry David Thoreau

When we've been conditioned to believe that being overweight is a moral issue, it's extremely difficult to overcome that self-defeating belief. However, there are steps we can take every day, as an integral part of a weight control program, that can make a dramatic difference in the way we feel about ourselves.

We can try to keep in mind that the reason we are losing weight has nothing to do with being good or no longer being bad. We are losing weight to improve our health and the quality of our life, and that's all there is to it.

We can stand on guard against cultural messages concerning the "desirability of thinness." Whenever a glamorous photo or advertising phrase triggers guilt feelings (the notion that we are "gluttonous sinners"), we can nullify the falsehood before it does any damage.

We can do our best not to focus negatively on our weight or size, but instead concentrate on such assets as our skills, our personality, our spiritual self.

We can remind ourselves as often as possible that we are entirely worthy in every respect, and that we deserve to experience and enjoy all the good that life has to offer.

THOUGHT FOR TODAY: It becomes easier to change me when I change my "idea" of me.

December 2

In a calm sea every man is a pilot.

—John Ray

Once, while bodysurfing near my home, I was caught off guard by an unusually large set of waves. The powerful walls of white water held me down and tumbled me head over heels. I struggled with all my might to reach calmer water, but soon was exhausted, out of breath, and panicked. A lifeguard became aware of my plight and pulled me back to shore.

Later, my rescuer patiently explained where I'd gone wrong. "When you get caught in the impact zone like that," he said, "the worst thing you can do is resist. It's impossible to overcome the ocean's power. What you should do is try to relax as much as possible, and save your energy."

It was a valuable nugget of advice. Indeed, the principle of nonresistance—of giving in to the natural flow—can be beneficially applied in any number of areas where we are powerless over forces in our lives.

No matter what we face—from a major disappointment or loss to an economic downturn—resistance invariably creates turmoil and exhaustion. Surrender, on the other hand, allows us to rely on our sensitivity, intelligence, and faith to carry us through.

THOUGHT FOR TODAY: Surrender can be my salvation.

There's always room for improvement—it's the biggest room in the house.

—Louise Heath Leber

We've all heard the expression, "Use it or lose it." Comedic connotations aside, there is much practical wisdom in the phrase. The truth of "use it or lose it" relates not only to our physical being, but also to our mental capabilities and inner spirit.

What actually happens to our body when we become inactive, either from illness or lack of motivation? We lose strength, flexibility, and coordination. Our lung capacity diminishes, and our circulatory system becomes less effective in doing its job.

What happens to our mind when we become isolated and stop learning? Our powers of concentration and memory suffer; we are generally less sharp. We become easily bored with ourselves and life in general.

What happens when we stop praying and meditating? We drift away from the attitudes and actions that keep us close to our Higher Power. We lose our sense of spiritual well-being.

Each of us knows from past experience that these setbacks can and will occur as the result of inactivity. That's why, day by day, we continue to seek new physical, mental, and spiritual challenges.

THOUGHT FOR TODAY: Action is the touchstone of growth.

December 4

There is one thing which gives radiance to everything.
It is the idea of something around the corner.
—G. K. Chesterton

Self-fulfilling prophecy—the phrase suggests that if we believe a certain outcome is inevitable, we will consciously or unconsciously act to bring about the expected result. We come down with a sore throat, for example. Although we're anxious to get over it as soon as possible, we're convinced deep down that the ailment will drag on and turn into something more serious. Sure enough, that's often what happens.

When we "prophesize" in this way, most of us tend to be negative in focus. However, self-fulfilling prophecies can work to our benefit rather than only our detriment—so long as we start out with as many positive expectations as possible, instead of dwelling on our doubts.

Indeed, there is growing evidence in the medical community that positive expectations by a patient can alter the course of even a serious illness, easing symptoms and actually speeding up recovery.

In other words, if we as patients—no matter what the illness—believe at the deepest level of our being that we will heal, our conviction will likely have a beneficial effect on the recovery process.

THOUGHT FOR TODAY: I expect to be well, to be fit—to be happy, joyous, and free.

It is a very hard undertaking to seek to please everybody.

—Publilius Syrus

As a teenager, and later as a young adult, I was willing to do just about anything to win approval. No mask or masquerade was too contrived or undignified. I would laugh at your jokes even when I found them tasteless and humorless; I would agree with your opinions even when I didn't understand them. I would be anything I thought you wanted me to be.

In recovery, I learned to stop compromising myself and worked toward gaining self-respect. It soon became clear that my people-pleasing behavior over the years had depleted me emotionally and brought on a tremendous amount of stress. I still get a pang when I remember the lengths I went to in order to fit in and be liked.

I'm so grateful that I'm now learning to accept myself as I am. The more self-accepting I become, the less concern I have with what others think of me or how I may appear to them. Life is so much less stressful and so much more comfortable now that I am my own person.

THOUGHT FOR TODAY: It's a lot easier to be myself.

December 6

Knowledge is the antidote to fear.
—Ralph Waldo Emerson

For quite some time we haven't been feeling well, so we finally get up the nerve to go to the doctor. After undergoing an examination and listening to the diagnosis, we can't wait to get dressed, head home, and put the whole experience behind us.

There are a lot of unanswered questions in our minds, but we don't ask them because we're afraid of what we might find out. If we're going to face any inconveniences or limitations, we'd rather not know about them.

The irony of our behavior—and the avoidance or denial which precipitates it—is that the more we learn about any ailment or injury, the sooner we are likely to get well. If we override our impulse to flee the doctor's office and, instead, try to educate ourselves to the greatest extent possible, we'll know what to expect and what healing actions we can take.

By becoming an informed patient, we can regain the feeling of control we may have lost when we were first diagnosed. Moreover, our fear and uncertainty will diminish, and we will be in the best possible position to help ourselves.

THOUGHT FOR TODAY: The more I know, the more I can do.

We never repent of having eaten too little.
—Thomas Jefferson

We've learned to stop eating when we are full. We've gotten to the point where we feel it's perfectly all right to leave food on our plate. For the most part, we've overcome parental admonitions that made us feel guilty when we didn't eat every single morsel. The echoes of such phrases as "Think of all the starving children" no longer cause us to overeat.

Nevertheless, it still makes us a little uncomfortable when a waitress scolds us for "not doing a better job." Sometimes we're embarrassed to split a meal with a friend, or ask for a take-home container. When we eat only half of a huge serving of food in someone's home, we may be concerned that we're offending our hosts.

There is no question that it's wrong and even immoral to waste food. But eating beyond our capacity when we're full—or eating more than we should when we're trying to lose weight—is certainly no solution to world hunger. It's not that we don't care; of course we do. But at this time in our lives we're trying to put first things first.

THOUGHT FOR TODAY: My first responsibility is to my own health.

December 8

Man, proud man! dressed in a little brief authority, plays such fantastic tricks before high heaven as make the angels weep.

—William Shakespeare

In years past, a major priority in my life was gaining control of other people. Sad to say, I became something of a master, exerting control by threatening or wheedling, rewarding or withholding, criticizing or complimenting, and so on.

The bottom line, when I was successful, was that I achieved compliance through fear of one kind or another. My manipulative behavior led to unhealthy, unharmonious, and strained relationships, not to mention bad feelings about myself. My goal was personal satisfaction, but I invariably ended up with a head full of remorse and a belly full of stress.

My narrow, self-centered approach to others has changed dramatically in recovery. Clearly, there's much more to relationships than control through domination. There's the satisfaction of working together to achieve mutual goals; the camaraderie and give-and-take of sharing responsibility; the good feelings that come from respectfully treating others as equals.

When it is sometimes necessary for me to temporarily exercise control—as a parent or an employer, for example—I've found that I can successfully do so by carefully deciding how and where to hold on, and how and where to let go and surrender.

THOUGHT FOR TODAY: Self-control is the only kind worth having.

*The old faiths light their candles all about, but burly
Truth comes by and blows them out.*
> —Lizette Woodworth Reese

When we meet someone new, isn't it true that we
usually want to find out right away what they do for a
living? There's really nothing wrong with that if we're
genuinely interested and want to strike up a conversation.

The problem is that many people tend to judge
and assess others—even put value on their potential
for friendship—by what they do and how much they
earn. On the scale of so-called "acceptability" in this
regard, a doctor is likely to rank higher than an
electrician, an electrician higher than a sales clerk, a
sales clerk higher than a janitor.

In the past, many of us judged and assessed
ourselves in the same manner. We either valued or
deprecated ourselves according to our job descrip-
tion, credentials, or salary level.

As we took actions to become emotionally and
spiritually whole—and our self-image improved—we
stopped equating ourselves with what we did for a
living. We discovered our true selves. And we became convinced that our worth is best measured by
who we are on the inside and by the way we treat
ourselves and others.

THOUGHT FOR TODAY: On what scale do I value
myself?

December 10

Joy, temperance, and repose, slam the door on the doctor's nose.

—Henry Wadsworth Longfellow

When my physician once tried to tell me that I had "participated" in all of my illnesses to one degree or another—by virtue of my attitudes, habits, and reactions—I became quite upset and insulted. Hadn't I spent years getting over the conviction that my "badness" was responsible for my health problems?

But when the doctor elaborated, and I reflected further, I began to put it together. Looking back over the previous year, I could see how many relatively minor ailments—colds, upset stomach, headaches—had occurred during times when I was run down or stressed out.

Then I began to think about major illnesses in my life, my heart attack in particular. Wasn't it true that I had become obsessed with money that year, and had been juggling four writing clients all at once? Wasn't it true that I had never been under more pressure?

Since that conversation with my doctor, I've become increasingly aware of the extent to which mental and emotional factors truly affect my health from day to day. When I fail to recognize my own limits and ignore such basic necessities as a proper diet, rest, relaxation, and exercise, there's no question that I put myself in jeopardy.

THOUGHT FOR TODAY: By changing my attitudes and actions, I can influence my health for the better.

On every occasion in which virtue is exercised, if something is not added to happiness, something is taken away from anxiety.

—Thomas Bentham

There are few feelings more satisfying than the sense of well-being that comes from doing what is good and right. That is why we try to put spiritual principles into action whenever and wherever we can.

When we carefully listen to another person's problems, putting ourselves in his or her shoes with understanding and compassion, we gain a sense of well-being.

When we act unselfishly by making choices not only in our own best interest, but also in the best interest of others involved in a project or situation, we gain a sense of well-being.

When we go out of our way to be kind and helpful to someone, without expectation of anything in return, we gain a sense of well-being.

When we promptly admit we are wrong and apologize, rather than stubbornly holding our ground or pretending that nothing has happened, we gain a sense of well-being.

When we forgive a person who has harmed us, putting aside our inclination to be resentful or even vengeful, we gain a sense of well-being.

When we practice spiritual principles in these ways, we feel right with the world, with God, with our fellows, and with ourselves.

THOUGHT FOR TODAY: Service to others benefits no one more than myself.

December 12

So much is a man worth as he esteems himself.
—François Rabelais

We have the best of intentions when we commit ourselves to a new health and fitness regimen. For a while we stick with it; we're enthusiastic and optimistic. Before long, however, we're back at square one: we're overeating, we've stopped exercising, we've gone back to smoking. And so on.

Anybody who has ever tried to lose weight, get in shape—who has pursued any health and fitness goal—is familiar with the start-stop syndrome. In my own case, I struggled fruitlessly for years to lose weight and get in shape. On different occasions I tried numerous diets, tennis, aerobics, swimming—you name it. The result was always the same. I took off like a rocket but fizzled in no time.

There are many causes for such frustrating setbacks, but low self-worth is frequently the most oppressive and most difficult to overcome. Many of us cannot meet our goals because, deep down, we are convinced we don't *deserve* to look good, feel good, be healthy.

To be successful, no matter what our goal, we must believe we are deserving of the good we set out to attain. Self-worth—even if only the germinating seed of self-worth—is always the starting point.

THOUGHT FOR TODAY: I deserve to be at my best.

Any one thing in the creation is sufficient to demon-strate a Providence to an humble and grateful mind.
—Epictetus

Some mornings when I step outside to pick up the newspaper, I see nothing but grit, grime, and the tips of my toes. Other mornings I automatically look skyward and feel overwhelmed by the beauty of the sunrise.

The way I look at things and what I see varies according to my frame of mind. Like most people, I can look at the same thing two days in a row and, depending on how I am feeling, experience it in two entirely different ways.

Because I'm aware of the way my perceptions can vary from day to day, I have the opportunity to make choices. When I am experiencing inner dis-quiet, for example, or when I feel distanced from God, I can choose to single out something in nature—a leaf, a distant stand of trees, the ocean, a child. I can focus on its splendor, uniqueness, and complexity—on the miracle of its very existence.

When I am able to do this, it takes me out of myself and away from the problems with which I've been preoccupied. It puts me in touch with the natural beauty and order of the universe. It rejoins me with my Creator.

THOUGHT FOR TODAY: By the way I choose to look at things, I can make today entirely different from yesterday.

December 14

Next to family, affection, health, and love of work, does anything contribute to the pleasantness of life, restoring and raising our self-esteem, as the traffic in kind speeches?

—Lucy Elliot Keeler

We don't usually think of communications as having any sort of impact on our health. The truth is, however, that our ability to communicate with others can affect physical and emotional well-being in a number of ways.

When we are under pressure, for example—as the result of a personal problem or outside event—simply "talking it out" can go a long way toward relieving stress. A close friend can help us see an issue in perspective, and provide support and encouragement.

Similarly, our willingness to listen can boost our sense of well-being. For those of us who have been highly self-centered in the past, our ability to "be there" for another person shows the progress we've made. Besides, it's a good feeling to know that others trust us enough to share their confidences.

We also benefit greatly when we tell others how we feel about them—by openly expressing love, concern, encouragement, or gratitude. This form of communication, perhaps more than any other, can have a profoundly beneficial effect on our sense of well-being.

THOUGHT FOR TODAY: Sometimes, all it takes to feel better is to "open up."

We would have much peace if we would not busy ourselves with the sayings and doings of others.
—Thomas à Kempis

One of the easiest ways to become sidetracked in our pursuit of health and well-being is to reject our own instincts and preferences in favor of what other people prefer and find beneficial.

We've chosen a particular diet, for example, and have begun to lose weight. But our next-door neighbor has just bought two bushels of grapefruits and insists that they are the ultimate answer. We feel obligated to try her new diet rather than stay on our own.

We've settled into a nice routine of biking—ten miles every other day. Then a co-worker convinces us that we won't get anywhere unless we lift weights too.

As for our spiritual life, we've become more comfortable than ever in our relationship with God. But we start doubting ourselves when a couple we know proselytizes us to seek God in *their* special way.

The point is, there's no single right or wrong way to achieve physical, emotional, and spiritual well-being. Each of us needs to choose what works best for himself or herself. While we should remain open-minded to new ideas and approaches, we should not allow ourselves to be swayed by fads or pressured by the preferences of other people.

THOUGHT FOR TODAY: I will choose what is best for me, and respect the right of others to do the same.

December 16

Self-respect is the noblest garment with which a man may clothe himself—the most elevating feeling with which the spirit may be inspired.

—Samuel Smiles

One night at a sharing group, I was telling some friends about my long-standing inability to fully accept myself. They knew exactly what I was talking about. Although a few of them acknowledged similar problems with self-acceptance and a poor self-image, none had experienced self-loathing at the deep level I described.

While I was driving home, I had a startling and revelationary thought. What arrogance on my part. What arrogance to cling so tightly to such a distorted and distasteful image of myself!

Certainly God didn't create a loathsome individual when He brought me into the world. Nor had He ever viewed me or treated me with loathing. To the contrary, when I welcome Him into my life He gives me unconditional love, guidance, and affirmation of my worth.

From that night forward, I've tried to keep the awakening (some might call it a spiritual experience) at the forefront of my consciousness. That way I can draw strength from it and utilize it whenever I begin to belittle and besiege myself. I must say, it has made a difference.

THOUGHT FOR TODAY: I will respect what God has created in me.

There is no great achievement that is not the result of patient working and waiting.
—Josiah Gilbert Holland

We are walking along the street late in the afternoon, eastbound. Behind us, the sun suddenly breaks through the clouds. In front of us, our own shadow appears. It is long and lean, just the way we'd like to be. If only we could reshape ourselves that quickly!

Nobody needs to be told that it doesn't work that way. We didn't become overweight in one day, between early morning and late afternoon. Those extra pounds didn't appear after a single Saturnalian meal. We might have discovered the weight suddenly, but we certainly didn't gain it suddenly.

For most of us, the simple fact is that we gained weight over a period of years because of poor eating habits, because of a sedentary lifestyle, and because we ate for reasons other than hunger.

Study after scientific study confirms—and we know from personal experience—that we are far more apt to be successful in achieving lasting weight loss if we go about it gradually. If we take weight off the way we put it on—a day at a time, a pound at a time—it's much more likely to stay off.

THOUGHT FOR TODAY: If there is a secret ingredient, it is patience.

December 18

Only those who risk going too far can possibly find out how far one can go.

—T. S. Eliot

At a meeting of cancer survivors I once attended, a man talked about the distinctions between "getting cured" and "recovering."

"Not long after I was diagnosed," he said, "it was brought to my attention that expecting to be *cured* is a passive approach. It implies standing on the sidelines, waiting for somebody or something to fix me. The idea of *recovery*, on the other hand, is active. It implies that I'm going to participate with my physician and do whatever I can to help myself get well."

I was impressed by what I heard that night. Later, it occurred to me that many of my friends and I had been taking the same approach regarding our substance and behavioral dependencies. From the very first day we sought help, we were steered in the direction of "recovering" rather than "getting cured." We continue to think of ourselves as recovering alcoholics, recovering addicts, recovering overeaters.

One day at a time, we actively participate in the healing process. And thank God we're taking that approach. Had we passively waited to be cured all at once, it's likely we'd still be seriously ill. Or worse.

THOUGHT FOR TODAY: I can and will participate in my recovery.

By mutual confidence and mutual aid,
Great deeds are done, and great discoveries made.
— Homer

Looking back, many of us can see that our festering mistrust contributed mightily to the malaise and disquiet we so often felt. We had somehow become convinced that most people were against us, that life was a losing battle, and that we would always be hard pressed to find peace of mind in such a world.

Thankfully, we eventually began to understand that the problem wasn't life, but ourselves, and that our negative attitudes were largely responsible for our discomfort. At that point, we made a conscious effort to put aside our cynicism and become more trusting. We gradually succeeded and, in the process, discovered that the world wasn't really such a bad place after all.

As we learned to trust ourselves—our motives, feelings, intuition, and actions—we became freer and more comfortable in most situations.

When we stopped doubting ourselves, we were able to become more trusting of others. Where once we had been constantly suspicious, we became increasingly secure in our relationships and interactions.

Our deepest feelings of security, comfort, and well-being grew out of our newfound trust in God. This commitment, more than any other, has turned our lives around.

THOUGHT FOR TODAY: My goal today is to trust myself, to trust others, and to trust God.

December 20

A diamond is a chunk of coal that made good under pressure.

—Anonymous

Here it comes again, out of the blue, that overpowering desire to overeat. We're not even really hungry, yet we suddenly crave every one of the foods we've been successfully avoiding. *Now* what do we do?

The one thing we don't want to do is sit still and *try not* to indulge the craving; the more we think about not overeating, the more the thought occupies our mind. Before long we're playing a form of Russian roulette, asking, "Should I—or shouldn't I?" By then it's usually too late.

But there are alternatives. An extremely effective one is simply to get busy, finding something to do that will channel our thoughts and energy toward recovery. Here are some activities that work for many of us. . . .

Take a nice long walk, preferably to a place you haven't been before. Spend some time on personal grooming: give yourself a manicure, get a haircut, have a leisurely bath. Catch up on chores or letter-writing. Do some exercise.

The action we choose will of course depend on what's quickly available as well as on personal interests. What matters most is that we get moving.

THOUGHT FOR TODAY: When a craving surfaces, the worst thing we can do is sit still.

'Tis cruel to prolong a pain, and to defer a joy.
—Charles Sedley

In my old life, I never would have admitted to myself that I welcomed physical pain. As a matter of fact, I usually became furious when an illness or injury caused me major discomfort. I've since come to realize that my relationship with pain in the past was far more complex and opportunistic than it appeared.

When pain came my way, it was frequently a timely diversion. It allowed me to temporarily avoid facing and dealing with all the other problems in my life. Indeed, physical pain almost always was more bearable than my ongoing emotional anguish.

I also received other "rewards" from pain—attention, sympathy, and care. Nor was I above exaggerating my pain in order to get out of trouble with my family.

Moreover, pain gave me permission to ease up on myself—to stop driving so hard, to relax, to become even more irresponsible than usual. My immaturity was such that pain even gave me a certain sense of self-importance.

Today when I'm occasionally in pain, I try to see it straightforwardly, as part of life. I try to find constructive ways to deal with it, to alleviate it, and to accept it.

THOUGHT FOR TODAY: When pain comes into my life, do I unknowingly seek "rewards" from it?

December 22

What other liberty is there worth having, if we have not freedom and peace in our minds—if our inmost and most private man is but a sour and turbid pool.
— Henry David Thoreau

Sometimes we don't have to look very far to find ways to enhance our emotional well-being. In my own case, simply becoming willing to fulfill my day-to-day responsibilities has made a world of difference in how I feel.

Prior to my recovery, I couldn't have been more *irresponsible* if I had tried. I had a reputation for failing to pay bills on time, for not returning phone calls, and for missing appointments and deadlines.

Less obvious expressions of my lack of responsibility centered around relationships. I couldn't be counted on to keep promises, to give my time, to show my feelings. I can only imagine how my behavior affected those around me. As for myself, I was in constant emotional distress, with knots in my stomach and a gnawing at the back of my mind.

I'm no longer willing to pay the price for irresponsibility. That's why, these days, I do my best to meet and fulfill my obligations. As a result, I'm able to enjoy my free time without anything hanging over me. On a broader scale, I feel good about myself and, more often than not, have a sense of inner peace.

THOUGHT FOR TODAY: Is there an action I can take, right now, to enhance my well-being?

Forget not that the earth delights to feel your bare feet and the winds long to play with your hair.
—Kahlil Gibran

Unlike most other forms of locomotion, walking puts us in touch with our own life-force by stimulating the senses. When we walk, the sights, sounds, odors, and textures of our environment are accessible and instantly perceptible.

No matter where we walk, in the country or in the city, there's always something new for us to notice, to touch, to smell, to hear. Even though we may take the same route day after day, the scenery around us changes continuously.

On city streets there is the diversity of people and their activities: a cacophony of talk, laughter, traffic, strife; a kaleidoscope of colors, textures, shapes. There can be a fascination in slowing down to observe other people—where they are going, what they are wearing, how they are negotiating crowds and crossings.

Seasonal and weather changes, in particular, keep our walks ever fascinating. All it takes is simple alertness to become aware of the beauty and aroma of flowering trees, the light and shadow of sun and clouds, the feel and taste of wind and rain.

THOUGHT FOR TODAY: Walking sharpens my appreciation of the world around me.

December 24

Friendship is a sheltering tree.
—Samuel Taylor Coleridge

On the second or third night of my sobriety, a new acquaintance in my support group pressed a dime and his phone number into my hand. "Call me before you take the first drink," he urged.

In the weeks that followed I was given numerous phone numbers by people who cared. On more than one occasion I made the call, and in doing so postponed taking the first drink long enough to think it through.

I can't count the times I've used the telephone in this way over the years, and not just for help in overcoming a rising obsession to drink, smoke, and binge on food. By calling friends for guidance and support during times of anxiety and fear, or while recovering from illness or surgery, I've been set straight, brought back into reality, and uplifted.

I've also had the pleasure of receiving phone calls along the same lines from others. It's gratifying to know that I can be counted on. And it's a great feeling to be able to slip a quarter and my phone number into a new friend's hand—to give back some of what was given to me.

THOUGHT FOR TODAY: I need not suffer in silence; help is close at hand.

All glory be to God on high,
   And to the earth be peace,
Good-will henceforth, from Heaven to men,
   Begin and never cease.

—Nahum Tate

Christmas is first and foremost a spiritual commemoration. It is a time when people gather together from near and far, in our households and in our communities. Christmas, then, is also a celebration of relationships.

For many of us, this day offers an opportunity to reflect on our progress along these lines. There was a time when our relationships were like crucibles in which our character defects bubbled to the surface. Today, in gratifying contrast, our interactions with others are positive indicators of our emotional growth and maturity.

In past years, how we dreaded family get-togethers! All too often on such occasions we hurt or were ourselves hurt by the very people we loved the most. This year we know how to handle ourselves and look forward to reunions. We've learned how to put aside unrealistic expectations of others, and how to be less sensitive and more accepting.

On this special day, we concern ourselves with what we can do for others, rather than what we feel should be done for us. We are motivated by the true spirit of Christmas—love, understanding, and service.

THOUGHT FOR TODAY: I celebrate love and joy; I celebrate progress.

December 26

Behold the turtle. He makes progress only when he sticks his neck out.

—James B. Conant

It's been some time now since we faced the fact that our nicotine addiction is ruining our health. We also know it's never too late to quit; most of the damage can still be reversed, and we'll benefit in many other ways. We know we have to quit, and we want to.

But we still haven't made the first move. We're afraid of putting on weight, of going through painful withdrawal, of sleepless nights and extreme nervousness. We've heard all the stories.

If we are among those trapped in such a fear-inspired limbo, several important considerations can help carry us out and forward. To begin with, everyone's experience is different; just because people we know had insomnia or gained weight doesn't mean we will.

More important, millions of other people have been able to muster the courage—on their own and with God's help—to do what it takes to quit smoking.

Once we make the initial move, we are on our way. Even if we don't succeed the first time, we are still on our way, and the odds for victory have shifted in our favor.

THOUGHT FOR TODAY: God grant me the courage to change the things I can.

Step after step the ladder is ascended.

—George Herbert

It's not uncommon to hold certain individuals in awe because they have turned some of our own long-held dreams into spectacular reality. We listen in amazement as a friend joyfully describes her latest triathlon. We secretly envy our co-worker's multilinguality. And we greatly admire a neighbor who has succeeded in a career we once dreamed of pursuing.

From our point of view, each of these achievements seems overwhelmingly difficult, if not impossible. Indeed, that is what has kept us from learning the new language or sport, or embarking on the new career.

But if we were to talk at length with those individuals we admire, we would find that the secret of their success is readily available. We would learn that virtually any large challenge can be broken down into a series of smaller ones. If we focus our energy on each step leading to the ultimate goal, we are likely to succeed. If, however, we focus on the overall "impossibility" of reaching our objective, we are bound to fail.

By approaching challenges step by step, just about anything we take on will become more manageable and enjoyable. We will make progress without realizing it and be amazed by our expanding capabilities.

THOUGHT FOR TODAY: One step at a time, one day at a time, my goal is achievable.

December 28

Patience and time do more than strength or passion.
—Jean de La Fontaine

The holiday season is winding to a close, and we've put on more than a few unwanted pounds. Once again we are annoyed and disappointed with ourselves, because now we are even further from our ideal weight. And once again we're determined to slim down by the end of January.

The problem is, seasonal, holiday, and crash dieting simply doesn't work. Those of us who finally have been able to reach our proper weight, and maintain it, know that it is a year-round proposition. Here are some of the things we've learned, from experts as well as our own experience. . . .

We start out with realistic goals. It's fine to have a long-term weight loss objective, but the only way to reach it is a day at a time.

We eat regularly rather than erratically. We used to think we were cutting calories by skipping meals, but we usually overcompensated later in the day.

We exercise regularly, but not obsessively. We lose the weight slowly, just as we put it on. We make our new eating habits a year-round part of our life. Our success is based not on one or more crash diets, but on lasting changes in our lifestyle.

THOUGHT FOR TODAY: A quick fix rarely lasts.

A good archer is not known by his arrows, but his aim.

—Thomas Fuller

On the beach one day, I ran into a friend whom I hadn't seen for a while. I remembered that he had taken up weight-lifting, but I had never seen him out of a business suit. When I complimented him on his muscle development and asked how his workouts were going, he answered cryptically, "Better than before."

He explained that he had recently undergone a major change in attitude about his training program. "Right from the beginning I was hooked on weight training," he told me. "I'd go to the gym almost every day after work and lift for hours, till closing time. And I developed a nice body.

"The problem was," he continued, "that I never thought it was good enough. And I never stopped to enjoy it. When I started to get burned out, I realized that my motivation for training so hard was all wrong.

"It's still sort of difficult to admit this," my friend said sheepishly, "but I was motivated more by my feelings of inadequacy than by anything else. When that sunk in, I was finally able to become a lot more relaxed about my workouts. And about myself."

THOUGHT FOR TODAY: If I'm not motivated for the right reasons, I won't recognize and appreciate my achievements.

December 30

What a searching preacher of self-command is the varying phenomenon of health.

—Ralph Waldo Emerson

For years and years, as far back as I can remember, one of the most self-destructive patterns in my life was the way I reacted to being ill. It didn't matter whether I had a cold or a slipped disk; I invariably felt that my affliction was a punishment for wrongs I had committed. And I would become extremely angry at the illness and myself.

On those occasions, my negativity would drag me deep into self-pity. At times I would sink so low as to abandon my spiritual beliefs, vowing to forsake God as He had forsaken me.

Even now, those same angry thoughts sometimes surface when I'm under the weather. But I try not to give power to such feelings, and refuse to indulge in them even momentarily. Thankfully, my old patterns are being replaced by new knowledge, new beliefs, and new reactions.

When I become ill these days, I know that my body is trying to tell me something—to slow down, to change my diet, to reduce stress. I know I heal more quickly when I send my immune system positive rather than negative messages. I believe that God wants me to be healthy and whole.

THOUGHT FOR TODAY: When I am sick I will be my ally, not my adversary.

Change in all things is sweet.

—Aristotle

On New Year's Eve, it is traditional if not obligatory to make resolutions of all the changes and corrections we intend to make in the year ahead. It may be our intention to quit smoking and drinking, or to lose weight and exercise regularly. We may want to become more tolerant and understanding of the people around us.

But there's a problem with New Year's resolutions when we make them thinking that a magical date—January 1—will provide the impetus for change that's been lacking during the previous 364 days. We make our resolutions, and within a few days or weeks we are back where we started. Our well-intended pledges bring about not instant success, but another layer of disappointment and guilt.

A change of behavior must be preceded by a change of heart, and this can occur on any day or night of the year, not just at the stroke of midnight on New Year's Eve.

Change of any kind, from putting down an addiction to taking up a new lifestyle, must begin with surrender and complete willingness on our part, followed by commitment and discipline that is renewed a day at a time.

THOUGHT FOR TODAY: Tomorrow morning can be the dawn of a new life if I'm completely willing and fully committed.

Index of Subjects

368

ABOUT THE AUTHOR

The author of *At My Best* chooses to remain anonymous, a practice consistent with recovery program philosophy. He has written several successful books with a combined total of more than 1 million copies in print, including *A Day at a Time,* a classic work in recovery literature, *A New Day* and *A Time to Be Free*